The
Last Crusade

Other Books by Michael A. Palmer

Guardians of the Gulf:
The Growth of American Involvement in the Persian Gulf,
1833–1992

On Course to Desert Storm:
The U.S. Navy and the Persian Gulf

The
Last Crusade

Americanism and the Islamic Reformation

MICHAEL A. PALMER

Potomac Books, Inc.
Washington, D.C.

Library of Congress Cataloging-in-Publication Data
Palmer, Michael, 1951–
   The last crusade : Americanism and the Islamic reformation / Michael
Palmer. — 1st ed.
      p. cm.
   Includes bibliographical references (p.   )
   ISBN-13: 978-1-59797-062-4 (alk. paper)
   ISBN-10: 1-59797-062-X (alk. paper)
   1. East and West. 2. Civilization, Islamic—Western influences. 3.
Islamic modernism. 4. Civilization, Western—20th century. 5.
Civilization, Western—21st century. 6. United States—Civilization—
20th century—Foreign public opinion, Muslim. 7. United States—
Civilization—21st century—Foreign public opinion, Muslim. I. Title.

   CB251.P274 2006
   909'.09821—dc22

                                             2006016477

Printed in the United States of America on acid-free paper that meets the
American National Standards Institute Z39-48 Standard.

Potomac Books, Inc.
22841 Quicksilver Drive
Dulles, Virginia 20166

First Edition

10 9 8 7 6 5 4 3 2 1

To Robert Dean Stethem, USN
1961–1985

Contents

Acknowledgments

I wish to thank many people for their assistance in conceptualizing, researching, writing, and publishing this book. Fritz Heinzen proved to be, once again, more than a mere literary agent. He was an important sounding board for ideas, read through several chapters, and helped me identify the most recent scholarship on the topics I addressed. Rick Russell, a friend of many years, helped me find a home for this work at Potomac Books. Wade Dudley, a friend and colleague at East Carolina University, read through the entire manuscript. Jonathan Reid, also a friend and colleague in ECU's History Department, brought me up to speed on my understanding of the Protestant Reformation before I began making comparisons to what I view as the Islamic Reformation. Tricia Dodds worked as my graduate research assistant during the fall 2005 semester. I also offer a special thank you to David Durrant, the Government Documents Librarian at the Joyner Library of East Carolina University. David, known in the Blogosphere as the "Heretical Librarian," took a leave of absence from his cushy, tenured academic job and joined the reserves, with the hope that he will end up seeing service in Iraq.

I would also like to thank three colleagues—Gerry Prokopowicz, Chad Ross, and David Long—for their willingness to discuss my work during innumerable lunch sessions. Their disagreements helped me temper or sharpen my argument (usually the latter).

Last, I wish to express my love and appreciation to my wife, Carol, and to my children, who were supportive and understanding while I was in "book mode."

If anything I have written in this work offends anyone's sensibilities, please note the views expressed in this book are my own.

Introduction:
The Death Throes of Political
Islam?

Imagine a civilization that once outstripped the West in virtually every measure before something "went wrong." Imagine that civilization victimized by Western encroachment, colonialism, and imperialism. Imagine some lands of that once-great civilization still occupied in the twenty-first century by Westerners or their proxies. Imagine a people who must still bear the presence of American naval vessels operating in local waters. Imagine the frustration of that civilization's people—men and women proud of their illustrious history and heritage—who see themselves and their culture derided in the West as somehow backward, something "other," something Oriental.

By this point you might have assumed that I am speaking of the Islamic world; actually, I am referring to China. The description does, of course, fit the Islamic world. And that is just the point: both of these once-great civilizations—the Chinese and the Islamic—fell behind the West, at least in the material sense, and were subsequently "victimized." But when was the last time that you read about young Chinese males strapping on suicide vests and blowing themselves up in a pizza parlor in Taipei? When was the last time young Chinese flew hijacked airliners into American landmarks? When was the last time that young Chinese blew themselves up in the London subway?

1

The efforts to explain and all too often to rationalize Islamist terror by tracing such actions to Western behavior miss an all-important point: if Western, and primarily American, behavior was *the* causative factor explaining the actions of those Muslims whom many in the West describe as terrorists, why is it that the Chinese, who suffered similarly, are not acting in a comparable fashion? This discrepancy suggests that something else, something internal to the Islamic world, is the causative factor prompting the actions of the Islamic jihadists.

In the fall of 2004, at the start of the Christmas buying season, a newspaper story noted that Wal-Mart had already imported more than $14 billion worth of Chinese manufactured goods. Chinese exports to the United States in 2004 approached $200 billion. In comparison U.S. petroleum imports from the Middle East that same year totaled about $30 billion; non-oil imports from the Arab world were statistically insignificant. In 1999 China's gross domestic product, despite the inefficiencies of its quasi-Communist political-economic system, was more than $1 trillion, or nearly twice that of the entire Arab world. China produces and exports textiles and consumer electronics; the states of the Middle East export raw materials—petroleum products—and terrorism.

While sinologists debate the nature, rate, and sustainability of China's modernization, no one doubts the country is rapidly transforming. China's consumption of petroleum products to feed its growing industrial sector currently grows at an annual rate of over 7 percent—seven times that of the United States—and was a major factor behind gasoline prices' steep rise in the West during 2005.

No such burst of economic activity is evident in the Middle East, where a once-great Islamic culture has failed the test of modernity, has sought solace in a politically correct state of victimhood, and has seen many of its adherents launch a militant *jihad* against "Jews and crusaders." This reality should be evident to any who bother to examine the historical record. Why does the Islamic world dwell on the relative pinprick of the European Crusades in the

Levant, an effort that pales when compared to the Mongol invasion and the swath of utter destruction that destroyed Iran and Iraq, areas that, even if considered "Oriental," had never been "Asian"? Why do Muslims deem a century (and in most areas far fewer years) of Western imperialism in the region to be more formative with regard to the current sorry shape of the Arab Middle East than the millennium of Turkish domination? I have no intention of arguing that the West is without guilt in its relationship with the Islamic world, but rather I contend Western transgressions were limited both in severity and longevity and, as is evident in the example of China, were insufficient as a causative factor to explain the landscape of the modern Middle East.

In the 1960s Princeton sociologist Cyril Edwin Black defined modernization as "the process by which historically evolved institutions are adapted to the rapidly changing functions that reflect the unprecedented increase in man's knowledge, permitting control over his environment, that accompanied the scientific revolution." Central to the concept of modernization is change, often rapid change. Concomitant to modernization are the weakening of tradition, shifts in economic and political power that have often led to bloody revolution, the always filthy process of industrialization and urbanization, more extensive education of the population, pressure on workers to produce economically, increased and more centralized governmental power, greater secularization as the laws of men displace the laws of the ordained (be they kings or priests), extension of life expectancy and the physical quality of life, a shift from the extended clan to the nuclear family, and marked changes in the relationship between and among the sexes. While most in the West consider many, although perhaps not all, aspects of modernization positive, each and every one involves a degree of real cultural pain—what Black termed "the Agony of Modernization"—rooted in change. In traditional societies men and women follow the footsteps of their parents. The son of a blacksmith could expect to become a smith himself. The sons and daughters of modern Western parents have no such expectation and cannot even be certain that they will have a single career in their lifetimes.

Secularism is often a particularly distressing aspect of modernization. Academics debate the causes of secularism. Is it rooted in the process of modernization itself? Or is it a by-product of the fruits of modernization? Whatever the cause, the fact remains that more modern societies tend toward the secular. Modernity does not turn people into avowed atheists — faith persists — but in secular societies religion's centrality to public life decreases.

In 1986 Richard John Neuhaus (then a Lutheran minister, but since 1990 a Catholic priest) coined the phrase *the naked public square)* which he defined as "public life stripped of all references to religion and religiously grounded morality." "Politics," Neuhaus argued, "is in largest part a function of culture, and at the heart of culture is morality, and at the heart of morality is religion." For many Americans the trend toward secularism is painful — agonizing enough for Neuhaus to term the present American government a "regime," in that federal authority has become "distinct from the system of government prescribed by the Constitution of the United States." My point is not to equate Father John with Islamists: he fights for his views with the pen and the spoken word, not the sword. But Father John expresses the sting people of faith in the West experience as their modernized societies increasingly take on a "godless" secular character.

Islamists likewise recognize the hard reality of modernity, and they understand and have seen that modernization inevitably leads to secularization. For Islamists, secularization conflicts with the central primacy of Islam in a Muslim's life. In a Qaeda al-Jihad tape obtained by ABC news in 2004, Azzam al-Amriki (or Azzam the American, most likely southern Californian Adam Gadahn) condemned the "people of America" for "your spreading of the false religions of Christianity, democracy, capitalism, and secularism to all corners of the globe." Earlier, in an October 2002 tape, Osama bin Laden advised listeners to submit "to Islam, . . . to the happiness of this world and the hereafter, and to escape your dry, miserable, materialistic life that is without a soul." Ayman al-Zawahiri, the Egyptian doctor who serves as bin Laden's chief lieutenant, noted in a video statement released in June 2005 that real reform in the region would have to be based on three principles, the first of which was

> the rule of Shariah [code of law based on the Qur'an; also spelled *Shari'ah*] because it is the Shariah revealed from the Lord to His servants and which ensures their interests, freedom, dignity, and pride. It also safeguards their honor. And because it is the Shariah, which the Islamic nation accepts no other, after having suffered from methods that are contrary to Islam, imposed on the Islamic nation through force and repression. [*sic*]

Some of the aims of Qaeda al-Jihad, as the organization after 2001 is properly named, can be considered traditional, albeit somewhat expansive, policy goals — for example, eliminating the state of Israel and forcing the withdrawal of Western forces and the end of Western influence on and within the entire Islamic world. Nevertheless, Qaeda al-Jihad's explanation for the weakness of the "Islamic nation" vis-à-vis the West is not relative economic or social backwardness; it is the division within the Islamic world fostered by Western policies and ideologies (nationalism) and the failure of the world's Muslims to live according to the true tenets of their faith. To Islamists, modernization *is* secularization and Westernization, and as such it represents yet another set of foreign and un-Islamic concepts foisted on the *ummah*, or the Islamic "nation."

Many in the West incorrectly share the assumption that modernization is synonymous with Westernization. What we often term "Westernization" is nothing more than a modernization process that first appeared in Europe. Westernization, which often accompanies modernization, involves nonwestern people adopting

Western ways. For example, constructing a modern auto-manufacturing plant in South Korea is an example of modernization; the fact that the senior plant managers wear suits and ties is that of Westernization.

The West may be said to have invented modernization; it certainly was the first region of the world to experience it, and not entirely by accident, as I will discuss. But the West has no monopoly on modernization, as assorted east and south Asian peoples have demonstrated. Japanese, Koreans, Chinese, Malays, Indians, and many other peoples beyond the West have modernized in an ongoing process that is nearly a thousand years old. As the centuries have passed, modernization's pace has hastened, its scope has broadened, and it has shown no sign of relenting.

Islamists, a fair number of other Muslims, and many Western academics reject the proposition that the current situation in the Middle East is the result of having missed the modernization boat. Nevertheless, few Muslims place the entire blame on the West—namely "crusaders" and the "Jews"—for the current situation; most also focus on the ummah's collective religious failings over the past several centuries. At its zenith, in their view, members of the Islamic world were motivated primarily by spiritual religious energy, guided by *Shari'ah* and united under God's banner by a successor to the Prophet Muhammad—a khalifa (caliph). Therefore their solution to current problems is to recapture not the past itself, but the ideal of the past.

An ever-growing number of Islamic organizations expect to reestablish—some locally and many globally—a "righteous khalifate" modeled on the rule of the four khalifas to succeed the Prophet Muhammad. Not all such groups advocate violence or jihad, at least not openly. Qaeda al-Jihad is but one of many organizations committed to establishing a global khalifate by means of jihad.

To achieve this end, al-Qaeda (shorthand) envisions a multistage campaign. The first phase is to energize the people of the ummah through teachings and the example of successful strikes against the West, especially the most powerful Western nation, the United States. The second stage involves driving the West from the Islamic world. Achieving this goal would secure

- the withdrawal of the Western military, political, economic, and diplomatic presence in the Middle East
- the destruction of the state of Israel
- the elimination of the various regimes currently ruling a divided Islamic world, be they monarchies, republics, or dictatorships
- the establishment of a true Islamic polity in a reformed khalifate, governed by Shariah
- the end of the West's "robbing" the region of its oil and other resources

At this point, following a defeat of the West comparable to that inflicted on the Soviet Union in Afghanistan in 1989, Islam and not American-style materialism would be the new beacon directing the world toward its future. Thus Islamic political control would spread as it did in the seventh and eighth centuries, either through the strength of its ideals and example or, more likely, through these means accompanied by force. As al-Zawahiri warned in a video released on June 17, 2005,

> What I also want to assert is that driving the invading crusader troops and Jews from the countries of Islam cannot be achieved only through demonstrations and chanting slogans in the street. We can achieve reform and drive the invaders out of the countries of Islam only through fighting in the cause of God. Almighty God says, "And fight them on until no more tumult or oppression, and there prevail justice and faith in Allah altogether and everywhere."

The brand of Islam al-Qaeda and other Islamist organizations offers is a formidable force. Any ideal that can motivate human beings to use their bodies as precision-guided munitions must be taken seriously. The failures of modernization, nationalism, secularism, socialism, and monarchies throughout the Middle East provide Islamist groups with fertile ground for recruitment, not only among the poor, but also among the disaffected middle and upper classes.

Note that I use the phrase "brand of Islam." The sentiment so often heard in the West, mouthed even by the likes of U.S. president George W. Bush and British prime minister Tony Blair, that Islamic radicals have somehow "hijacked" Islam is false. The interpretation of Islam formulated by men such as bin Laden, al-Zawahiri, Sayyid Qutb, and Sayyid Abul A'la Maududi is no less a legitimate interpretation of Islam than any other. That very legitimacy makes this Islamist ideal so compelling and powerful. The first step to understanding the homicide bomber is to recognize this (albeit uncomfortable) fact.

Nevertheless, the force of the ideals underpinning the West, and especially the United States, is no less formidable and incorporates the momentum of several centuries of history. From its inception, the political experiment that became the United States has embraced a sense of exceptionalism and, since 1776, universalism. Americans proclaimed their political and economic truths to be "self-evident" and applicable to everyone, not just to the inhabitants of the British Empire in North America. The birth of the United States, celebrated in the nation's Great Seal, marked a "New Order of the Ages" ordained by "Providence."

Americanism can be defined as "a universal civic creed." Its politics were embodied in the Declaration of Independence; its economic ideals were evidenced in American eagerness to shed the shackles of mercantilism and to establish a universal system of freer trade. As Abraham Lincoln spoke at the Springfield Lyceum in January 1838,

Let reverence for the laws, be breathed by every American mother, to the lisping babe, that prattles on her lap — let it be taught in schools, in seminaries, and in colleges; let it be written in Primers, spelling books, and in Almanacs; — let it be preached from the pulpit, proclaimed in legislative halls, and enforced in courts of justice. And, in short, let it become the *political religion* of the nation; and let the old and the young, the rich and the poor, the grave and the gay, of all sexes and tongues, and colors and conditions, sacrifice unceasingly upon its altars. [italics in the original]

Americanism's continuity is evident throughout history, for example, in the philosophy of the Manifest Destiny, Lincoln's "the last best hope for mankind," Franklin Delano Roosevelt's "arsenal of democracy," the "new world order" of the 1980s, and Francis Fukuyama's "End of History."

Fukuyama, who at the time of the publication of his 1989 article was head of the Policy Planning Section of the Department of State, made the case for the "triumph of the West, of the Western *idea*," concurrent with what he saw, somewhat prematurely, as "the total exhaustion of viable systematic alternatives to Western liberalism." Fukuyama wrote that we were witnessing the

end of history as such: that is, the end point of mankind's ideological evolution and the universalization of Western liberal democracy as the final form of human government. This is not to say that there will no longer be events to fill the pages of *Foreign Affair*'s yearly summaries of international relations, for the victory of liberalism has occurred primarily in the realm of ideas or consciousness and is as yet incomplete in the real or material world. But there are powerful reasons for believing that it is the ideal that will govern the material world *in the long run*. [italics in the original]

Unfortunately, the Islamists are not totally exhausted, nor are they willing to accept as fact that Islam had become a relic of the past, or a less than viable alternative to traditional Western liberalism. But if Fukuyama was precipitate in his pronouncement, his analysis will prove itself, as he wrote, "in the long run." And it has been "in the long run" that Americanism has proved its worth.

In 1776 the American revolutionaries thought that they were turning the world upside down. They expected monarchism and mercantilism to wither away. They also expected the world to cry out for their formula for life, liberty, and happiness. In this belief the Americans were naive, but that naïveté was rooted in an overly expectant time frame and not the general march of history. By the end of the nineteenth century, the global economic system had moved in the direction the Americans had pioneered during and immediately after their revolution. Democracy and republicanism *were* on the march. In a mere century the thirteen colonies grew from a struggling confederation to the strongest industrial power on the planet. The twentieth was an American century, replete with deadly struggles but also another series of American successes. Monarchism, aristocracies, mercantilism, fascism, and communism had all fallen prey to the West and, specifically, to Americanism.

And now it is the turn of Islam, the last levee of the traditional world still standing against the rising tide of modernization, Westernization, and Americanism. The jihadists hope to build their traditionalist past into a bulwark against a wave of modernization that, if not repulsed, threatens to destroy Islam, not because it is a weak religion, but because it is central to the entirety of the lives of its believers. Whereas the majority of Christians and Jews preserved the basics of their faiths while surrendering the "public square" to modernity, whether such a retreat is possible for Islam has yet to be determined. And, to be sure, if bin Laden and men like him have their way, it will never be necessary. Modernity shall be Islamized, rather than Islam modernized.

But if the Islamists fail—this book's central thesis is they will—Islam's shift from the center to the periphery of the "public square" will be excruciating. Perhaps we are already witnessing that agony: just as in its war with America, Japan's kamikazes were desperate harbingers of the empire's end, the homicide bombers herald the death throes of political Islam.

A note on definitions is appropriate. The use of Western terminology to describe Muslims is inexact and leaves one open to such charges as "Orientalism." What, after all, does it mean to say that someone is a "Muslim fundamentalist"? Would that person call himself or herself a "fundamentalist"? A terrorist? A radical? Should one simply identify all Muslims, individually and collectively, as nothing but Muslims? To do so would undoubtedly lead to accusations of the broad-brush treatment of an enormous community, failing to differentiate between those who murder the innocent and those who do not.

So, I offer these definitions:

Islamism: the ideal of reestablishing the khalifate and
   its global dominion
Islamist: one who believes in that ideal
Jihadist: one who believes in the ideal and is willing
   to kill (perhaps even himself or herself) to achieve it

Each chapter begins with a quotation from the Egyptian Sayyid Qutb (1906–66). A political philosopher and member of the Muslim Brotherhood, he earned a master's degree in education from what is now the University of Northern Colorado. He was hanged in Egypt in 1966. Most specialists and jihadists consider Qutb one of the fathers—"the Godfather" to some—of the Islamist movement.

Chapter 1
"Slay the Idolators
Wherever You Find Them"

Can anyone say that if [the seventh-century khalifas]
Abu Bakr, 'Umar or 'Othman had been satisfied that the Roman
and Persian powers were not going to attack the Arabian
peninsula, they would not have striven to spread the message of
Islam throughout the world? How could the message of Islam
have spread when it faced such material obstacles as the
political system of the state, the socio-economic system based
on races and classes, and behind all these, the military power
of the government?

—Sayyid Qutb, Milestones

The Near East was the world's first region to achieve a level of "civilization." The great river valleys of the Nile, Tigris, and Euphrates were the sites of the first great states of the ancient world. Social scientists offer various theories for these developments. Some suggest that great civilizations began along rivers because of the farmers' need to work collectively to irrigate fields. Others argue that the rise of the early states reflected man's insatiable quest for power over his fellow human beings. Still others propose that the need for collective defense against marauders led to the creation of the ancient state. Whatever the causes, civilization in western Eurasia began in the Fertile Crescent, the region stretching from the head of the Persian Gulf in the east, northwestward along the valleys of the Tigris and Euphrates rivers, then south

13

and west through the Levant—now Syria, Lebanon, Palestine, Israel, and Jordan—and then across the Sinai to the Nile and south along that great river.

If warfare was not the driving force behind creating the Fertile Crescent's states, it most certainly played a significant role in their development. Empires rose and fell, succumbing most often to invasion by those with more advanced techniques and tools of warfare. Egyptians, Babylonians, Mesopotamians, Assyrians, Persians, Greeks, Macedonians, Romans, and others rose to dominance and then fell from power.

As these states grew, styles of warfare changed. Spearmen and archers dominated the Early Bronze Age; during the High Bronze Age (1600 BC–1200 BC), the domestication of the horse made war chariots bearing archers the dominant military weapons system. The Iron Age briefly witnessed a revival of the infantry, but by 1000 BC, Assyrian cavalry—mounted soldiers armed with spears or bows—swept all before them. Their principal weapon was the short, composite recurved bow constructed of wood, animal horn, and tendon. The mounted archer gave the Assyrians an impressive combination of mobility and firepower and for more than a millennium remained the symbol of Eastern warfare.

The first of the great Eastern empires to rule the entire Fertile Crescent was that of the Achaemenids. In the mid-sixth century BC, Cyrus "the Great," the first conqueror-king to be so named in western Eurasia, established the Persian Empire. By the 520s Cyrus and his sons had spread their dominion to Ionia along the western coast of the Anatolian Peninsula, south to Egypt, north to the Eurasian steppe, and east to India.

The Achaemenids' accomplishments were many. Cyrus was the first conqueror to contemplate the conquest of the entire world. He died trying in fact, fighting the Scythians in the Jaxartes River valley in 530 BC. The Achaemenids were in the forefront of state administration. Cyrus divided his huge kingdom into satrapies, each ruled by a satrap, or king. Cyrus and his successors ruled as *shahnshah* (king of kings). The Achaemenids also sought to tie their domain together with a system of roads; Cyrus is often reputed to have established the world's first postal system.

Cyrus also embraced the reality of a multicultural empire. A cuneiform cylinder discovered in Iraq in the late nineteenth century chronicled Cyrus's 539 BC conquest of Babylon and his respect for the city's people and their religious faiths and customs. For example, he liberated the Jews, ending their Babylonian captivity, and allowed them to return to Jerusalem. The document is the oldest extant record of what could be considered a declaration, however limited, of human rights.

The dominant religion of the Achaemenids' era was Zoroastrianism. Zoroaster, the founder of the religion, lived in what today is northeastern Iran centuries, perhaps as much as a millennium, before the advent of the Persian Empire. Zoroastrianism was initially monotheistic. Its followers worshiped Ahura Mazda, a deity who communicated with humans through Attributes (Angels), termed "Amesha Spenta," or Bounteous Immortals, that sometimes took the forms of spirits and at other times took the human form. The sacred texts of Zoroastrianism, the Gathas, related how Ahura Mazda created the world and all that was in it, including men and women, who, like the supreme deity, were fundamentally good. Zoroastrians believed they had to strive constantly in their lives to reach heaven by accepting Ahura Mazda's revelations and acting accordingly. People faced judgment on the third day after their deaths, when Ahura Mazda weighed their good thoughts, words, and deeds against the bad ones. The souls of those who possessed a positive balance went to heaven; the rest went to an underworld, a place of punishment and retribution. Zoroastrian beliefs also included a judgment day, the resurrection of the good, and the coming of a messiah—the Saoshyant—who would be born miraculously of a virgin.

The Achaemenids accepted Zoroastrianism, which could be considered the Persian state religion. Darius, a somewhat distant

Achaemenid cousin who in 522 BC succeeded Cyrus's son Cambyses II, proclaimed, "I worshipped Ahura Mazda. I am the King by grace of Ahura Mazda."

Nevertheless, by the sixth century BC a religion that was initially a monotheistic creed had become polytheistic, perhaps because of its connection to, and the needs of, a multicultural empire. The Persians allowed subject peoples to worship their own gods, and a few of these, most notably Mithra, found their way into the Zoroastrian pantheon. In fact by the time of Cyrus, the religion included a powerful new deity — Angra Mainyu, the Satan-like god of darkness and evil who possessed his own corps of demon-like servants. Nonetheless, to the extent that Zoroastrianism was a state church, the state, not the church, was dominant.

Despite the Achaemenids' relative tolerance, the empire was not without problems or internal tensions. While various ethnic and religious groups retained certain rights, individuals remained subject to the monarch's will. The huge treasuries Alexander's conquering Macedonians discovered suggest that not only was Persian taxation substantial, it was heavier than necessary and may have throttled economic development. While the satrap system was a notable administrative advance, the empire was far too extensive to be run either efficiently or securely. Corruption was rampant and rebellions frequent.

The main strength of the Persians' army lay in its sheer numbers; at sea they relied on subject peoples — primarily the Phoenicians of the Levant coast and the Ionian Greeks — for ships and crews. The Persian navy's loyalty and effectiveness were thus suspect, and the Phoenicians' reluctance may have prevented Cambyses II, after his conquest of Egypt, from advancing farther westward to attack Carthage, which had begun as a Phoenician colony. The Persian army was huge by contemporary standards and included spearmen, swordsmen, cavalry, chariots, and swarms of the kind of mounted archers who had long dominated Eastern warfare. Despite these strengths, by the late sixth century the Persians realized

that they needed (and lacked) an effective heavy infantry component and began to recruit and increasingly rely on Greek mercenaries.

The Greek style of warfare had developed along markedly
different lines from those pursued in the East. The Greeks were
weak in cavalry but strong in heavy infantry and sea power.

Initially, as had been true in the East, horsemen dominated
warfare in the Aegean basin. Aristotle noted in *Politics* that the
Greeks had relied "for strength and superiority in war . . . on cavalry; indeed, without discipline, infantry are useless." But by the
sixth century BC the mounted arm had lost its primacy around the
Aegean to disciplined, heavily armored, spear-armed infantry—
hoplites—fighting in a tight rectangular formation called the "phalanx." Militarily, the phalanx formation had few strengths and many
weaknesses. Defensively, the formation of massed spearmen was
virtually impregnable to cavalry attacking from the front; offen-
sively, the combination of mass and momentum made the phalanx
difficult to stop when it thrust forward. But the phalanx possessed
dreadful battlefield mobility, and large formations were hard to
maintain in the confusion of battle. Well-handled mobile cavalry
could crush the flanks and rear of any spear formation.

The Greeks' adoption of the phalanx grew as much, and perhaps more, from political necessity than from military requirements.
The geography of Greece—mountains cut by valleys—did not lend
itself to the cavalry warfare tactics used in the Fertile Crescent's
largely open plains. When a given Greek city's manpower reached
the point where it could field a large phalanx, the formation could
usually master the threat posed by enemy cavalry, which was usually small in number. But the driving force behind the shift to the
phalanx was the desire of a growing segment of the population,
broader than the old cavalry aristocracy, to defend their towns
and their own interests and thereby acquire political power. By
agreeing to shoulder the responsibilities of military service these
citizens gained political rights in their polis, a change that led to

developing the concepts of politics and democracy. This ideal of "civic militarism"—acceptance by a broad segment of the population of the responsibility to fight in return for political rights and power—was absent in the vast expanse of the Persian Empire.

Reliance on the hoplite phalanx had another major impact on Greek warfare. Since the soldiers doing the fighting were citizens, they sought victories that would allow them to return to their homes more quickly. As a result, the Greeks fought decisive, climatic battles that could effectively end struggles in a single day.

Commanders of the fleets of the larger Greek city-states, most notably Athens, used these same concepts. Triremes—war galleys with three tiers of oars on each side, rowed by free citizens—formed the core of the Athenian thalassocracy's sea power. These Greek sailors knew they were fighting for home and city, giving them far greater motivation than the coastal regions' subject peoples who contributed forces, at times under duress, to the Persian Empire.

In the early fifth century BC, the Persian *shahnshah* Darius decided to extend his empire to include Greece. In 498 the Athenians had captured and burned Sardis, the capital of the Persian satrapy of Lydia. In 494 Darius suppressed an Ionian Greek rebellion that the Athenians had supported.

Darius launched two invasions of Greece; both failed. The first ended in 492 when a storm destroyed the Persian fleet off Cape Athos. The second attempt, a cross-Aegean amphibious effort that lacked cavalry, failed at Marathon in 490 when an Athenian phalanx easily destroyed a large force of Persian infantry. Athenian casualties were about 200; the Persians lost more than 6,000 men.

In 488 Xerxes, Darius's son and successor, launched a huge invasion by land and sea. In a feat of engineering brilliance, the Persians bridged the Hellespont and crossed from Asia into Europe. After a small force of Spartan hoplites and other Greeks delayed them at the narrow pass of Thermopylae, it was too late in the campaigning season when the Persians took Athens to complete the victory over the Greeks. Xerxes attacked at sea, but the Athenians and the other Greek naval contingents defeated the Persian fleet at Salamis.

Xerxes withdrew with the bulk of his army to Asia, leaving behind General Mardonius and 40,000 men, the most that could be sustained over the winter in Thessaly. When the campaigning season opened in the spring of 479, the Greeks maneuvered Mardonius into a position where his cavalry could not dominate the battlefield, and they destroyed the Persian army at Plataea.

Over the next 150 years the Greek city-states fought each other while a new threat rose to the north in Macedon. The Macedonian rulers were monarchs in the old style. By the reign of Philip II (359–336) the Macedonians had adapted the best elements of Eastern and Western warfare into their army. They vastly improved the power of the Greek phalanx; developed an effective cavalry force, which the Greeks had always lacked; and adopted the Persian concept of world conquest into the vision for their empire. Philip meant to use this force to subjugate outright and intimidate into submission the Greek city-states and then to conquer the vast Persian Empire. Unfortunately for Philip, an assassin ended his dream in 336.

The throne passed to his son, Alexander the Great. After securing his rear in campaigns in Thrace, Illyria, and Greece, the twenty-two-year-old Macedonian king crossed the Hellespont in 334. In less than four years and against long odds, Alexander's army won a series of battles that effectively destroyed the Persian Empire, overrunning Anatolia, the Levant, Egypt, and the area we know now as Iraq. He continued his advance to the east for three more years before he was checked in 327 along what is now the Jhelum River in Pakistan. Four years later Alexander died in Babylon.

Alexander's empire was short lived. After his death it quickly disintegrated into "Hellenic" successor states centered in Macedonia, Iraq, and Egypt and ruled by Alexander's former generals. Many of the Persian Empire's fragmented eastern parts eventually coalesced under Parthian rule. That empire lasted from 250 BC to AD 226. The Hellenism Alexander bequeathed to the world was a fusion of Greek and Persian concepts, and more of the latter than the former influenced the political realm. Hellenic armies looked quite a bit like those Alexander had fielded, but they lacked the ideal of "civic militarism" that had once been so dominant in Greece. The Parthians were purely Eastern in both their political and military spheres. On the battlefield they relied on heavily armored cavalry, or cataphracts, and swarms of mobile, mounted archers.

To the west, in Rome, the Greek tradition of civic militarism reappeared. Roman soldiers were citizens who marched under the banner SPQR, or *Senatus Populusque Romanum* (the Senate and people of Rome). Their governmental system rested on the concept of the people's sovereignty; Rome was a republic—a term derived from the Latin *res publica* (public thing).

Rome's disciplined legions conquered the entire Mediterranean basin. They were ultimately checked in the east by the Parthians, who defeated Crassus at Carrhae in 53 BC, and in the north by the Germans, who destroyed Consul Varus's army at the Teutorburgerwald in AD 9.

At first glance, the history of western Eurasia during the ancient period might well seem undifferentiated. In both the East and the West, empires and states rose and fell. Monarchy was the most prevalent form of government. Religion, whether Zoroastrianism or the myth-based pantheons of the Greeks or Romans, served the state.

But already there were themes evident in the West that set it apart from the East. Greece and Rome bequeathed to the world the ideal that "civilized" and expansive governments, and not only small tribal communities, could embrace the concepts of democracy, republicanism, civic militarism, and the rights of the individual. While in the West these concepts did not fully mature by twenty-first-century standards and during long stretches of history such ideals were not to be found, in the East they were entirely absent among the ruling elites of large states. Further, in the West the military tradition focused on disciplined heavy infantry, shock tactics, and decisive battles. In the East cavalry predominated; archers on foot or horseback softened up an enemy before the mounted arm completed his destruction. When Eastern armies did field heavy infantry, the units usually consisted of mercenaries, hirelings from the West. The Greeks and Romans developed their own sea power, both military and commercial, and Athens became the world's first thalassocracy. The Persians relied on subject peoples and never fully exploited the opportunities offered at sea. Thus there were no Eastern thalassocracies.

The rise of Christianity during the first through the sixth centuries and of Islam during the seventh through the tenth centuries widened and deepened the divide between East and West. Although both religions began in the same region—what we now consider the Middle East—Christianity shifted its center of gravity westward and developed within a Greco-Roman tradition. Islam remained an Eastern religion.

Space prohibits an in-depth discussion of the three great monotheistic religions—Judaism, Christianity, and Islam—born in the Near East. I will limit my discussion to certain aspects of their nature and development: universalism, the concept of heaven, the ordained use of violence, the notion of "neighbor," and the relationship between the church and the state.

The biblical account of the Jews offers a glimpse into humankind's early history in the Fertile Crescent. Peoples shifted from a nomadic to a settled agricultural existence, then fled famine in one region and relocated to another. When Yahweh demanded that Abraham kill his beloved son Isaac but then prevented the death at the last moment, the transition changed from human to animal sacrifice. Elsewhere in the Torah conquerors came and went, states rose and fell, and peoples were enslaved and liberated.

One notable aspect of Judaism involved universality, or rather the lack thereof. Judaism was monotheistic; there was only one

God—Yahweh—and the Jews were his "chosen people," bound by belief and ethnicity. As such, Judaism had no universal impulse, akin to Christianity or Islam, and no desire to either proselytize or conquer the world.

Nevertheless, the Jews were prepared, at God's direction, to conquer their small corner of the globe—their "promised land"—and woe to those who stood in their path. The Jews, given their special covenant relationship with the Almighty, looked somewhat askance at non-Jews. Leviticus 19 commanded, "Thou shalt not avenge, nor bear any grudge against the children of thy people, but thou shalt love thy neighbor as thyself." How broadly the ancient Jews defined the term "neighbor" remains a subject of scholarly debate, but the reference to "thy people" suggests a certain narrow outlook.

The ancient Jews of the Torah did not believe in the existence of a heaven. Judaism was a religion focused on *mitzvah,* or actions performed in accord with one's religious beliefs. Jews believed in earthly rewards and punishments.

Among the Jews the relationship between what we today term "the church" and "the state" varied over their long history. There were times, under kings such as David and Solomon, when the church and the state were intertwined. But throughout most of Jewish history, especially the early formative period, the Jews often lived as a people ruled by non-Jews and, after the days of the Roman Empire, as part of a global Diaspora.

While Christianity evolved from Judaism, the new faith differed markedly from its antecedent. Unlike Judaism, Christianity was, or at least quickly became, a universal creed. Anyone could become a Christian, and the early fathers of the church made every effort to spread the faith.

Christianity was also, at least initially, pacific. In the Gospel of Matthew, Jesus informed his audience, "Blessed are the peacemakers: for they shall be called the children of God." (Matt. 5:9) He then superseded an Old Testament directive: "Ye have heard that it hath been said, An eye for an eye, and a tooth for a tooth: But I say unto you, That ye resist not evil: but whosoever shall smite thee on thy right cheek, turn to him the other also." (Matt. 5:38–40) In the Garden of Gethsemane after Judas's betrayal, Peter drew his sword and sliced off the right ear of Malchus, a servant of the high priest; Jesus healed the man before being led off to trial, torture, and crucifixion. (John 18:10)

Christianity further expanded the Jewish concept of "neighbor" beyond the bounds of the group. The Letter of Paul to the Romans commanded, "Owe no man any thing, but to love one another: for he that loveth another hath fulfilled the law. . . . Love worketh no ill to his neighbour: therefore love is the fulfilling of the law." (13:10)

Christianity, unlike Judaism, embraced the concept of an afterlife, although the image of heaven was less of an earthly paradise than of a spiritual state. Matthew related,

> The same day [Jesus] came to the Sadducees, which say that there is no resurrection, and asked him, saying, Master, Moses said, If a man die, having no children, his brother shall marry his wife, and raise up seed unto his brother. Now there were with us seven brethren: and the first, when he had married a wife, deceased, and, having no issue, left his wife unto his brother: Likewise the second also, and the third, unto the seventh. And last of all the woman died also. Therefore in the resurrection whose wife shall she be of the seven? for they all had her. Jesus answered and said unto them, Ye do err, not knowing the scriptures, nor the power of God. For in the resurrection they neither marry, nor are given in marriage, but are as the angels of God in heaven. [Matt. 22:29]

The new faith also contained important elements that would later prove critical in the relationship of the church and the state in the West. Again Matthew:

Then went the Pharisees, and took counsel how they might entangle him [Jesus] in his talk. And they sent out unto him their disciples with the Herodians, saying, Master, we know that thou art true, and teachest the way of God in truth, neither carest thou for any man: for thou regardest not the person of men. Tell us therefore, What thinkest thou? Is it lawful to give tribute unto [Tiberias] Caesar, or not? But Jesus perceived their wickedness, and said, Why tempt ye me, ye hypocrites? Shew me the tribute money. And they brought unto him a penny. And he saith unto them, Whose is this image and superscription? They say unto him, Caesar's. Then saith he unto them, Render therefore unto Caesar the things which are Caesar's; and unto God the things that are God's. When they had heard these words, they marveled, and left him, and went their way. [Matt. 22:21]

There are, in fact, different ways to interpret Jesus's response. Under contemporary Jewish law what was due Caesar was, in fact, nothing. Nevertheless, Christ's admonition has generally been interpreted to allow a separation of church and state in the Christian community.

Another important gospel passage relating to this theme is also found in Matthew.

When Jesus came into the coasts of Caesarea Philippi, he asked his disciples, saying, Whom do men say that I the Son of man am? And they said, Some say that thou art John the Baptist: some, Elias; and others, Jeremias, or one of the prophets. He saith unto them, But whom say ye that I am? And Simon Peter answered and said, Thou art the Christ, the Son of the living God. And Jesus answered and said unto him, Blessed art thou, Simon Barjona: for flesh and blood hath not revealed it unto thee, but my Father which is in heaven. And I say also unto thee, That thou art Peter, and upon this rock I will build my church; and the gates of hell shall not prevail against it. And I will give unto thee the keys of the kingdom of heaven: and whatsoever thou shalt bind on earth shall be bound in heaven: and whatsoever thou shalt loose on earth shall be loosed in heaven. Then charged he his disciples that they should tell no man that he was Jesus the Christ.

The instructions Jesus gave to Simon-Peter provided Christianity with an enormous flexibility to meet the demands posed by a rapidly changing world. Whatever the church's teachings, the popes were later free to reinterpret doctrine, and if necessary even dogma, and to determine what would be "bound" or "loosed" not only on earth but also in heaven.

The admonition to "render unto Caesar" proved particularly useful to Christians; for most of Christianity's first three centuries of existence, while it thrived and expanded, it did so as an at-best tolerated yet often persecuted alien sect within the Roman Empire. By Constantine's time about a quarter to a third of the empire's 60 million people were Christians, but they held no temporal power. Only in 313 did Christians find relief in the Emperor Constantine's Edict of Milan, which ended persecution of Christians in the Roman Empire. The emperor's Christian mother, Helena, traveled to the Holy Land and searched for the sites of Jesus's crucifixion, an effort that reconnected a church centered in Rome to Jerusalem. In 375 the Emperor Gratian shifted his responsibilities as Roman *pontifex maximus* (supreme pontiff) to the pope.

By the eighth century the pope had become a temporal as well as a spiritual authority. He ruled the papal states in central Italy and proclaimed the doctrine of *plenitudo potestatis*—literally, a plenitude of power that enabled the pope to tell monarchs how to run their domains—throughout the Christian world.

This rise to papal authority did not last. Kings and princes had little desire to do the pope's bidding. By the early sixteenth century, when Martin Luther began the process that would become known as the Protestant Reformation, the Roman Catholic Church had already lost most of its temporal power. What remained would be gone by the end of the Thirty Years' War in 1648. Today the temporal rule of the Roman Catholic popes is confined to tiny Vatican City with its nearly 1,000 inhabitants.

Whereas Christianity began as a set of beliefs divorced for centuries from political power, Islam's purely religious phase was short lived. A dozen years after the Prophet Mohammad received his first revelations, his Medina-based followers began their war against the Meccans; a decade later the Muslims began to raid the territories of the Byzantine and Sassanian (Persian) empires.

The Prophet Muhammad was born in Mecca, in the Hijaz (the western Red Sea coast of Saudi Arabia), about AD 570. At the age of forty he began to receive revelations from Allah via the Angel Gabriel. The revelations—known as the suras (chapters) of the Qur'an—continued until the Prophet's death in 632.

While Islam claims to be built on the foundations of Christianity and Judaism, the Qur'an does not include any texts from the Christian New Testament or the Jewish Torah. Nor do Muslims read these books or accept them as entirely truthful. Muslims reject the divinity of Jesus, deny that he was crucified, and do not believe in his resurrection. The Jesus of the Qur'an is a prophet, one in a long line leading to Muhammad. Some Muslims believe that New Testament's references to the Second Coming of the Holy Spirit (or Holy Ghost) are, in fact, prophecies of the coming of Muhammad. In effect Muslims believe that the Jews and Christians are guilty, at the minimum, of the misinterpretation—perhaps even the willful misrepresentation—of their own sacred texts.

Like Christianity, and unlike Judaism, Islam quickly became a universal creed. Anyone could become a Muslim—that is, someone who submits to Allah's will and pursues the Five Pillars of Islam: the profession of faith (*shahada*), prayer (*salat*), almsgiving (*zakat*), fasting (*sawm*), and, if at all practical, pilgrimage (*hajj*).

As was true of Christianity, Islam also envisioned an afterlife. But the heavenly rewards awaiting Muslims were more physical than spiritual. The fifty-sixth sura, "The Event," relates the following:

> When the great event comes to pass, there is no belying its coming to pass—abasing (one party), exalting (the other), when the earth shall be shaken with a (severe) shaking, and the mountains shall be made to crumble with (an awful) crumbling, so that they shall be as scattered dust. And you shall be three sorts. Then (as to) the companions of the right hand; how happy are the companions of the right hand! And (as to) the companions of the left hand; how wretched are the companions of the left hand! And the foremost are the foremost, these are they who are drawn nigh (to Allah), in the gardens of bliss. A numerous company from among the first, and a few from among the latter. On thrones decorated, reclining on them, facing one another. Round about them shall go youths never altering in age, with goblets and ewers and a cup of pure drink; they shall not be affected with headache thereby, nor shall they get exhausted, and fruits such as they choose, and the flesh of fowl such as they desire. And pure, beautiful ones, the like of the hidden pearls: a reward for what they used to do. They shall not hear therein vain or sinful discourse, except the word peace, peace. And the companions of the right hand; how happy are the companions of the right hand! Amid thornless lote-trees, and banana-trees (with fruits), one above another. And extended shade, and water flowing constantly, and abundant fruit, neither intercepted nor forbidden, and exalted thrones. Surely We have made them to grow into a (new) growth, then We have made them virgins, loving, equals in age, for the sake of the companions of the right hand.

A numerous company from among the first, and a numerous company from among the last.

The definition of "neighbor," which had broadened from Judaism to Christianity, took a backward step with Islam. Sura 48:29 reads in part, "Muhammad is the Apostle of Allah, and those with him are firm of heart against the unbelievers, compassionate among themselves."

Nor did Islam continue the trend away from vengeance, or the notion of "an eye for an eye," and toward the New Testament's admonition "to turn the other cheek." For example, verses thirty-three and thirty-four of the fifth sura state,

The punishment of those who wage war against Allah and His apostle and strive to make mischief in the land is only this, that they should be murdered or crucified or their hands and their feet should be cut off on opposite sides or they should be imprisoned; this shall be as a disgrace for them in this world, and in the hereafter they shall have a grievous chastisement, except those who repent before you have them in your power; so know that Allah is Forgiving, Merciful.

The question of religiously sanctioned violence also relates to conversion. Sura 2:256 reads:

There is no compulsion in religion; truly the right way has become clearly distinct from error; therefore, whoever disbelieves in the *Shaitan* [the Adversary or Satan] and believes in Allah he indeed has laid hold on the firmest handle, which shall not break off, and Allah is Hearing, Knowing.

But verse eighty-nine of the fourth sura suggests a quite different approach to nonbelievers.

They desire that you should disbelieve as they have dis-
believed, so that you might be (all) alike; therefore take
not from among them friends until they fly (their homes)
in Allah's way; but if they turn back, then seize them and
kill them wherever you find them, and take not from
among them a friend or a helper.

Likewise in the fifth verse of the ninth sura:

So when the sacred months have passed away, then slay
the idolaters wherever you find them, and take them captives and besiege them and lie in wait for them in every
ambush, then if they repent and keep up prayer and pay
the poor-rate [*jizya*], leave their way free to them; surely
Allah is Forgiving, Merciful.

Such evident contradictions may well bring to mind the admonition in the Judeo-Christian tradition that "you can justify virtually any action using the Bible." But Islam is somewhat different.
Innumerable inconsistencies, often linked to a given time's circum-
stances, exist within the narrative. Muslims address this problem
partly through interpretation but also by the application of *naskh*—
a doctrinal abrogation based on sura 2:106 combined with the
chronological order of revelation. The verse in question from the
second sura reads, "Whatever communications We abrogate or
cause to be forgotten, We bring one better than it or like it. Do
you not know that Allah has power over all things?" Because
the suras of the Qur'an are traditionally arranged by length
and not by the order of their revelation, one cannot determine
their chronology from their order. The three verses quoted above
from suras 2, 4, and 9 are Medinan suras and were, in fact, revealed in that relative order. Scholars of the Qur'an consider sura
2 to be the 87th of the 114 suras revealed to Muhammad, sura 4
to be the 92nd, and sura 9 to be the 113th. In other words, to

the extent that inconsistencies exist, the violent suras 4 and 9 take precedence over the oft-quoted tolerant sura 2 because they were revealed later.

That does not mean that all or most Muslims think that non-believers should be crucified or forced to convert or to pay the *jizya*—a head tax levied on Christians and Jews living under Islamic rule. Nevertheless, the Qur'an offers those so inclined, through the application of the *naskh* doctrine, the option of taking a rather forceful and violent line toward nonbelievers.

One of the most significant differences between Christianity and Islam involves the relationship of the church, or mosque, to the state. With regard to scripture, no sura in the Qur'an offers the comparable flexibility of Jesus's admonition to "render therefore unto Caesar the things which are Caesar's; and unto God the things that are God's." We find the reasoning behind such a division of sovereignty in John's (18: 33–37) account of the passion.

> Then Pilate entered into the judgment hall again, and called Jesus, and said unto him, Art thou the King of the Jews? Jesus answered him, Sayest thou this thing of thyself, or did others tell it thee of me? Pilate answered, Am I a Jew? Thine own nation and the chief priests have delivered thee unto me: what hast thou done? Jesus answered, My kingdom is not of this world: if my kingdom were of this world, then would my servants fight, that I should not be delivered to the Jews: but now is my kingdom not from hence. Pilate therefore said unto him, Art thou a king then? Jesus answered, Thou sayest that I am a king. To this end was I born, and for this cause came I into the world, that I should bear witness unto the truth. Every one that is of the truth heareth my voice.

Conversely, Allah's kingdom was most definitely "of this world" and the next, and his followers were prepared to fight. Sura 2:107

reads, "Do you not know that Allah's is the kingdom ["dominion" or "sovereignty" in some translations] of the heavens and the earth, and that besides Allah you have no guardian or helper?" Sura 3:26 continues the theme: "Say: O Allah, Master of the Kingdom! Thou givest the kingdom to whomsoever Thou pleasest and takest away the kingdom from whomsoever Thou pleasest, and Thou exaltest whom Thou pleasest and abasest whom Thou pleasest in Thine hand is the good; surely, Thou hast power over all things."

The combination of sacred texts and the historic fact that the Prophet Muhammad, unlike Jesus, assumed the religious, political, and military leadership of his people ensured that the practice of Islam, far more than Christianity, demanded of its followers a holistic approach to life. In many ways, this integration of religion into politics makes Islam such a powerful faith. Unfortunately, that same holism makes it more difficult for those in the Islamic world to adjust to the process and pressures of rapid modernization.

In AD 622 Muhammad fled with his followers from Mecca to Medina and opened his campaign against his enemies. Despite often being outnumbered, the Muslims won most of the battles and by 627 had secured Mecca.

Amid the turmoil of Islam's first war, a rift developed between Muhammad and the Jews of Medina. The Prophet changed the direction he faced when praying from Jerusalem to Mecca, and at the war's end he began a campaign of what would today be termed "ethnic cleansing." According to the *Hadith* (sayings of the Prophet collected by a follower) of Salih Muslim (Book 19, #4364 and #4366):

> It has been narrated on the authority of Ibn Umar that the Jews of Banu Nadir and Banu Quraizi fought against the Messenger of Allah (may peace be upon him) who expelled Banu Nadir, and allowed Quraiza to stay on, and granted favour to them until they too fought against him. Then he killed their men, and distributed their women,

children and properties among the Muslims, except that some of them had joined the Messenger of Allah (may peace be upon him) who granted them security. They embraced Islam. The Messenger of Allah (may peace be upon him) turned out all the Jews of Medina. Banu Qainuqa' (the tribe of 'Abdullah b. Salim) and the Jews of Banu Haritha and every other Jew who was in Medina.

It has been narrated by 'Umar b. al-Khattib that he heard the Messenger of Allah (may peace be upon him) say: I will expel the Jews and Christians from the Arabian Peninsula and will not leave any but Muslims.

Muslims beyond the Arabian Peninsula did not observe such practices. Muhammad considered Jews and Christians "people of the book," and as such they were preferred over polytheists and pagans. Jews and Christians could accept a protective covenant (*dhimma*) that allowed them to practice their religion, albeit in an unassuming manner. Sura 9:29 directed Muslims to

fight those who believe not in Allah nor the Last Day, nor hold that forbidden which hath been forbidden by Allah and His Messenger, nor acknowledge the religion of Truth, (even if they are) of the People of the Book, until they pay the Jizya with willing submission, and feel themselves subdued.

While Jews and Christians were better off than other religions' followers, the "people of the book" were nonetheless subjects inhabiting a lower rank. Their treatment varied over time, but the fundamental nature of the *dhimma* (contract) is evident in the infamous "Pact of Omar," a template for Muslim-*dhimmi* (Christian or Jewish subject) relations drafted during the khalifate of Umar, probably between 717 and 720.

In the name of God, the Merciful and Compassionate. This is a letter to the servant of God Umar [ibn al-Khattab], Commander of the Faithful, from the Christians of such-and-such a city. When you came against us, we asked you for safe-conduct (aman) for ourselves, our descendants, our property, and the people of our community, and we undertook the following obligations toward you:

We shall not build, in our cities or in their neighborhood, new monasteries, Churches, convents, or monks' cells, nor shall we repair, by day or by night, such of them as fall in ruins or are situated in the quarters of the Muslims.

We shall keep our gates wide open for passersby and travelers. We shall give board and lodging to all Muslims who pass our way for three days.

We shall not give shelter in our churches or in our dwellings to any spy, nor hide him from the Muslims.

We shall not teach the Qur'an to our children.

We shall not manifest our religion publicly nor convert anyone to it. We shall not prevent any of our kin from entering Islam if they wish it.

We shall show respect toward the Muslims, and we shall rise from our seats when they wish to sit.

We shall not seek to resemble the Muslims by imitating any of their garments, the *qalansuwa* [conical cap worn under the turban], the turban, footwear, or the parting of the hair. We shall not speak as they do, nor shall we adopt their *kunyas* [nickname such as Abu ____].

We shall not mount on saddles, nor shall we gird swords nor bear any kind of arms nor carry them on our persons.

We shall not engrave Arabic inscriptions on our seals.

We shall not sell fermented drinks.

We shall clip [the hair on] the fronts of our heads.

We shall always dress in the same way wherever we
    may be, and we shall bind the *zunar* [sash] round our
    waists.

We shall not display our crosses or our books in the
    roads or markets of the Muslims. We shall use only
    clappers in our churches very softly. We shall not
    raise our voices when following our dead. We shall
    not show lights on any of the roads of the Muslims
    or in their markets. We shall not bury our dead near
    the Muslims.

We shall not take slaves who have been allotted to
    Muslims.

We shall not build houses overtopping the houses of
    the Muslims.

(When I brought the letter to Umar, may God be pleased
    with him, he added, "We shall not strike a Muslim.")

We accept these conditions for ourselves and for the
    people of our community, and in return we receive
    safe-conduct.

If we in any way violate these undertakings for which we
    ourselves stand surety, we forfeit our covenant
    [dhimma], and we become liable to the penalties for
    contumacy and sedition.

Umar ibn al-Khittab replied: Sign what they ask, but add
two clauses and impose them in addition to those which
they have undertaken. They are: "They shall not buy anyone made prisoner by the Muslims," and "Whoever strikes
a Muslim with deliberate intent shall forfeit the protection of this pact."

Christians and Jews formed a distinct minority within the Arabian Peninsula, but that would change dramatically as Islam began
to spread. In 628 the Prophet Muhammad addressed letters to his

neighbors, including the rulers of the Byzantine and Sassanian empires. The letter to the Byzantine emperor Heraclius read as follows:

> In the name of Allah, the Beneficent, the Merciful. This letter is from Muhammad the slave of Allah and his Apostle to Heraclius, the ruler of the Byzantines. Peace be upon him who follows the right path. Furthermore, I invite you to Islam and if you become a Muslim you will be safe, and Allah will double your reward, and if you reject this invitation of Islam you will be committing a sin by misguiding your subjects. And I recite to you Allah's statement: "O followers of the Book! Come to an equitable proposition between us and you that we shall not serve any but Allah and (that) we shall not associate aught with Him, and (that) some of us shall not take others for lords besides Allah; but if they turn back, then say: Bear witness that we are Muslims." [Qur'an 3:64]
>
> —Muhammad Rasul-ullah
> [Muhammad the Messenger of Allah]

What if Heraclius refused to "become a Muslim"? Was the message from the Prophet nothing more than a spiritual calling, or was it a not-so-veiled physical threat? The subsequent course of events indicates that it was the latter. Even before Muhammad's death in 632, Arab forces initiated a series of raids into Byzantine and Persian territories. Following the Prophet's passing his successor, the khalifa Abu Bakr, primarily resolidified Muslim control within the Arabian Peninsula in campaigns collectively known as the *ridda* (apostasy) wars. The first khalifa nevertheless found the time and resources to set in motion an outright invasion, and in 634 the Muslims defeated the Byzantines at Ajnadayn in Palestine.

The Muslims were coming! And the question of what drove them forward is critical, but scholars often gloss over it. Historians often portray the trans-Arabian military offensives that followed

Muhammad's death as unplanned extensions of the *ridda* wars. Albert Hourani wrote in *A History of the Arab Peoples*, "The momentum of action carried . . . into the frontier regions of the great empires and then, as resistance proved weak, into their hearts." As if the successes of Arab-Muslim conquests that stretched from the Pyrenees to the Hindu Kush in a century were not spectacular enough, we are asked to believe that they were wholly serendipitous. Nevertheless, only a few scholars argue otherwise. Patricia Crone, in her *Meccan Trade and the Rise of Islam*, concluded that "Muhammad had to conquer, his followers liked to conquer, and his deity told him to conquer: do we need any more?"

Whatever the truth, the important point is that the interpretations of modern-day Islamists are more in line with Crone's than with Hourani's. In *Milestones* Sayyid Qutb rejected the idea that "*jihaad bis saif* (striving though fighting)" was "merely for the defense of the 'homeland of Islam.'" Qutb argued that if the seventh-century Islamic warriors had been asked, "'Why are you fighting?' they would not have answered: 'My country is in danger; I am fighting for its defense' or 'The Persians and the Romans have come upon us,' or 'we want to extend our dominion and want more spoils.'" How *would* they have answered? Qutb quoted the Arab declarations made to the Persian commander Rustam shortly before his great defeat at Qadisiyyah in 637:

> God has sent us to bring everyone who wishes from servitude to men into the service of God alone, from the narrowness of this world into the vastness of this world and the Hereafter, and from the tyranny of religions into the justice of Islam. God raised a Messenger for this purpose to teach His creatures His way. If anyone accepts this way of life, we turn back and give his country back to him, and we fight with those who rebel until we are martyred or become victorious.

While we in the West may feel more comfortable — particularly with our Muslim neighbors — when we argue that jihad is a purely defensive phenomenon, it is difficult to make that case for Islam in its first century. Nor does it matter what we think if the Islamists and jihadists, such as Qutb, view that early history as a precedent for violent action.

While Crone and Qutb differ in their assessments of the motivations behind the Arab invasions, with Crone focusing on conquest and booty and Qutb on service to Allah, they both agree that the political unity that Islam offered to the Arabian Peninsula's tribes underlay those early successes — victories achieved against all odds and expectations. For the would-be jihadists, the unity of the world's Muslims is thus a prerequisite for a new and hopefully final campaign to rid the world of *jahiliyyah*, or ignorance.

Chapter 2
"The Ruin of Civilization"

The Islamic Jihaad has no relationship to modern warfare, either in its causes or in the way in which it is conducted. The causes of Islamic Jihaad should be sought in the very nature of Islam and its role in the world, in its high principles, which have been given to it by God and for the implementation of which God appointed the Prophet—peace be on him—as His Messenger and declared him to be the last of all prophets and messengers.

—Sayyid Qutb, Milestones

For believers, Allah's will may sufficiently explain the Muslim armies' remarkable advance following the Prophet's death. In fact anyone reviewing the course of those early campaigns cannot but be impressed by their speed and relative ease. Nevertheless, such successes were not without precedent in the ancient world. Alexander the Great crushed the enormous and seemingly powerful Persian Empire and reached India in less than a decade.

In the seventh century, the major empires bordering on the Arabian Peninsula—the Byzantine and Sassanian—were exhausted. Between 602 and 624 they waged a devastating drawn-out war against each other in the Near East. By the 620s excessive taxes and manpower levees, physical destruction, floods, plague, and conflict had drained both empires. Concurrently, in the Arabian Peninsula a belief structure united the Arab tribes under the banner

38

of a single God—Allah—and, through that unity and in service to this new religion, they spread his message at the expense of the weakened empires to the north.

The Muslim armies' religious fervor, viewed in military terms as superior morale, played a crucial role in their success. But so too did their mobility, their leadership, their enemies' outright terror that followed the sacking of towns that resisted their advance (a common tactic for all that era's armies), the prospect of lower taxation, and their enemies' exhaustion.

The Arab armies' rate of advance was phenomenal. In 634 they defeated the Byzantines at Ajnadayn; Damascus fell in 635, Basra in 636; they routed the Sassanian army at Qadisiyyah in 637; and Antioch fell that same year, Jerusalem in 639, Alexandria in 642, and Cappadocia in 650. By 688 Muslim armies and fleets were at Constantinople's gates, but there they faltered, as they did again in 717. One of their commanders, Tariq ibn Ziyad, crossed the straits from Morocco to the Iberian Peninsula in 711. The mountain where his troops landed still bears his name—Jebel Tariq, anglicized as Gibraltar. By the 730s Arab armies were deep into central France, where Charles "the Hammer" Martel checked them at the Battle of Tours in 732. Other Muslim forces from the Maghreb—the Mediterranean coast of North Africa—landed in Sicily in 827. Advance raiding parties threatened Rome in 846 and for a time held a lodgment in southern Italy. In 859 the Muslims captured the Sicilian city of Enna and slaughtered several thousand inhabitants. In 870 after a month-long siege, Syracuse fell. In 884 the Muslims burned the monastery at Monte Cassino. Finally, in 902 the last Christian stronghold on Sicily—Taormina—fell, ending seventy-five years of Christian opposition. Organized resistance in the Iberian Peninsula began in 718 and never ceased until Granada's destruction in 1492.

Despite this record of success, strains quickly became evident in the new Islamic empire. For more than a century after the Prophet's death, infighting and intrigue were endemic, starting with the *ridda* wars in the peninsula. Abu Bakr, the first khalifa, may well have been poisoned. A disgruntled Christian slave assassinated the second khalifa, Umar, in 644. Uthman, the third khalifa, likewise fell to an assassin, and succession struggles erupted into open civil war. Ultimately, Ali, Muhammad's son-in-law, became khalifa. His succession led to the creation of a reactionary splinter group, the Kharijites, a member of which assassinated Ali in 661. His son, Hasan, proclaimed himself the new khalifa, but rival factions centered in Damascus declared for Muawiyah of the Umayyad clan in 661 and Hasan relinquished his power. Thus began the short dynasty of the Umayyads, who moved the capital from Medina to Damascus and made the succession hereditary. Yazid succeeded his father Muawiyah, but Husain, Ali's other son, declared himself the rightful khalifa. Open rebellion followed. In 680 Umayyad forces defeated Husain's army and killed their rival at Karbala in present-day Iraq. Thus the split within Islam between the Shia, or those who had supported Husain, and the more numerous Sunni was widened.

The Umayyad khalifas were notoriously unfaithful to Islam. Al-Walid II, for example, consumed forbidden alcohol as he swam in a wine-filled pool. The political rivals of the Umayyads, most notably the al-Abbas family in the east, portrayed the khalifal administration as un-Islamic. The Abbasids drew their support from among several disgruntled factions and staged a revolt in 747. By 750 they had defeated the Umayyads and captured Damascus. In a feigned gesture of reconciliation, the first Abbasid khalifa invited about eighty leading Umayyad notables to a banquet near Jaffa, but then he had them murdered. One of the Umayyads, Abd al-Rahman, escaped and reached Cordoba, where he proclaimed himself khalifa. Meanwhile the Abbasids shifted the capital eastward to Baghdad.

While internal tensions did not prevent Islam's continued expansion, it must have retarded it. One can only wonder how far Muslim forces might have advanced had it not been for political divisions, infighting, and, at times, outright civil war. Amid the turmoil, the taxation burden steadily rose. The Arab tribesmen, who bore the weight of fighting the conquests, were increasingly spread ever more thinly as their new empire stretched from the Atlantic to south Asia. As early as Umar's khalifate, Syrian converts to Islam had been conscripted to fill out the armies' ranks.

Muslim forces also met increasing difficulties as they advanced more deeply into the heart of Europe. Part of the reason for the early Muslim successes, according to the fifteenth-century polymath Ibn Khaldun, was the Arabs' willingness to combine their traditional and mobile cavalry-based "attack and withdrawal" tactics with the disciplined "closed formation" style of infantry warfare preferred in the West, a style of fighting that he personally considered best suited for "one willing to die." Nevertheless, once beyond the open areas of the Fertile Crescent and North Africa, Islamic armies stumbled. As preoccupation with their newly conquered lands, treasures, and female slaves increased, their enthusiasm for battle waned. According to Ibn Khaldun, the Arabs reverted to more mobile tactics but were often defeated, as they were at the Battle of Tours, by their enemies' heavy infantry. As had the Achaemenids centuries earlier, Arab rulers in the Maghreb began to recruit Western—that is, Christian—heavy infantry as mercenaries to fight in their civil wars. Such measures were not, of course, workable for campaigns against European Christian nations.

In the East, the Abbasids turned to the Eurasian steppe for their manpower. An army of Christians, Jews, and Zoroastrians could hardly be depended on to spread the Prophet's message. By the time the first Abbasid, Abul Abbas as-Saffah (750–54), became khalifa the days of rapid advances and unlimited booty were past. The Abbasids began to disband the existing armies and in their place created a new force of paid soldiers—a mix of Syrians, Persians, and Turks. Heavy cavalry, supported by lighter horse archers, became their decisive arm on the battlefield. Khalifa al-Mutasim ibn Harun (833–42) removed the remaining

Arab soldiers from the army rolls because of their unreliability, in both political and military terms, and transitioned to yet another system, which relied primarily on Turkish slaves from the steppe—Mamluks (one who is a possession).

The Abbasids' system of military slavery—single generation and self-eliminating—was unique. Agents purchased young Turkish males from along the Transoxanian frontier or black Africans from the upper Nile regions. These men were forcibly converted to Islam, trained as soldiers, and paid for their services. Women were likewise purchased to serve as their wives. Those soldiers who survived retired with pensions. Their offspring, because they were born of Muslim parents, were free men and women.

While the Abbasids' approach was effective, it was not without drawbacks. The system, far removed from the Western ideal of civic militarism, was in a sense almost the complete opposite. Society virtually divorced itself from the military that served it. The Mamluk system drew the Turks into the Muslim orbit and involved the risk that Turkic groups would move south on their own, which they ultimately did. Moreover, as the system progressed for several generations, it led to another unforeseen development: it established a Mamluk faction, or an aristocracy composed of retired warriors and the former slaves' families.

Muslims also faced problems at sea. While Arab seafaring had a long tradition along the Arabian Peninsula's southern and eastern coasts, Muhammad's tribesmen-followers were strangers to the oceans. As had the Achaemenids before them, the early khalifas relied on subject peoples, primarily the dhimmi Christian populations of the Levant and the North African coast, who were familiar with shipbuilding, navigation, and seaborne commerce. These methods worked well enough in the western and central Mediterranean basins, where the Roman Empire's remnants lacked any effective naval power. Ibn Khaldun wrote, "[The Arabs] fell upon the European Christian rulers and made massacres in their realms." But the same was not true in the eastern Mediterranean, where the Byzantines had a powerful fleet. Naval deficiencies contributed to the Arab defeats before Constantinople in the late seventh and early eighth centuries. Nor did Muslim dominance of the Middle Sea last. By the eleventh century the Christians were challenging the Arabs at sea from Gibraltar to the Levant, and this trend continued into the fourteenth century. Ibn Khaldun noted, "The Muslims came to be strangers to the Mediterranean. The only exceptions are a few inhabitants of the coastal regions, who are active on the sea."

The maritime shortcomings of the Arabs raise a broader question about the nature of the dhimma system. Most discussion about the dhimmis' role in the Islamic world focuses on ethical questions concerning equal rights or on how well—or how poorly—Muslims behaved toward the "people of the book." But a more important question is rarely asked: Was it sensible long-term policy to treat such a significant proportion, and in some areas a majority, of the khalifate's subjects as lesser peoples? Depending on one's point of view, either Muhammad or Allah dictated the dhimma scheme at a time when Islam was confined to the Arabian Peninsula and the Muslim-Arab element represented the population's overwhelming majority. In that situation, such a structure's long-term impact was minimal and could be considered a marked improvement over the ancient world's prevalent systems of outright slavery. But as the Arabs advanced in the late seventh century, the dhimmi populations under their control formed a majority. Islam gradually became the dominant faith in the Levant and the Maghreb, but Muslims were either a bare majority or in some areas a minority in the Iberian Peninsula, Sicily, much of the Balkans (during the Ottoman period), or Anatolia (until perhaps the sixteenth century). As late as the nineteenth century a third to a quarter of the Ottoman Empire's subjects remained Christians. Moreover, in the medieval era the dhimmis were concentrated in the very sectors of society that, beginning in the late Middle Ages, would become the dynamic elements driving the

West's economic, military, and political development—namely, the maritime, commercial, industrial, and banking sectors.

By maintaining the prescribed dhimmi system, the khalifas also denied themselves access to a significant potential source of manpower for their armies and thus relied increasingly on Turkish slaves. Armies posed a political threat in a way that navies did not. As a result, Islam waged war with one hand tied behind its back, a hand whose loyalty was suspect and could quickly turn subversive.

Nor were the Muslims' problems confined to the military, naval, and ethnic spheres. There are clear indications that Arab rule, at least until the Abbasids and probably beyond, if to a lesser degree, was an administrative disaster. The amount of land under cultivation decreased in many areas. And as the steady stream of booty dried up and the Khalifas sought cash, taxes rose. Eliyahu Ashtor wrote, "The tax system of the caliphs brought disaster to the peasantry of Upper Mesopotamia, and there is no reason to believe that the plight of peasants in other Near Eastern countries was better."

By the eleventh century the Arabs were losing their imperial grip. In the West the Christian areas of the Iberian Peninsula began to coalesce into more powerful political entities, even if they could not yet be termed "states," and challenged the Umayyads. The Muslims had also been driven out of the Italian Peninsula. In the East the Turkic groups from the central Eurasian steppe posed a threat by moving south and west into Muslim lands.

In 711 when Tariq's army crossed the strait that would one day bear his name and attacked al-Andalus (southern Spain), Europe west of the Byzantine Empire's frontiers was devoid of anything approaching a kingdom, let alone a state. Tribal elements were still on the move. Western kingdoms had no strictly defined borders or administrative systems; kings were little more than senior lords, with limited authority and less power. Only the Catholic Church possessed a hierarchical structure and administrative network, but Europe was still in a process of Christianization that would take two more centuries. The West proved to be such an easy mark for the invaders, because the Muslims, whatever their shortcomings, were unified politically and religiously, possessed a common Arab-Muslim identity, were well motivated, and relatively speaking were more disciplined militarily.

But the West slowly began to recover from its "Dark Ages." The church continued to expand and to provide administrative functions for Catholic monarchs. Kings brought weaker lords under control and extended monarchical powers over their lands. Incomes rose, economies grew, trade expanded, and the ability to exert military power increased.

In the early 720s, the Christians of the Iberian Peninsula won their first victory at Covadonga. The *Reconquista* (reconquest) had begun. The military advantage in Iberia shifted back and forth between the Christians and the Muslims during the eighth and ninth centuries, but gradually the former's domains grew and the latter's frontier moved inexorably southward. In 1031 the last of the Umayyad khalifas' rule came to an end amid rebellion and civil war. Muslim Iberia shattered into a bevy of separate petty kingdoms, more akin to city-states, known as the *taifas*. Political division and an inability to rely on their non-Muslim population (or even on the native Iberian converts to Islam) led to further defeats. The taifas often relied on mercenaries—Berbers, Serbs, and at times even Christians—but to no avail: in 1085 an army led by King Alfonso VI of Castile captured Toledo.

The weak taifa kingdoms sought help from the Almoravids, frontier Berbers who in the 1070s had overrun Morocco and established their capital at Marrakesh. Help arrived and checked the Spanish advance, although Toledo remained in Christian hands. As soon as the immediate Christian threat ended, the Almoravids turned on the taifas and established their own khalifate over the petty kingdoms.

Within a half century the Almoravids themselves faltered. They faced major revolts in Morocco and Iberia because of their heavy-handed rule, clannishness, and insistence on an extreme interpretation of Islam. In the early twelfth century, Alfonso I "the Warrior," king of Navarre and Aragon, regained the initiative for the Christians on the battlefield, helped by the defection of as many as 14,000 Mozarabs—those Iberian Christians whom the Almoravids had threatened with deportation to Morocco. Amid the struggle, rebellion spread to the Arab Muslim population of al-Andalus, who considered themselves cut out of the khalifate's affairs by virtual barbarians. In 1147 they invited another force from the Maghreb frontier—the Almohads (Unifiers)—to intervene in the affairs of al-Andalus.

The arrival of the Almohads, who like the Almoravids sought a purer form of Islam, followed a similar course. By 1174 they had checked the Christian advance, but along the way they had also eliminated the Almoravids and established themselves as the ruling regime in Muslim Iberia.

The Almohads, once in control, moderated their behavior and oversaw a rebirth of scholarship, art, and architecture in what remained of al-Andalus. Among the scholars the Almohads patronized was Abul Walid Muhammad Ibn Rushd al-Qurtubi (1126–98), generally known as Ibn Rushd or in the West as Averroës. Many consider him the first rationalist philosopher. He struggled to define reason and belief as separate spheres. His works were influential in the West in the twelfth and thirteenth centuries and served as a preface to the thinking that became prevalent in the Renaissance. Unfortunately, he was not as well received within the Islamic world. Under extreme pressure from the Christian kingdoms, the Almohads could ill afford the animosity of the religious scholars, who considered ibn Rushd's works as veritable attacks on Islamic dogma. Ultimately, the Almohads banished the philosopher to Morocco, declared his teachings anathema, and banned or burned his books.

Almohad rule was short lived. In 1212 Spanish and Portuguese forces defeated the Almohad army at las Navas de Tolosa, ending their power in Spain. In 1236 an army led by Ferdinand III of Castile captured Cordoba. The Almohads survived until 1269, when they lost control of Morocco to yet another Berber dynasty. By that point the Muslim position in al-Andalus was in steady decline and its days were numbered.

For the Muslims, events in the central Mediterranean were not going any better than those farther west. About 1050 the Fatimid khalifa al-Mustansir, faced with the defection of the Zirids who ruled much of the Maghreb, decided to punish them and reestablish control over his western territories. He turned to an Arab tribe—the Banu Hilal, who had recently migrated from the Arabian Peninsula to southern Egypt—to bring the Zirids back into line.

The Banu Hilal struck west and decisively defeated the Zirids in 1052. Unfortunately, they sacked the towns of the Maghreb as they advanced, including the Zirid capital, al-Qayrawan, in 1057.

Al-Qayrawan was one of the intellectual centers of the Islamic world. It drew scholars and students, including women, from throughout the Maghreb and al-Andalus. The study of medicine at its ad-Dimmah hospital was perhaps the most advanced in the world. The city was also blessed with a library with extensive manuscript holdings.

All that changed with the Banu Hilal's arrival. They destroyed the city as well as the other major urban center in Tunisia. According to Ibn Khaldun, "[The Banu Hilal] destroyed all the beauty and all the splendor of the monuments of Qayrawan. Nothing that the [Zirid] princes had left in the palaces escaped the greed of the brigands. All that there was in the town was carried off or destroyed." Neither the city nor Tunisia recovered from the blow; Islam had lost another intellectual center.

Tunisia had been the base from which the Arabs had launched their attacks against Sicily in the ninth century. Christian efforts to retake the island had been thwarted, often by reinforcements sent from the Maghreb. But in 1061, amid the turmoil along the North African coast, the Christians struck once again at the island.

By the mid-eleventh century, Drogo, Humphrey, and William

"Iron Arm"—Norman mercenaries and the elder sons of Tancred de Hauteville, a member of the lesser Norman nobility—had established themselves in power in southern Italy. In 1046 a third brother, Robert Guiscard (alternately translated as "the Resourceful" or "the Weasel"), joined the family and helped extend Norman rule. To deflect the Normans' ambitions to the south lest they continue to encroach on papal lands, the pope acknowledged the Hautevilles' rule of Apulia and Calabria in southern Italy and of Sicily, then in Muslim hands.

The work of "liberating" Sicily fell to Robert and the youngest of his brothers, Roger, who in 1060 began his invasion of the island. Aided by political divisions among the emirs, the willingness of some Muslims to serve as mercenaries, and the unhappy Christian population, Roger managed to wrest the island from the Muslims and captured the capital, Palermo, in 1071. It took another two decades to complete the reconquest, but by 1091 the Normans controlled the entire island and threatened Ifriqiya—modern-day Tunisia.

Only a handful of Normans—according to some contemporary accounts numbering only in the hundreds—served the de Hautevilles in Sicily. To rule, the Normans preserved much of the Muslim administration and allowed the local populations throughout the island to retain their laws, traditions, language, and culture. Muslims were required to pay a special tribute—the *jizya* in reverse. Latin, Greek, and Arabic became the official languages of the realm.

The Arab-Norman kingdom was short lived. In the twelfth century, Sicily was one of the richest and most enlightened realms in the West. The Norman rulers' tolerance allowed them to draw upon the strengths of the Latin, Greek, Jewish, and Arab cultures. Norman administrative advances came not from Christendom, for example, but from the Fatimids in Egypt. But by 1194 pressures caused by increasing intolerance, the discomfort of Muslims living under Christian rule, and the vagaries of European power politics led to the collapse of Norman rule and ultimately to the latinization of the island and its culture.

To the east, the Islamic world of the tenth and eleventh centuries was also in turmoil. The Abbasids oversaw a revival of Islamic power, moving the capital from Damascus to Baghdad. The intellectual center of gravity also shifted eastward to Iran. The Abbasids adopted Persian influences; increasingly, Persians organized and ran the civil administration. The Abbasids also codified many important Islamic elements, for example, a formal concept of jihad and the division of the world into *dar al Islam* (the abode of Islam) and *dar al Harb* (the abode of war, where Islam did not reign).

Abbasid authority quickly waned. Civil war, coups, revolts, and a resurgent Byzantine Empire threatened the khalifate throughout the ninth century. Claiming to be a descendant of Fatima, Muhammad's daughter and the wife of Ali, the fourth khalifa, a Shia Abbasid pretender seized power in Tunisia. In the mid-ninth century, the Abbasids lost control of Egypt, first to Ibn Tulun of the Tulunids, the son of a Turkish slave, and ultimately to Gawhar, a Fatimid general and former Christian slave from Sicily who had converted to Islam. Conflict and periodic misrule did little to further economic development.

During the tenth century Turkic groups, in part because of their acceptance of Islam, began to form larger allegiances along the frontier in Transoxania. In 999 the Ghaznavids gained control of Khurasan from the khalifate, but they focused their attentions eastward into northern India. By 1040 the Seljuks had displaced the Ghaznavids, broadened the Turkic power base, and moved toward the southwest into the khalifate's lands. Persia was soon in their hands, and Damascus fell in 1055. While the Seljuks remained nominally loyal to the Abbasids, they completed the shift from Arab-Persian to Turkish control in the region—a shift that would not be reversed until 1923. In 1050, the Seljuk leader, Tughril Beg, was the first to receive the title of sultan from the Abbasid khalifa.

In the mid-eleventh century, the Seljuks began to raid Byzantine territory in eastern Anatolia. In 1071 Sultan Alp Arslan (Valiant Lion) commanded a heavily outnumbered Seljuk force, defeated a Byzantine army at Manzikert, and captured Emperor Romanus IV. Following that victory the Seljuks extended their control to the shores of the Aegean. In 1078 the Seljuks established their new capital in Nicaea (now Iznik), less than a hundred miles southeast of Constantinople.

The Seljuks' arrival from the northeastern frontier rejuvenated Islam in the East, much as the influx of the Berber Almoravids and Almohads from the southwestern frontier had, albeit temporarily, shifted the balance between Christianity and Islam in al-Andalus. But the Turks' thrust into Asia Minor at the very moment when Christendom seemed to have finally gained the upper hand against the Muslims elsewhere in the Mediterranean basin prompted a strong reaction in the West. In 1095 at the Council of Clermont, Pope Urban II issued his call for what became known as the Crusades.

Many histories of Muslim-Christian hostility begin their tales of woe in 1095—for example, Amin Maalouf's *The Crusades Through Arab Eyes*. In his *The Shade of Swords: Jihad and the Conflict Between Islam and Christianity*, after discussing Islam's rise and its early struggle in the Arabian Peninsula, M. J. Akbar conveniently passes over the entire history of the Arab conquests and four centuries of interreligious warfare in his haste to get to the Crusades and his splendidly told account of Christian butchery and blood lust. Of the five extant accounts of Pope Urban's speech, Akbar chose to quote the one that was recorded decades after the event by someone who may not even have been in attendance and is thus the least likely to be accurate. Nevertheless, it has the advantage of being the only one of the five that could be deemed overtly sensationalist.

The Crusades should be viewed within their historical context and not as a starting point for what followed. The Crusades did not start in 1095, nor did they end in 1221. Warfare between Christendom and the Islamic world had been continuous for more than 400 years—since the first Islamic raids of 633—and would continue almost without cease until 1923. The pope's call for a crusade was a direct response to Christian Anatolia's invasion by the Seljuk Muslim Turks, who had then set up their capital in Nicaea—the town that in 325 had been the site of the important Council of Nicaea and from which came the "Nicene Creed" that hundreds of millions of Catholics recite at Mass each week. By 1095 between a half and two-thirds of Christian lands had fallen into Muslim hands. The reports of Seljuk outrages and massacres of the Christian population, exaggerated or not, prompted the papal call. In short, the Crusades were a reaction—a counterattack—to Islam's latest expansion into what had been for nearly a millennium Christian domains. What made the Crusades so notable was not their brutality, but that Muslims were on the receiving end and the Christian assaults drove into the Islamic heartland. While the crusading effort ultimately failed, that the West had progressed so that it could project such force into the Levant and sustain it there by sea for more than a century boded ill for the Muslims in the shifting balance of power between them and the western Europeans.

Depending on one's definition of the term "crusade" there were either five or seven, beginning in 1097 and ending in either 1221 or 1250. The Western effort did fail. Muslim forces bested their Christian opponents. And Christians did, on occasion, inflict terrible massacres on the Muslim and the Jewish populations.

The cities and towns captured by the Christian armies were hardly the intellectual or commercial centers of the Islamic world. Jerusalem, Acre, and the other towns that came under the Crusaders' control were veritable backwaters. The Christians never captured the main hubs of Islamic learning in the East: Damascus, Alexandria, Baghdad, or in Persia.

Unfortunately for the Muslims, as the crusading impulse lessened, a new threat emerged in the east—the Mongols. In 1218

Genghis Khan, after uniting the Mongol tribes and conquering much of China, learned that the emissaries he had sent to the shah of the Transoxanian Muslim empire of Khwarizam had been executed. The Great Khan struck with as many as 200,000 men. The Mongols made quick work of the Khwarizam armies and captured Bukhara, Samarkand, Merv, Nishapur, and Balkh. They massacred the Muslim population, sparing only technicians useful to their continued conquests.

The Mongols resumed their advance in 1253 under the leadership of Hulagu, overrunning the rest of Persia, destroying its centers of learning, and executing those scholars who had the misfortune to fall into their hands. In 1255 they captured Alamut, from whence the infamous Assassins had operated. They continued southwestward into Iraq, aided along the way by those oppressed by Sunni Islam—namely, Christians and the Shia.

In 1258 following Khalifa Musta'sim's refusal to surrender, the Mongols besieged Baghdad. Although the Abbasids had long been aware of the Mongols' approach, their military preparations were woefully inadequate. After a fifty-day siege the city fell, according to some accounts because of the treachery of the khalifa's Shia vizier, Ibn al-Alqami. (In May 2005 Abu Musab al-Zarqawi, the late Qaeda al-Jihad leader in Iraq, referred to the Iraqi Shia working with the Americans in a statement titled "The Return of Ibn Al-Alqami's Grandchildren.") The Mongols pillaged the city for forty days. Accounts vary, but the khalifa was either locked in his storeroom of treasure and starved to death or wrapped in a carpet and crushed by horses lest his blood be shed. Some accounts place the dead at 2 million, although 800,000 is more likely and more than sufficient evidence of the extent of Mongol devastation. They vandalized Baghdad's three dozen libraries and threw the manuscripts into the river, along with enough bodies that it was said the Mongols could ride their horses across the Tigris. The stench of death was horrible, and pestilence followed, spreading as far as Syria.

Hulagu continued his advance westward and by 1260 had captured Aleppo and Damascus. As he prepared a new advance to the south—Egypt—fate intervened. Islam was saved, in the same fashion that the Europeans had been saved twenty years earlier. In 1241 following Mongol victories in Poland and Hungary, the khan had died and all the Mongol royal princes had had to return to Karakorum to elect a new khan, saving Europe from further invasion. In 1259 the successor and Hulagu's brother, Mongke Khan, died. Hulagu cancelled his invasion plans, returned to Mongolia with the bulk of the army, and left his chief lieutenant, the Christian Kitbuqa Noyen, in command with orders to conquer Egypt.

During the Crusades control of Egypt had passed from the Fatimids to the Kurdish-Turkic Ayyibids, who were led by the Kurd Salah al-Din, better known in the West as Saladin. By 1171, while he dueled with Christian Crusaders, Salah al-Din had managed to wrest control of Syria and Egypt from the Fatimids and established his own dynasty.

In 1249 the Ayyubid Sultan Salih Ayyub died. His wife, Shajarat al-Durr, concealed his death for several months until she had secured her own position through cooperation with senior Mamluk commanders.

Shajarat, who started her career as a harem slave of Turkish or Armenian origin, was an extremely capable woman and one of the few ever to rule a Muslim state. After the Mamluks assassinated her husband's heir, perhaps with her cooperation, she assumed the role of sultana, ruled effectively, and defeated a French invasion, capturing and ransoming King Louis IX.

Despite her successes, pressures demanding a male ruler mounted. Shajarat responded by marrying the Mamluk general Aybek, who became the nominal sultan. But Aybek had his own ideas. In 1257 Shajarat learned that her husband was planning a new marriage and had him assassinated. The outraged Mamluks arrested and imprisoned the Sultana and subsequently beat her to death before assuming power themselves in 1259.

Saif ad-Din Qutuz led the Mamluk army from its cantonments in Cairo north into Palestine to meet the Mongols. The two armies sparred throughout the summer of 1260 before they finally met on the Ain Jalut (Spring of Goliath) battlefield on September 3. The Mamluks destroyed the Mongol Army and captured and executed Kitbuqa, but Qutuz's glory was short lived. On the march back to Egypt a disgruntled subordinate, Baibars, murdered his commander and seized power. Over the next few decades the Mamluks drove the remaining Mongols and crusaders from the Levant.

Any objective examination of the history of the Middle East reveals that the Crusades' impact on the Islamic world paled when compared to that of the Mongol invasions. While the crusaders never advanced far beyond the Levant coast, the Mongols destroyed the better part of six centuries of Islamic development in Persia, Iraq, and Syria. Millions died as a result of their conquests. The Mongols destroyed irrigation systems developed over the course of centuries in Persia and Iraq, and some historians argue that agricultural recovery came only in the twentieth century. Under the short-lived Mongol rule in Persia, they introduced worthless paper money that undermined whatever economic activity had survived the initial assault.

The Mongols' administrative incapacity and their lack of cultural sophistication did result, however, in new converts. Within a half century the surviving Mongols in the Middle East had accepted Islam and adopted local languages and cultures.

Unfortunately, no sooner had the Middle East begun to recover than a new wave of invaders swept out of the steppe. Timur-i lang (Temur the Lame, better known in the West as Tamerlane) was a Sunni Muslim Turk intent on world conquest. Between 1398 and 1402 his army swept through Persia, Iraq, Syria, and Anatolia. He sacked Isfahan, Aleppo, Baghdad, Damascus (another 20,000 massacred), and Ancyra. At Isfahan he built a pyramid out of 40,000 severed human heads. Timur's empire in the Near East did not long survive his death in 1405. The Persians reestablished their control in the east and the Mamluks in the west.

Nevertheless, by the early fifteenth century the Middle East had been in turmoil for more than 500 years. Since the waning of Abbasid power in the late tenth century, the intellectual centers of Toledo, Cordoba, Palermo, al-Qayrawan, Damascus, Baghdad, and Isfahan had been destroyed or pillaged (many several times). The last remnants of Arab rule were history. The Persians rebuilt their own Shia empire in the east.

In the west Turkic groups were the beneficiaries of centuries of instability and destruction. The Mamluks gained power in Egypt and the Levant. Seljuk rule ended in 1307, largely as a result of the Crusades and the Mongol invasions. In 1402 when Timur marched into central Anatolia, he was met on the Ancyra battle-field by a Turkish force led by the Ottoman Sultan Bayezid I. Timur defeated the Ottomans and captured Bayezid, who subsequently committed suicide to avoid a more unpleasant fate. Nevertheless, after Timur's death ended the threat from the east, the Ottomans were able to resume their drive toward power.

As the Seljuks weakened, assorted Turkic groups filled the vacuum. A chieftain named Osman led one of these groups in western Anatolia. In 1299 Sultan Osman I captured the Byzantine city of Bilecik and began to expand his rule throughout the peninsula. By the 1330s the Ottomans had established a veritable state, with their own currency, administration, and an effective army that incorporated the best of the many styles of warfare then prevalent in the Near East. Orhan, Osman's son, married the daughter of a Byzantine prince and supported the coup that brought his new son-in-law, John V Palaeologus, to the throne. The new emperor turned to Orhan for help in the Balkans and permitted the Ottomans to establish a bridgehead in the Gallipoli peninsula—in Europe proper.

The Ottomans, like their Seljuk Turkish brethren before them, rejuvenated Islam in the East. They embraced their religion and considered themselves *gazis*—a Turkish term derived from the Arabic *ghazi*—Muslim frontier warriors who raided infidel lands and prepared the way for the spread of Islam by force, or, through a fighting jihad.

A 1337 inscription from the mosque Orhan constructed in the then Ottoman capital of Bursa described the sultan thus: "The mujahid [one who wages jihad], Sultan of the gazis, gazi son of a gazi [Osman] . . . march lord of the horizons." As Turkish professor Mehmet Ipsirli of Fatih University, Istanbul, concluded, "The Ottoman state originated as a state geared towards conquest and gaza, preserving this character throughout six centuries. In that context, it would not be a mistake to call the Ottoman state as an expedition lasting for six centuries."

We ought not make too much of the self-proclaimed ghazi status of the Ottoman sultans. They were pragmatic in the extreme, willing to work with a Christian power when it served their purpose, even to the extent of marrying a Byzantine princess. Orhan's description of himself was nothing more than a conventional assertion of his legitimacy as an Islamic ruler. Nonetheless, Ibn Khaldun, Orhan's near contemporary, writing in fourteenth-century Tunisia, considered the connection between Islam and jihad self-evident. He wrote:

> In the Muslim community, the holy war is a religious duty, because of the universalism of the (Muslim) mission and (the obligation to) convert everybody to Islam either by persuasion or by force. Therefore, caliphate and royal authority are united in (Islam), so that the person in charge can devote the available strength to both of them at the same time.

The Ottomans revived sagging Islamic fortunes in the East and resumed their advance against Christendom. From their bridge-head in the Balkans, they began to expand northward until they had the rump of the Byzantine state surrounded. Constantinople fell in 1453, bringing an end to the Roman Empire. The Ottomans continued their advance and overran the area that today comprises

Greece; Bulgaria; Romania; Serbia; Albania; Bosnia; Hungary; the major islands of the eastern Mediterranean; the Crimean Peninsula; a large swath of the southern Eurasian steppe in what is now Ukraine; Iraq; the Levant; Egypt; the east and west coasts of the Arabian Peninsula, including the Hijaz and the holy cities of Mecca and Medina; and eventually the coast of North Africa as far as, but not including, Morocco. They twice besieged Vienna, Austria, in 1529 and 1683 and came close to breaking into the heart of central Europe.

The rise of the Ottomans marked a resurgence of Islamic power and placed political control firmly in Turkish hands. But the Ottomans absorbed fundamental Islamic beliefs and practices that boded ill for their future. The sultans initially ruled as autocrats, their authority unchecked by any sector other than the religious one in an age (the fifteenth century) when political and economic pluralism were already on the rise in western Europe. They expanded on the dhimmi system, segregating those ruled into *millets*, separate courts for recognized religious communities. The Arabs, who had once been the champions of Islam, were but one of several ethnic or religious millets, all of whom were along for the ride. Christian and Jewish groups remained under the dhimmi system, subject to discriminatory practices and the *jizya*. Unfortunately, within the core Ottoman areas in the Balkans and Anatolia, the Greek, Armenian Christian, and Jewish millets dominated many of the economic sectors that in the West were leading the way out of feudalism. In fact as the West began to dismantle feudalism in the fifteenth century, the Ottomans were busily establishing a comparable structure in their own realm.

The Ottomans adopted the *timar* (fief) system, which was similar to that established by the Mamluks in Egypt. Seeking to avoid the pitfalls of the European feudal system, in which hereditary local lords gained sufficient power to challenge the central monarch, the Ottomans periodically shifted their *sipahis* — the equivalent of European knights — from fiefdom to fiefdom. Politically, the system could be considered an improvement compared to European feudalism, but the political gains were counterbalanced by negative economic ramifications. Since the sipahis knew that their control of a given timar was temporary, their only incentive to do anything was to extract as much wealth as possible from it before they moved on to the next.

To avoid reliance on unruly and unreliable tribal elements, the Ottomans mimicked the Abbasids and turned to slavery to man their new army. As early as the 1330s the Ottomans faced manpower shortages and began to rely on enslaved Christians and prisoners of war. This force became known as the *jeniceri* (new army) corps — the janissaries (new soldiers). By the 1380s to fill out their standing army the Ottomans had developed a conscription procedure known as the *devshirmeh* (Turkish *devisrme*), a form of human tax on the empire's Christian subjects in the Balkans. The system was, as can be imagined, not well appreciated among the Christian population of the empire. Most, but by no means all, families were less than eager to have their young male children hauled off by Ottoman officials, never to be seen again and only to become lifelong slaves to the sultan. The janissaries did have some privileges: their children were born free, and while devshirmeh often converted to Islam, they were not always forced to do so. Those found to be intellectually gifted moved into an administrative track that led to the position of grand vizier, or the sultan's chief of staff. Those in the military track could likewise progress to high command. Those who survived their ordeals or became invalids received pensions. The downside to such service was that devshirmeh possessed few rights. If they fell out of favor — an increasingly likely outcome as they rose in power — they were subject to punishment at the sultan's will.

The system had many strengths. The janissary corps pioneered the use of gunpowder weapons in the Ottoman army. Nevertheless, before long the janissaries began to demand ever more from the sultan. By the late fifteenth century they had staged their first major revolt, demanding and receiving higher pay and quicker promotions. By the mid-sixteenth century they had secured the right to marry, thereby creating a janissary class. In 1622 when they saw their interests threatened by Osman II's reform efforts, they stormed the palace. The sultan tried to save himself by executing the unfortunate grand vizier and allowing the rebels literally to tear apart his chief eunuch, but to no avail. Osman was deposed and subsequently assassinated.

By 1453, when Mehmet II "the Conqueror" captured Constantinople, the balance of power between West and East had already begun to shift. Within fifty years the Portuguese would be sailing the Indian Ocean and the Spanish would be exploring the New World. But the trends working against Islam were not evident to contemporaries, be they Muslims or Christians. For another two centuries after the fall of Constantinople the Ottomans seemed to be on the verge of conquering Europe. And it was only through military conquest that they could have averted their demise.

The Islamic world saw incredible advances in the areas of science, literature, the arts, architecture, and social sciences. The Arabs had rediscovered the works of the Greeks and Romans, absorbed them into their own canon, and passed them on through the portals of Sicily and Spain to the Europeans, helping to fuel the Renaissance. But what had Muslims done with those ideas? Why did Islam not progress the same way as the West? The West did not steal Islamic ideas; it copied them. Both Islam and Christianity had access to the same pool of ideas, and while the West built upon those ideas, Islam did not.

While it might be tempting to dismiss such a conclusion as an "Orientalist" interpretation intent on minimizing Muslim accomplishments, one of the earliest critical accounts of the Islamic system's shortcomings was written by the best-known Arab scholar of the medieval world, Ibn Khaldun, who published his *Muqaddimah* in 1377. Many scholars, both Muslim and European, consider him the prototypical modern historian, economist, and sociologist. If modern Western scholars penned what Ibn Khaldun wrote about his own society, they would be branded, at best, as politically incorrect.

As a good Muslim, Ibn Khaldun attributed the Arabs' loss of power to their unfaithfulness to their religion: "They became enmeshed in worldly affairs of no value and turned their backs on Islam. Therefore, God permitted them to be ruined, and He permitted the Arabs to be completely deprived of their power, which He gave to others [the Turks]." But Ibn Khaldun was perceptive enough to realize that more than Islamic infidelity lay behind the Arabs' failings. He wrote that regions "that succumb to the Arabs are quickly ruined." Nor were the Arabs, in his view, particularly productive compared to others: "The Arabs, of all people, are least familiar with crafts [industry]." Even in the realm of scholarship he was critical: "Most of the scholars in Islam have been non-Arabs." While some writers today interpret this remark to mean that most Islamic scholars were Christians or Jews, Ibn Khaldun was actually referring to Persian Muslims.

In his economic analysis, Ibn Khaldun was particularly harsh, maintaining the khalifas often spent themselves into "financial straits" over luxuries. While he avoided directly attacking the rulers of his day even after they lost political power to the Turks, Ibn Khaldun's general criticisms of their economic policies, suggest that he was commenting on what he observed within the Islamic realm for he knew nothing of the world beyond the frontiers. He noted the long-term economic dangers inherent in the tendency of cash-starved rulers to seize the property of those who required the government's protection, calling these subjects "capitalists." He maintained such attacks "on people's property remove the incentive to acquire and gain property" and ultimately led to "the ruin of civilization." Here Ibn Khaldun, citing a Hadith tradition and quoting the Prophet, pointed his finger at the khalifas: "Muhammad said: 'The caliphate after me will last thirty years; then, it will revert to being tyrannic royal authority.'" Presaging U.S. economic policy by 600 years, Ibn Khaldun also explained how raising taxes could actually result in lower tax yields by slowing down economic activity. Conversely, he noted, when

> tax assessments and imposts upon the subjects are low, the latter have the energy and desire to do things. Cultural enterprises grow and increase, because the low taxes bring satisfaction. When cultural enterprises grow, the number of individual imposts and assessments mount. In consequence, the tax revenue, which is the sum total of the individual assessments, increases.

Despite these problems, the Islamic world *was* significantly ahead of the West in terms of culture, education, architecture, the sciences, and governmental administration until the late Middle Ages. This gap was especially marked when compared to Europe north and west of the Byzantine Empire. Islamic science was built on the foundation of the Greek and Roman past, one lost, destroyed, and ignored in the Christian world. Muslim scholars recovered, expanded, and then transmitted advanced scientific and philosophical ideas to the West. As T. E. Lawrence noted of the Arabs, "They had performed a real service in preserving something of a classical past for a mediæval." Muslim scholars shaped mathematics, philosophy, science, medicine, and surgery. They gave the West its system of numbers and the word "algebra." They formed the first universities as centers of learning and undertook massive programs of translation into Arabic. Ibn Khaldun's commentaries on money and other aspects of economics predated similar ideas published by Adam Smith by four centuries. Muslim cities were cleaner and better run than smaller European towns. The main streets in Toledo, which along with Cordoba was one of the intellectual capitals of al-Andalus, were paved and lit. When Norman soldiers of fortune drove the Muslims from Sicily, they inherited an efficient Arab administration.

Nevertheless, something was going wrong. Today's Muslim Web sites touting Arab scientists' achievements frequently cite few or none who lived after the fourteenth or fifteenth centuries. Here again, Ibn Khaldun, who wrote in the fourteenth century, offered interesting insights that are somewhat out of character for a man of such intellectual breadth and depth. For example, he noted that Islam "cultivated" the "traditional legal sciences . . . in a way that permitted no further increase. The students of those sciences reached the farthest possible limit in knowledge of them." Could he have believed that knowledge was finite? Perhaps, for he considered "the great number of scholarly works available" to be "an obstacle on the path to attaining scholarship." Ibn Khaldun noted early Islamic scholars' efforts to translate Greek and Latin texts into Arabic, but subsequently those manuscripts "were forgotten, abandoned, and scattered. All the sciences came to exist in Arabic. . . . [Scholars] could dispense with all other languages, because they had been wiped out and there was no longer any interest in them." For all his brilliance, Ibn Khaldun believed that there was little or nothing to learn from the world beyond Islam. He wrote,

> We further hear now that the philosophical sciences are greatly cultivated in the land of Rome and along the adjacent northern shore of the country of the European Christians. They are said to be studied there again and to be taught in numerous classes. Existing systematic expositions of them are said to be comprehensive, the people who know them numerous, and the students of them many. God knows better what exists there. "He creates whatever He wishes, and His is the choice."

This damning indictment reflects a lack of interest among Muslim scholars of the late Medieval period, especially when one realizes that Ibn Khaldun's definition of "the philosophical sciences" included mathematics, algebra, business, inheritance law, geometry, trigonometry, surveying, optics, astronomy, logic, physics, medicine, agriculture, and metaphysics. He also, somewhat curiously, noted that the

> intellectual sciences and their representatives succeeded to some degree in penetrating Islam. They seduced many people who were eager to study those sciences and accept the opinions expressed in them. In this respect, the sin falls on the person who commits it.

Nor was Ibn Khaldun alone in his approach to philosophy. Al-Farabi, writing several centuries before, had predicted that intellectual development would come to a halt when it reached "the stage where it was with Aristotle." He continued, "Scientific investigation will then cease, and all methods will be fully worked out. Theoretical philosophy as well as popular universal philosophy will be perfected, and there will be no more room for any further investigation. It will then become a craft, to be taught and learned only." As Tarif Khalidi once noted, with regard to the concept of progress, there is something inherently limiting within "any ideology claiming to embrace the whole of knowledge."

The Mongols' swath of destruction across Persia and Iraq and the loss of Sicily and much of al-Andalus to the Christians were heavy blows to the Islamic world. But the Islamic states also fell victim to their fellow Muslims—for example, the Banu Hilal, who pillaged al-Qayrawan in 1057, and Timur-i lang, who replayed the Mongol invasion in the late fourteenth century. Moreover, in terms of relative power vis-à-vis the Christian West, the Arabs were falling behind by the eleventh century. Thus, through the Crusades, the West was able to project power into the Levant and sustain it there.

While the Turks energized Islam in the East, just as the Berbers had done in the West, the fix would be temporary unless serious changes were made within the system. In a sense, the Ottomans' battlefield successes masked the need for adjustment until it was too late. The Ottomans gave new life to Islam as a military force, but politically they remained trapped by their religion, established traditions, and modus operandi.

At the heart of Islam's failure as a world system was its treatment, as mandated by the Qur'an, of nonbelievers. No global empire that subjected such a large proportion of its population, the dhimmis, to second-class status with limited rights could compete with the rise of the West, any more than the slave-holding states of the American Confederacy could long cope with the power of the industrializing states of the North. "Injustice," Ibn Khaldun wrote, "brings the ruin of civilization." Unfortunately, he and other Islamic thinkers failed to consider their system's impact on the dhimmi and, in the long run, on themselves.

Chapter 3
The Rise of the West

If . . . we rely on Western ways of thought, even in teaching the Islamic sciences, it will be an unforgivable blindness on our part. Indeed, it becomes incumbent on us, while learning purely scientific or technological subjects for which we have no other sources except Western sources, to remain on guard and keep these sciences away from philosophical speculations, as these philosophical speculations are generally against religion and in particular against Islam. A slight influence from them can pollute the clear spring of Islam.

—Sayyid Qutb, Milestones

No one doubts that the West dominates the world today and has for several centuries. But why and how did the West rise to prominence?

Scholars offer many reasons for the rapid ascent of western Europe. Some argue that the West has long been an aggressive culture that advanced through exploiting its own people and those whom it was able to subject to slavery and colonialism. While true to a degree, it still does not answer the question. The Europeans were not alone in exploiting their own people during the Middle Ages. What was the Islamic world's dhimmi system—the Islamic law governing the treatment of conquered non-Muslim communities—if not an exploitative system? Nor was slavery solely a Western institution. While slavery did become part of some Western legal codes,

65

it was never hard coded into Christianity the way it was into Islam. The only aspect of slavery that the West can claim as its own is abolition. But regarding colonialism and imperialism, certainly, the West was guilty of both. But did the Chinese and the Ottomans not build vast empires? In fact world history shows that the West began its rise when it was both smaller and weaker than the Ottoman and Chinese empires.

And that is just the point: how was it that the weaker West outperformed these empires? In 1900 the strongest European nation was Hohenzollern Germany. Until the late nineteenth century Germany had no imperial or colonial past; nor had it participated in the institution of slavery as had many of its European neighbors. Further, no one would claim that the rise of the Kaiser's Germany was the result of acquiring the Bismarck Archipelago and Cameroon.

Serendipity is another often-suggested cause for the rise of the West, and a degree of good fortune was involved, just as there was in Islam's initial spread. But when we speak of developments that persisted over the course of several centuries, luck is an inadequate cause. History suggests that it is the *duration* of historical outcomes that allows us to discern their causes in the import of good fortune or bad, wise policies and foolish ones.

What of science? Many Muslims like to point to the West's "theft" of Islamic science. The Islamic world had, and continues to have, access to Western thinking, so why did the Islamic world's sciences not progress at a comparable pace? Science is a human resource and, like natural resources, serves as a tool for advancement. The West, the Islamic states, and China had abundant human and natural resources, but they each made use of them in different fashions and to various degrees. Science, in isolation, does not provide a sufficient cause for the rise of the West.

Several interrelated factors did propel the West forward. Thanks in part to the Arabs, Westerners rediscovered their own classical foundations and the myriad improvements to them developed in the early Islamic world. Among these ideas were rationalism and open inquiry, the dominance of the state over the church, democracy, republicanism, civic militarism, and the geopolitical importance of the sea. The West, to varying degrees, embraced these ideals and attitudes and, over the course of several centuries, began to employ them. Western society became increasingly open to innovative and inventive applications of science. As economies began to recover and expand in the wake of the Dark Ages, weak Western monarchs desperate for cash allowed their commercial sectors to expand more freely in exchange for the right to tax profits. They also championed these productive sectors against the church. Invention and innovation in the commercial sector further enhanced the power of both the markets and the monarchy in the long run. As the commercial elements of society—the bourgeoisie—expanded, economic pluralism became a central element of western European life. Economic pluralism led inexorably to either repression or political pluralism, and in the West the latter predominated.

In the Islamic world, conditions were completely different. The Arabs discovered the foundations of Greco–Roman culture and never fully incorporated many of its elements. Islam always struggled with the concepts of rationalism and open inquiry; rejected the idea of a division between church and state, let alone of the predominance of the state over the church; viewed democracy and republicanism as infringements on God's sovereignty; preferred military slavery to civic militarism; and did not fully appreciate the importance of sea power until the rise of the Ottomans in the fifteenth century. As a result, by the fifteenth century innovation and invention were beginning to lag in the Islamic world. Powerful and rich (compared to Western monarchs) Eastern khalifas and sultans saw no need to permit economic pluralism, especially in commercial sectors often dominated by Greeks, Armenians, and Jews—dhimmis, all. Nor could Eastern rulers favor the interests of such groups against the state religion, because those rulers were in a sense part of the "church" in the Islamic world. Members of the commercial sectors found themselves struggling to protect their property from their rulers while simultaneously competing with more aggressive European merchants who were supported by powerful ocean-going navies. Since economic pluralism failed to develop fully, political pluralism remained an ideal, one many Muslims still reject as anti-Islamic. Subhi Labib, in a survey of Islamic capitalism's development during the medieval period, identified a vibrant but unstable system of "commercial and consumer-credit capitalism" marked by the domination of the elites — princes and tax farmers — who were "bad debtors." "Confiscation in times of unrest and invasion," Labib wrote, "was the order of the day." Another Western innovation, insurance for the merchant's undertakings, "remained practically outside the scope of Islamic economic thought."

In the early seventh century when Islam swept out of the Arabian Peninsula, western Europe was totally disorganized. Petty kings ruled loose confederations and had little legitimacy or identity with the people they ruled. Monarchs ruled from their saddle or their keep, with only a handful of retainers to assist them. Defense and security were local concerns. Given this weak starting point, inevitably as western Europe recovered it gradually gained strength vis-à-vis the Islamic world. The Catholic Church's hierarchical organization and clergy offered the budding monarchs an example of a suitable structure and an immediate means of support. As a result the church and the state, once entwined by Constantine and his imperial Roman successors, grew together once again. The clergy often doubled as civil administrators; to this day we still use the terms "clerical" and "white collar" to describe the tasks Catholic priests once performed. But interconnection came with a price: the nobility increasingly intervened in the church's affairs, most notably in appointments and the investiture of local bishops.

In the eleventh century, Pope Gregory VII worked to free the church from monarchical meddling. His efforts led, somewhat indirectly, to a growing separation of the church and the state. The ensuing struggle between the pope and European monarchies, especially in the Holy Roman Empire, ended in victory for the papacy and in Germany's political splintering until the nineteenth century. But while the crisis strengthened the church, it did so by separating it from the political realm. A clearer line of division served to demarcate the responsibilities of the church and of the lay rulers. As a result, as Joseph R. Strayer wrote in his *On the Medieval Origins of the Modern State*, "the Gregorian concept of the Church almost demanded the invention of the concept of the State."

Beginning in the eleventh century European monarchs began to develop structures to perform the essential functions of dispensing justice through lawyers and court systems and of managing the realm's affairs by proto-bureaucracies. Gradually these developments spread outward from the monarchs' courts into the provinces. Europeans rediscovered Roman law, political administration improved, tax revenues increased, and the people progressively regarded their monarchs as legitimate rulers of their kingdoms.

By the thirteenth century the western European monarchies could properly be termed "states," at least of the pre-Westphalia variety. And such development came just in time because Europe, and the Islamic world, faced a series of near-cataclysmic events caused by climate change — global cooling — and recurring outbreaks of plague.

Despite these problems, Western states survived and grew in power. Instead of confiscating property and money during its economic depression, monarchs yielded degrees of power to various groups. Among those accorded greater influence were the nobility, the merchants, and others in the commercial sector. The forty-first section of the *Magna Carta* (1215) declared,

> All merchants shall have safe and secure exit from England, and entry to England, with the right to tarry there and to move about as well by land as by water, for buying

and selling by the ancient and right customs, quit from all evil tolls, except (in time of war) such merchants as are of the land at war with us. And if such are found in our land at the beginning of the war, they shall be detained, without injury to their bodies or goods, until information be received by us, or by our chief justiciar, how the merchants of our land found in the land at war with us are treated; and if our men are safe there, the others shall be safe in our land.

Many monarchs granted varying degrees of consulting power to newly created assemblies. England's parliament grew in importance and served to support or, on occasion, block the king's efforts to raise cash from taxes in lieu of relying on money drawn from royal properties. In the absence of an effective bureaucracy in a port, the king would appoint a merchant to serve as the tax collector, and the merchants were expected to pay their taxes in return for ever-greater protections and support for their activities.

As the state's infrastructure grew, its balance of power with the church shifted. The Catholic Church viewed itself as morally and spiritually superior to the state, with the pope serving as the "vicar of Christ" on earth. The church's view of its importance was rooted partly in traditions dating back to Constantine's conversion and partly to its philosophical foundations. In the early fifth century Augustine, who began his adult life as a teacher of rhetoric and philosophy before converting to Catholicism and entering the priesthood, wrote *De civitate Dei* (The city of God) in response to accusations that the rise of Christianity had precipitated the barbarians' capture of Rome. Augustine countered that Rome fell because it was not Christian enough. He warned that Christians should look to heaven (or the city of God) for salvation and should expect to find only temptation in the city of man. His arguments could be, and often were, construed as a claim of moral superiority for the church. But Augustine's writings offered several other concepts. He suggested that the pre-Christian Roman Republic's rise was the result of its superior morality compared to the empire's decadence. This position implied that the state's relative morality rested less with its chosen faith than with its behavior. Augustine also viewed government as an evil, a form of moral slavery inflicted upon mankind as a punishment for original sin. Nevertheless, to Augustine government was thus necessary, something mankind had to endure along the road to salvation. Given the nature of the city of man, he felt the Catholic Church should distance itself from civil government. Thus while Augustine's philosophy supported the idea of the church's spiritual primacy, it also envisioned a separation of the church from the state.

Catholic religious philosophers of the eleventh and twelfth centuries may have treaded a narrow path at times, but they nonetheless sketched out lines of argument that embraced reason as well as faith in the search for answers to religious questions, even the existence of God. The writings of Anselm and the unfortunate Peter Abelard best exemplify these views.

In the thirteenth century Thomas Aquinas struggled to combine Aristotelianism, then under attack from the church, and Christian thought. He likewise embraced a rational approach to his thinking, suggesting the existence of something akin to natural law in which men could see the workings of God. He wrote,

> Since the principles of certain sciences — of logic, geometry, and arithmetic, for example — are derived exclusively from the formal principles of things, upon which their essence depends, it follows that God cannot make the contraries of these principles; He cannot make the genus not to be predictable to the species, nor lines drawn from a circle's center to its circumference not to be equal, nor the three angles of a rectilinear triangle not to be equal to two right angles.

Aquinas, despite his influence within the church, did not offer the last word in the debate. Until the sixteenth century the struggle between belief and reason continued, often with belief holding the upper hand.

In the mid-fifteenth century, a technological innovation undermined the Catholic Church's ability to contain thought within what it considered acceptable bounds. The new technology, built on Chinese (moveable type) and Islamic (paper) foundations, was the printing press. The new printed works were cheaper, more accessible, and less likely to introduce errors into texts than handwritten manuscripts. The printed word became the "information revolution" of the age, an innovation that deepened and broadened the Renaissance's impact and strengthened the concept of Western "progress." A historian of printing, Elizabeth L. Eisenstein, wrote that it was "the duplicating process that made possible a continuous accumulation of fixed records," and that "permanence . . . introduced progressive change." The new technology led to the publication of religious and other materials in the Europeans' vernacular tongues, paving the way for the refinement of national languages, literatures, and identities. Less expensive books led to greater literacy, expanded educational opportunities, and social mobility. Mass production and consumption of the written word also shattered the church's monopoly on learning and belief. Martin Luther noted, "Printing was God's highest act of grace," and undoubtedly the new process maximized the impact of his *Ninety-five Theses* and paved the way for the Protestant Reformation's success. By the early sixteenth century more than 2,000 European cities and towns had presses, and printers had produced as many as 10 million copies of more than 40,000 pamphlets and books.

The Dutch humanist Erasmus (1456–1536) was an early beneficiary of the printing age. He considered the pre-Christian classics a "natural gospel," writing that he could "hardly refrain from saying, St. Socrates, pray for me." But Erasmus found his humanistic and secular worldview under siege amid the tumult of the Reformation.

Copernicus's heliocentrism "offended the medieval sense that the universe was an affair between God and man." Copernicus sought to discover the unity of nature, albeit a unity that evidenced God's handiwork, but the Polish astronomer waited until he was near death in 1543 to publish his theory of how the solar system worked.

While the "Copernican Revolution" in scientific thought is often portrayed as a paradigm shift in Western thinking, the Catholic Church's grip remained a threat to open debate, as epitomized in the problems Galileo faced in the early seventeenth century. He wrote to a patron in 1615, "Nor does God less admirably discover himself to us in Nature's actions, than in the Scripture's sacred dictions." The infamous Inquisition forced Galileo to defend his dialogue of heliocentrism, and he subsequently recanted, apologized, and lived under house arrest.

Nevertheless, the struggle between reason and belief in the West ended with the triumph of the former. Jacob Bronowski and Bruce Mazlish in *The Western Intellectual Tradition* defined the scientific method as

> the idea that nature — physical nature and human nature — follows consistent and permanent laws. To the medieval mind, nature had been in some sense a constant miracle: it was sustained and renewed from each moment to moment by a divine intervention. The Renaissance mind and the modern mind also find nature wonderful, but for a different reason: they find it wonderful that nature consistently follows the same laws. The rise of the scientific method rests on our conviction that nature is not arbitrary, but is profoundly lawful.

Medieval Islam underwent a comparable struggle between belief and reason, between the anti-rationalists, such as al-Ghazali and the Ibn Rushds. The problem was not that the Islamic practitioners of the scientific method were less capable or imaginative than their Christian brethren; instead they lost their debate and the lineage of Muslim scientists died after the fifteenth century.

The Islamic world admittedly faced difficult times between the eleventh and fifteenth centuries. Recurring bouts of plague, the loss of Toledo and Cordoba in Iberia and Palermo in Sicily, the crusaders' inroads in the Levant, the Arab tribesmen's sacking of al-Qayrawan, and the Mongols' and Timur-i lang's swath of destruction in Iraq and Iran—all did little to facilitate intellectual or material progress. The climate change that accompanied the "Little Ice Age," which began about 1300, caused crop failures and famines and exacerbated this era's troubles.

The West also had its travails: famines, the Hundred Years War (1337–1453), and the Black Plague, which killed a third of Europe's population starting in the mid-fourteenth century. Moreover, Christendom was besieged by its own enemies: Berbers and Mamluks in the south, Turks in the southeast, and the Tatars (Mongol descendants now converted to Islam) in the eastern steppes. Constantinople fell to the Ottomans in 1453, and there were prospects of further Muslim advances into central Europe.

Both the Christian West and the Muslim East experienced difficult times. The question is, how did the respective systems respond to these challenges?

European feudalism peaked in the twelfth century and began to decline in the thirteenth century. (The Ottomans did not adopt their feudal system until the fifteenth century.) The feudal system in the West was hierarchical and oligarchic; the nominal monarch had little sense of ownership of all his lands and people, and they had little if any attachment to him. Economies were overwhelmingly agriculturally based, but economic power rested with the church, the lords of the manor, or the guilds in the towns. Thus the terms of economic exchange were determined not by the market but by custom, usage, and law. Nevertheless, the hereditary nature of feudal control did foster a sense of ownership among the tenants of a fief and the need to improve the value of one's holdings as a family legacy.

By the fifteenth century Europe had greatly changed and not solely in terms of its intellectual tradition. The Black Death made the labor of the survivors, be they farmers or townspeople, more valuable, and inventors looked to science and technology to compensate for labor shortages. Towns grew and on occasion converted their economic strength into political power that afforded them autonomy as city-states, while monarchies also grew in strength, although not yet overly bureaucratic or static. Europe remained politically fragmented and competitive, whereas Islamic states became increasingly unified under the Ottomans and Islam. Intellectually, Europe was vibrant, the church was waging a losing battle against the state, and the West had rediscovered its classical history and heritage.

While Europe remained predominantly agricultural, the commercial sector was undergoing a metamorphosis. Science, technology, innovation, market expansion with new sources of wealth and investment, and myriad legal procedures designed both to tap and to protect this new wealth spurred dynamic processes that hastened change in the West. A revolution in the maritime sphere either reflected or drove development in the West and led in a few short centuries to global hegemony.

In western Eurasia, from the ancient period until the Renaissance, ships came in two basic forms. Commercial types were beamy, or broad, vessels termed "round ships." They were fair conveyors of cargo but were unwieldy and incapable of sailing with anything other than a trailing wind. Warfare was the responsibility of the "long ship"—or the galley—sleek vessels propelled by oars in battle. They carried large crews for their size but few provisions, limiting their range of operation. Their low freeboards made them dangerous in heavy seas. Both the round and long ships of the period were weakly built, constructed shell first and then framed internally for support. Navigation was also primitive. Mariners often "piloted"; that is, they remained near, if not within sight of, the shore and judged their position and course accordingly. The maritime season was also limited to the months of March through October. As a result, until the rise of the West, sea power—a combination of military and commercial capabilities at sea—was regional and seasonal. Because of sea power's limitations, blockading a distant enemy port was virtually impossible. Only if a friendly army encamped on a nearby stretch of coast, could a galley squadron attempt to blockade an enemy city. Thus navies, leashed as they were, generally operated as flanking forces for the armies to which they were attached. Until the sixteenth century, naval operations were extensions of land warfare with what could best be considered amphibious maneuvers.

The peoples whose coasts fronted the Atlantic faced a more difficult environment than their cousins in the Mediterranean basin. Strong currents and heavy weather were a challenge to long ships. The Gauls used their round ships to fight the Romans in the first century BC without success. The rowed galley remained the superior fighting platform, especially in the Mediterranean.

In the late medieval period, several developments revolutionized sea power. Ship production techniques improved, with ships constructed frame first and then externally planked, resulting in larger, more strongly built vessels. The development of the sternpost rudder and the bowsprit improved ship handling and enabled round ships to work their way more closely to the wind. Several navigational advances reached northern Europe from the Mediterranean—the astrolabe, compass, and improved charts.

The advances in ship design, navigation, cartography, and armaments that occurred between the fourteenth and sixteenth centuries engendered a maritime revolution. By the mid-seventeenth century, the nature, scope, and scale of both maritime commerce and naval warfare had changed dramatically. Heretofore, only states with large and mighty armies—such as those of the Macedonians, Romans, Arabs, and Mongols—had possessed the power to forge global domains. But now the world's new empires were maritime based, with states more akin to Athens than to Rome. Sea power was no longer an adjunct but had become a rival to land power. "The sea," in the words of Fernand Braudel, had become "the gateway to wealth."

Northern shipbuilders enjoyed no monopoly on design improvements. Shipwrights in the Mediterranean also refined their round ships, incorporating ideas imported from the north and devising their own advances in construction techniques and rigging (the lateen sail), advances northerners were more than ready to adopt. Shipbuilding know-how flowed freely between the Atlantic- and the Mediterranean-based builders.

Northern Europeans owed their ultimate global maritime dominance to superior ship designs and a pair of interrelated developments. First, the northerners quickly adopted, by necessity rather than choice, improved round ships as war platforms; the Christian and Muslim states of the Mediterranean did not. Second, the northern Europeans' refinement of the sailing man-of-war in the fourteenth and fifteenth centuries positioned them, unlike their southern neighbors, to take full advantage of the cheap iron cannon's development late in the sixteenth century.

As a platform for ship-to-ship fighting, the galley did not fare as well in the rougher northern waters as it did in the Mediterranean. When northern shipwrights constructed larger, more strongly built, and more maneuverable round ships in the thirteenth century, states fronting the Atlantic began eagerly, though gradually, to incorporate these new vessels into their naval forces. For example, in the late twelfth century the English navy consisted principally of assorted galley types, by the early thirteenth century powerful round ships formed the core of English battle fleets, and by the early fourteenth century galleys had all but disappeared from English orders of battle. Conversely, well into the sixteenth century, Mediterranean navies clung to their battle-proven galleys, which continued to hold their own against round ships.

As a result, northern shipbuilders had a three-century head

start in the refinement of the round ship as a fighting platform. While most sailing ships taken into the fleet in wartime were still merchant vessels pressed temporarily into service, northern European states began to look to shipwrights to design and build sailing vessels specifically for wartime use. These new ships incorporated several prominent design features, such as towering fore and aft "castles," or fighting platforms, from which soldiers could rain projectiles down onto their less fortunate opponents. Gradually, the recognizable design of purpose-built sailing warships began to emerge.

Nevertheless, these early sailing men-of-war, even when armed with the primitive gun-powder weapons of the day, did not yet ensure technological superiority for northern navies beyond their home waters. Until the sixteenth century reliable cannon remained too expensive to be used extensively in the field, whether on land or at sea. States generally consigned their heavy guns to siege trains, and the Muslim Ottomans, not the Christian Europeans, had the most powerful weaponry. Both northern and Mediterranean navies mounted only small numbers of expensive, mostly bronze heavy cannon in the bows of their ships.

The great guns' expense masked the true nature of the technological changes taking place in the maritime world and lulled the Mediterranean powers into a false sense of complacency. As long as fiscal concerns limited the naval use of artillery, the galley remained a viable fighting platform. Since bow-mounted guns fired forward, in battle they could be used more efficiently by the highly maneuverable galleys than by sailing ships. Thus in 1500, no one recognized that the war galley had reached the end of its development. No one foresaw that the fighting round ship would continue to evolve as a weapons system for another 350 years; nor that by the century's end the advent of cheap iron cannon would allow the larger, longer-ranged round ship to carry powerful broadside batteries to the four corners of the globe. No one suspected that the age of galley warfare was about to draw to a close.

Only in the fifteenth century did shipbuilders begin to mount guns broadside. Not until 1501 did a Frenchman cut gun ports in a ship's hull. Only a few men-of-war, such as the English *Harry Grace à Dieu* and the French *François,* mounted large batteries with numerous broadside cannon. And of the *Harry*'s 141 guns, only twenty-one were all brass and rather expensive heavy cannon.

In the late sixteenth century the English developed cheap cast-iron cannon, thus signaling the end of the galley's long reign and ensuring the round ship's preeminence as the state-of-the-art man-of-war. Iron cannon were inferior to brass or bronze guns. Cast-iron guns weighed more, did not last as long, and were more apt to explode. But the development of new casting methods enabled English iron smiths to produce large numbers of admittedly inferior but very cheap cannon. The northern navies quickly adopted the use of both English construction methods and guns. As a result, northern Europeans suddenly possessed both the raw materials and the technological know-how to furnish enough guns to line the decks of their men-of-war.

Early in the seventeenth century, the Mediterranean powers awoke to discover that their navies were obsolescent, if not obsolete. Refinements could no longer make the galley a viable warship. The southern Europeans, Turks, Arabs, and the rest of the world had fallen, and would remain, behind.

The maritime revolution's economic impact was no less dramatic. Reduced transportation costs meant lower prices, especially in the Atlantic, while the cultural and violent frontier aspect of the Mediterranean generally sustained upward pressures on prices. The Atlantic region—stretching from the Bay of Biscay through the North Sea to the Baltic—became a single integrated market. The same did not occur in the Mediterranean, even within Muslim-controlled areas. Continued innovation in northern Europe led to reduced prices of many items, while in the Near East prices either remained stable or increased. Extending commerce into the

Baltic region offset crop yield losses in western Europe that were caused by climate change, but no such expansion was possible within the Mediterranean. Moreover, within the Atlantic region, the expanding trade volume demanded increased production and economic development and efficiency. The integration of prices undermined the medieval reliance on custom and usage and fostered the shift to market pricing.

The quantitative and qualitative expansion of Western commerce led to numerous societal and institutional adjustments. Profitable merchants became bankers and charged interest, despite the church's prohibitions against usury. The danger and difficulty of moving large sums of money over great distances led to developing bills of exchange and to expanding the banking system. Armed with cheap paper (based on a manufacturing technique from the Islamic world) and a new decimal system (that we still term "Arabic") complete with a zero, European bankers developed a system of double-entry bookkeeping that made it easier to monitor business activity and determine profitability.

The most important changes accompanying the West's commercial expansion also fostered its continuation—namely, changes in the area of law. Commercial enterprise is by nature fraught with risk. War, piracy, weather, accidents, theft, unforeseen market changes, and other factors can lead a merchant to loss or ruin. The natural tendency of any human being so situated is to attempt to minimize the risks involved. Developing insurance for ships and cargoes was one method of reducing risk. Establishing a predictable system of laws, especially one that protected life and property, was yet another Western development that accompanied commercial expansion. New laws recognized the rights of nonfamily economic associations, or corporations. Merchants also agreed to pay regular taxes in exchange for legal changes that protected their wealth from confiscation.

As these taxes filled the European monarchs' coffers, the

monarchs made it their policy to protect and to assist their merchants in finding new markets. The merchants then would generate greater wealth, riches that could be taxed. This new system of mercantilism marked a partnership between the state and the merchant class and a transitional stage between feudalism and capitalism.

While both commerce and knowledge passed freely between the people of the Atlantic and the Mediterranean coasts, their worlds remained quite separate. Merchants traded, but the major markets—for example, for grain—were not integrated.

As for shipping, several factors worked against the Islamic world. For the most part, their Mediterranean coast formed a lee shore that was quite dangerous in the age of sail, given the basin's prevailing winds. The winds themselves tended to blow in cycles and in directions favorable to the southern Europeans. The Islamic world's coastline was shorter than Europe's and broken by fewer major rivers, which meant fewer ports and especially fewer deepwater entrepôts than the Europeans had. The almost continual state of corsair and pirate activity in the Mediterranean drove up prices and hindered the Muslims' and the southern Europeans' efforts to develop integrated markets.

In the mid-fifteenth century, the Ottomans began to reverse the Islamic world's fortunes at sea. They built up a capable naval force and developed its requisite leaders, who at worst held their own with the Christian naval powers in the Mediterranean. By the late seventeenth century, as Andrew C. Hess demonstrated, the Ottomans had forged their own seaborne empire.

But several factors, in addition to those listed above, worked against the Ottomans. Their use of maritime muscle differed markedly from that of the Atlantic naval powers. The Ottomans used their navy in conjunction with their land forces to gain territory for their feudal timar system. More land meant more fiefdoms, more mounted sipahis, and more tax revenues. Western Europeans used their sea power to open or gain markets in hopes of increasing trade volumes and producing greater wealth and revenues for the state. The sectors that led commercial expansion in the West were often occupied by dhimmi—or the Christians (Greeks and Armenians) and Jews—within the Ottoman Empire. The dhimmi chafed under religious and political limits beyond which they could not rise. While they often gained "influence," Greeks, Armenians, and Jews still could not secure codified political power or legal protections for their wealth until the Ottoman *Tanzimat* (reorganization) reforms of the mid-nineteenth century. Whereas in the West economic pluralism developed into political pluralism, within the Ottoman realm economic pluralism led instead to envy among the Islamic population and a desire for independence among most Greek and Armenian millets.

Despite the improvements evident during the Ottoman Empire's halcyon days (the fifteenth, sixteenth, and seventeenth centuries), the East was not keeping pace with the West economically, either in terms of production or rates of growth. Increasingly the Islamic world, once the purveyor of manufactured goods such as carpets, sold its raw materials to the West and purchased foreign textiles.

Militarily, the Ottomans held their own. As Gábor Ágsoton noted in his *Guns for the Sultan,* the Ottoman army remained more than competitive. The army and the state it served proved capable of adopting new technologies, such as firearms and cannon; developing the industry to mass-produce them; and using them effectively on the battlefield. At sea the Ottoman galleys matched Italian and Spanish galleys into the early seventeenth centuries. But Ottoman successes at sea against the Christian powers of the Mediterranean basin concealed the extent to which both were falling woefully behind the maritime developments taking place in the Atlantic world. Finally, in the mid-seventeenth century, what John Francis Guilmartin has termed "the Mediterranean system of warfare at sea" collapsed. He wrote, "The fiscal and logistic burden of maintaining a galley fleet powerful enough to accomplish anything of note strategically had grown so large as to be prohibitive." While

Ottoman galley fleets waged a successful but expensive twenty-four-year-long campaign to gain Crete (1645–69), the English and the Dutch fought massive battles in the Channel and the North Sea with their sailing men-of-war in a struggle for global maritime supremacy.

Ultimately, one of the major factors in the Ottoman Empire's downfall was its *timar* system, adopted at the time that most of Europe had already shed feudalism, and retained well into the eighteenth century. As Cicero noted more than two millennia ago, "The sinews of war are infinite money." By the eighteenth century the Ottoman Empire's feudal tax base could not generate the cash necessary to compete with the commercially oriented European powers, not even with the relatively backward Russia.

Religion also played a role in the Ottoman Empire's failure. In Islam science never fully evolved as a discipline free from the influence or outright control of religion. Arab–Persian science peaked in the fourteenth and fifteenth centuries, just at a time when European thinkers were beginning to free themselves from their church's grip. In the Ottoman Empire, neither a scientific revolution nor a paradigm shift of thinking occurred. The mosque and the state remained intertwined within the Ottoman bureaucracy, primarily in the role of the *ulema*, which served as an advisory body for the sultan. Historians of the institution note its qualitative decline as early as the sixteenth century, evident in a narrowing of the curriculum at the *madrasas*, where young would-be scholars were trained; the disappearance of philosophy courses; the transfer of positions from father to son; and the body's concurrent bureaucratization.

Perhaps the most telling event that demonstrates the extent to which the Islamic world suffered from self-inflicted wounds occurred during the rule of Sultan Beyazid II (1481–1512). Early in his reign news of the printing press's invention reached Istanbul. Beyazid's initial reaction to this new technology was positive. But the ulema decreed that using such a device to print Turkish or the Arabic of the Qur'an would be sacrilege. As a result, the sultan outlawed printing in Turkish and Arabic, a ban that would not be lifted, and then only partially, until 1729. Oddly, the ulema did not restrict the dhimmis from printing in their own languages. As a result the Greeks, Armenians, and Jews were able to benefit from the advance, while the ruling Muslims were not.

Sir Francis Bacon considered the printing press one of the three major inventions that shaped his world. In Aphorism 129 of his 1620 *Novum Organum,* he wrote:

> Again, it is well to observe the force and virtue and consequences of discoveries, and these are to be seen nowhere more conspicuously than in those three which were unknown to the ancients, and of which the origin, though recent, is obscure and inglorious; namely, printing, gunpowder, and the magnet [compass]. For these three have changed the whole face and state of things throughout the world; the first in literature, the second in warfare, the third in navigation; whence have followed innumerable changes, insomuch that no empire, no sect, no star seems to have exerted greater power and influence in human affairs than these mechanical discoveries.

While the West advanced with gunpowder, the compass, and the printing press in tow, the Islamic world denied itself the last invention. When considering the monumental importance of the printing press—after language and writing, *the* major communications advance until telegraphy—for disseminating knowledge and transforming the world of ideas, the Islamic authorities' decision to deny themselves the fruits of such progress for almost four centuries is difficult to comprehend. So, too, is the decree's long-term impact in the Islamic world.

By the seventeenth century the gap between the West and the East was rapidly becoming a chasm. Across Eurasia, from England in the west to China in the east, populations increased, placing major demographic pressures on all the world's states. The population of Istanbul, for example, grew from about 100,000 in 1520 to 700,000 in 1600. Prices, especially of foodstuffs, increased by as much as 500 percent as agricultural production failed to keep pace with population growth. The resultant strains tore especially at the still feudal Ottoman Empire. The *timar* system began to collapse. Many of the *sipahis* could not afford to outfit themselves and their retainers for service. The state began to switch from a feudal force, backed by a smaller group of troops controlled by the sultan, to an army that it raised, maintained, and controlled. To meet the rising costs of such a force, the Ottomans reduced the troops' pay and saw the loyalty of those who served plummet. When rumors reached the janissaries in 1622 that the reforming Sultan Osman II planned to replace them with a militia, they rose up and murdered him. Other sultans raised taxes on the dhimmi by as much as 600 percent and in the countryside began to rely even more heavily on "tax farmers," a practice universally loathed throughout history by adherents of all religions. While the Ottoman Empire did not collapse under these pressures, it did begin to show signs of stagnation and rapid decay.

The West likewise underwent a period of great difficulties. For example, the population of London — 50,000 in 1500 — ballooned to 400,000 by 1650. The Stuart monarchy of the early seventeenth century struggled to find the funds it needed to operate, an effort that led to civil war, regicide, and, temporarily, the Commonwealth. Religious and political division and dissent tore at the body politic. But whereas the strains of the era weakened the Ottoman state internally without shaking its deadening autocratic grip, England's restored now-constitutional monarchy emerged strengthened, in large part because of the increased revenue flow funneled to London by mercantilism and its associated navigation acts. Overseas settlement, an option unavailable to the Ottomans, permitted England's political and religious dissidents to emigrate and make a fresh start in the New World.

By the seventeenth century the West had become an economically pluralistic society. This pluralism fostered greater innovation, production, lower prices over the long term, greater and broader wealth, a focus on the material, the state's financial enrichment, and the churches' loss of political power (and after 1648 the end of religious wars). As the rate of advance increased, the bulk of Western society embraced change and formed what could be termed a "progressive" — that is, adapted to the concept of progress — culture. Economic pluralism led to efforts to protect lives and wealth through the law. This movement strengthened the concept of "natural rights," such as those outlined by John Locke in his *Second Treatise of Civil Government* — "life, liberty, and property." Protecting these rights from the state led inexorably to the extension of political pluralism and the rise of the bourgeoisie.

In the Ottoman Empire, economic pluralism was slow in developing and handicapped by the dhimmi system. The absence of pluralism had stifled innovation. The Ottomans did copy Western technologies, but they developed few if any of their own. Efforts to increase production often failed. They generated wealth at a slower pace than in the West and struggled under increasing financial burdens that left them unable to meet their enemies on equal terms. The political power of Islam, however, remained strong. Major segments of the population resisted change, leaving Ottoman culture grounded in tradition. Limited economic pluralism did not, nor could it, lead to identifying any "natural rights" beyond those identified in the Qur'an. Accordingly, then, laws to protect these nonexistent rights were unnecessary. To the extent that economic pluralism existed, when denied a political outlet, it led instead to discontent and revolution.

Chapter 4
"God's American Israel"

Man cannot understand all the laws of the universe, nor can he comprehend the unity of this system; he cannot even understand the laws which govern his own person, from which he cannot deviate by a hair's breadth. Thus he is incapable of making laws for a system of life which can be in complete harmony with the universe or which can even harmonize his physical needs with his external behavior. This capability belongs solely to the Creator of the universe and of men, Who not only controls the universe but also human affairs, and Who implements a uniform law according to His will.

—Sayyid Qutb, Milestones

The forces at work in early modern Europe shaped the evolution of England's American colonies. Demographic developments ensured the growing population's existence. The maritime revolution provided the means to shift people across the Atlantic and to exert power once there. A Puritan theme — namely, that the Old World was hopelessly corrupted whereas the New World presented the righteous with a fresh opportunity to make things right — gave an important and novel shape to the English plantations in North America. John Winthrop's "A Model of Christian Charity," penned on the *Arbella* in 1630 en route to the New World, epitomized that view:

> The Lord will be our God, and delight to dwell among us, as His own people, and will command a blessing upon us in all our ways, so that we shall see much more of His wisdom, power, goodness and truth, than formerly we have been acquainted with. We shall find that the God of Israel is among us, when ten of us shall be able to resist a thousand of our enemies; when He shall make us a praise and glory that men shall say of succeeding plantations, "may the Lord make it like that of New England." For we must consider that we shall be as a city upon a hill. The eyes of all people are upon us.

From the beginning of U.S. history, this theme of exceptionalism has run through the American collective mind. Not all Americans in every age have been so moved. Some have always refused to accept the view that their country was somehow different, somehow unique. Nevertheless, the thread remained, weaving its way throughout U.S. history. A "crusading" element in the American psyche—be it military, republican, democratic, liberal, progressive, reformist, or some combination—has always existed.

The American historical experience has done little to weaken this sense of exceptionalism. As Walter A. McDougall noted in *Freedom Just Around the Corner*, the most significant difference between the world of 1601 and that of 2001 was the development of North America, a wilderness in 1607 that "today hosts the mightiest, richest, most creative civilization on earth—a civilization, moreover, that perturbs the trajectories of all other civilizations just by existing." Many may well dismiss such sentiments as "triumphalism," but that does not change the facts of history.

In the century before the American Revolution (1663–1763), seventeenth-century ideals combined with the eighteenth-century political concepts of the Enlightenments, for a movement that, as Michael Howard pointed out in *The Invention of Peace*, rejected "traditional authority in church and state" and elevated "reason and individual judgement as the only acceptable basis for intellectual and political authority." While the roots of the various Enlightenment movements—be they French, English, or Scottish—lay in Europe, their core principles resonated strongly in the American colonies.

A scholar in England reading John Locke's *Second Treatise of Civil Government* (1690) could reflect on his theory of the origins of private property.

> Though the earth, and all inferior creatures, be common to all men, yet every man has a property in his own person: this no body has any right to but himself. The labour of his body, and the work of his hands, we may say, are properly his. Whatsoever then he removes out of the state that nature hath provided, and left it in, he hath mixed his labour with, and joined to it something that is his own, and thereby makes it his property. It being by him removed from the common state nature hath placed it in, it hath by this labour something annexed to it, that excludes the common right of other men: for this labour being the unquestionable property of the labourer, no man but he can have a right to what that is once joined to, at least where there is enough, and as good, left in common for others.

To Americans, however, Locke might as well have outlined the settling of the New World. The colonists "mixed their labour" with the land and made their property from what had heretofore been held in common (in their view) by the native population *and* the Europeans.

A French scholar reading Jean-Jacques Rousseau's *The Social Contract* (1762) might experience the excitement of a new, secular political theory.

What man loses by the social contract is his natural liberty and an unlimited right to everything he tries to get and succeeds in getting; what he gains is civil liberty and the proprietorship of all he possesses. If we are to avoid a mistake in weighing one against the other, we must clearly distinguish natural liberty, which is bounded only by the strength of the individual, from civil liberty, which is limited by the general will; and possession, which is merely the effect of force or the right of the first occupier, from property, which can be founded only on a positive title. We might, over and above all this, add, to what man acquires in the civil state, moral liberty, which alone makes him truly master of himself; for the mere impulse of appetite is slavery, while obedience to a law which we prescribe to ourselves is liberty.

But if the "social contract" concept as the origin of the state was only a theory in Europe, it was history to many Americans, especially those whose ancestors had crossed the Atlantic on the *Mayflower* and signed their famous "compact."

In Europe the French physiocrats, among them François Quesnay, and the early classical economists—such as Marie Jean Antoine Nicolas Caritat, marquis de Condorcet—philosophized against the concepts and strictures of the prevalent imperial structure. The dominant European system of political economy was mercantilism, an arrangement that stressed developing industry, establishing colonies, and creating a merchant marine supported by a strong navy, all designed to ensure a favorable balance of trade in order to accumulate specie—gold and silver—and the national wealth assumed to accompany it. On the eve of the American Revolution Adam Smith made his case for freer markets and trade when he wrote *The Wealth of Nations* (1776). But in the North American colonies, the virtues of freer trade were a reality, not a theory. Merchants and traders ignored mercantilist restrictions and practiced freer-trade because the English (after 1707, known as the British) government so often lacked the resources, the ability, or the desire to enforce the Navigation Acts in much of the New World.

Philosophy alone did not shape the new republics. So, too, did history. Many early Americans were acquainted with the writers of the Classical Age. Educated colonists were familiar with Greek history and their democracy and with the Romans and their republicanism. Greek historian Polybius, in his *Histories,* had addressed the question of governmental separation of powers.

> The three kinds of government that I spoke of above [monarchy, aristocracy, and democracy] all shared in the control of the Roman state. And such fairness and propriety in all respects was shown in the use of these three elements for drawing up the constitution and in its subsequent administration that it was impossible even for a native to pronounce with certainty whether the whole system was aristocratic, democratic, or monarchical.

Likewise, in *The Spirit of Laws* (1752), the French Enlightenment philosopher Charles-Louis de Secondat, baron de Montesquieu, argued for a separation of governmental powers. Yet, here again, the Americans had their own experiences with these issues. The British political system involved a separation of authority, as did the colonial governments with their elected assemblies but appointed councils and governors.

Americans knew from their study of history, particularly of the ancients and of England, that all three traditional forms of government—monarchy, aristocracy, and democracy—had both advantages and disadvantages. All could become tyrannical. To Americans the problem with government was less its type than the very fact that it was government at all. As the Declaration of Independence proclaimed:

That whenever any Form of Government becomes de-
structive of these ends [right to life, liberty, and the pursuit of happiness], it is the Right of the People to alter or
to abolish it, and to institute new Government, laying its
foundation on such principles and organizing its powers
in such form, as to them shall seem most likely to effect
their Safety and Happiness.

Nor was the distaste for "Divine Right," shared by most sev-
enteenth- and eighteenth-century political philosophers, necessary
to convince Americans of a monarch's shortcomings. The English
monarchy was quite remote to the American colonists: no king or
queen had ever set foot on American soil. In the two centuries
before the American Revolution, England had been a monarchy, a
commonwealth, and then a monarchy (albeit constitutional) once
more. The English had overthrown, beheaded, and then invited
kings to assume the throne, often on a contractual basis.

When the American colonies sought and won independence in their Revolution (1775–83), the political effect was
to create thirteen new countries and a new type of state based
on revolutionary Enlightenment ideals, the impact of which are
still felt today. As Michael Howard noted, the initial cadre of
American leaders represented something new — "an oligarchy
that, uniquely, did not justify its ascendancy by its past or
present military activities." We can say the same of that
oligarchy's lack of religious legitimacy, meaning it did not use
the church to establish the state. Howard continued:

The ruling philosophy of the generation that established
the independence of the United States was the very quin-
tessence of the Enlightenment, with its beliefs in the rights
and perfectibility of man and his capacity for peaceful
self-government once the artificial barriers to his freedom—

monarchy, aristocracy and established church—had been destroyed.

Many of the American founders were Deists, men who believed in the existence of God, or of a supreme being, but who rejected the centrality of formal religion. To them the Almighty was the superlative inventor—a rational being who had fashioned the universe and set it in perpetual motion as only he could. As the Americans declared in July 1776:

> We hold these truths to be self-evident, that all men are created equal, that they are endowed by their Creator with certain unalienable Rights, that among these are Life, Liberty and the pursuit of Happiness. —That to secure these rights, Governments are instituted among Men, deriving their just powers from the consent of the governed—

What was it that Americans expected from their revolution? Certainly, they sought to gain their political and economic independence. They intended to establish republican governments to protect their life, liberty, and property. They understood that political rights rested on a foundation of economic rights. After all, one must first own a newspaper before one can have a free press. Americans hoped to secure the freedom of the individual to worship as well as an increasing degree of separation between the church and the state, because they understood that religious persecution was most likely where there was a link between the two. They were committed to avoiding entanglement with the Old World power system, although the course of the war for independence forced them to accept a "perpetual" alliance with France.

They also anticipated many more changes to their own station and to the state of the world. They declared that all men, and not just Englishmen, possessed basic rights (although not to the extent that they were willing to grant those rights to their own slaves). They believed that freer commerce and the end of mercantilism would herald an age of greater toleration and peace. In fact as Michael Howard argued, the concept as understood in the West came from the Enlightenment.

The revolutionaries' experiences, beliefs, desires, and expectations resulted in a unique vision of the future—Americanism, which is evidenced in the adoption of the Great Seal of the United States on June 20, 1782, more than a year before the Treaty of Paris ended the war. The colonists believed that they had uncovered a revolutionary approach to government that was timeless, potentially boundless (*novus ordo seclorum,* or a new order of the ages), and ordained by the Almighty (*Annuit cœptis,* or Providence has favored our undertakings). Many Americans considered their nation "God's American Israel." As Yale graduate and war veteran David Humphreys wrote in his 1804 "Poem on the Future Glory of the United States":

> Progressive splendors spread o'er evr'y clime!
> Till your blest offspring, countless as the stars,
> In open ocean quench the torch of wars:
> With God-like aim, in one firm union bind
> The common good and int'rest of mankind;
> Unbar the gates of commerce for their race,
> And build the gen'ral peace on freedom's broadest base.

Americanism was the modern world's first secular creed. As was true of Christianity and Islam, anyone could become an American provided he or she accepted certain principles, the most important of which was the people's sovereignty and power to form governments that protected their (God- or nature-given) rights through laws made by men (and now women). In a mere century the American unleashing of Western capitalism through free (or at least freer) trade, more open markets, and republican government made the United States the most materially successful of the Western capitalist nations and the most powerful state worldwide.

In the interim, however, the new American republic remained fragile—politically, economically, and militarily. Its reach beyond its own shores was nonexistent as the European mercantilist powers did not share America's vision and failed to throw open their empires for trade. Nor did many of the world's minor powers respond as expected. In fact America's economic recovery, not to mention the glorious and prosperous future it sought, met its first external challenge from a set of minor powers situated along the Mediterranean coast—the Barbary Coast—of North Africa. The Barbary States played a formative role in shaping the new American republic.

Americans often have difficulty describing the perpetrators of the Barbary peril. Were they pirates, privateers, or state-sponsored terrorists? Actually, none of these terms adequately describes the threat U.S. shipping confronted in the Mediterranean in the late eighteenth and early nineteenth centuries. The Americans and the Barbary States operated within distinct intellectual worlds. This asynchronicity lies at the root of our frequent misunderstanding of the problem.

The creation of the United States stemmed from the rise of the West, the European Enlightenment, and a concept of statehood rooted in political assumptions and developments that had evolved since 1648 and the Treaty of Westphalia, which ended the tumultuous and bloody Thirty Years' War. Westphalia established the foundations for the sovereign nation-state, with its fixed boundaries and clearly defined political responsibilities. The savagery of the war, rooted largely in sectarian divisions, reduced central Europe's population by as much as a fifth and convinced most Europeans that conflict offered little solution to their religious disagreements. Moreover, mercenary units, which made up major elements of the armies fighting the Thirty Years' War, committed outrages that sparked widespread revulsion and led the strengthened state to rely increasingly on regular, better-disciplined, national armies.

After 1648, European warfare evolved toward the form that Carl von Clausewitz attempted to define in *On War* (published posthumously in 1832) and that Martin van Creveld described in 1991 as "trinitarian." The "trinity" in question consisted of the state, its military, and its people. The trinitarian state sought to monopolize the use of war — defined by Michael Howard as "armed conflict between organized political groups" — to serve political ends. For example, in the maritime arena, as the trinitarian state evolved after 1648, it worked to eliminate random violence at sea — piracy — and ultimately the public's participation, or privateering. Ashore, the state moved away from relying on mercenaries and toward establishing regular armies. These new forces, in the ideal, would avoid plundering the countryside and committing violence against civilian populations, be they friendly or enemy. The state's monopolization of warfare would also preclude the civilian population from joining the fight.

This distinction between soldiers and "innocent civilians" is thus a construct of recent historical vintage. Throughout the five millennia of recorded human history, the clear divide between civilians and the military is a Western development of the past four centuries and one never entirely adhered to even within Europe and honored less frequently outside Europe. Historically, civilians generally were considered fair game for plunder, rape, slavery, and slaughter. In the seventh century, Islam, with its clearly defined rules for a conquered population's treatment, represented an improvement on contemporary practices.

In the West, we prefer to believe that we wage "total war" and that before the rise of the great states conflict was somehow "primitive" — a lesser form of the art. Nevertheless, as Lawrence H. Keeley argued in his *War Before Civilization*, "primitives" waged true "total war."

Primitive war was not a puerile or deficient form of war-fare, but war reduced to its essentials: killing enemies with a minimum of risk, denying them the means of life via vandalism and theft (even the means of reproduction by the kidnapping of their women and children), terrorizing them into either yielding territory or desisting from their en-croachments and aggressions. At the tactical level, primi-tive warfare and its cousin, guerrilla warfare, have also been superior to the civilized variety. It is civilized warfare that is stylized, ritualized, and relatively less dangerous. When sol-diers clash with warriors (or guerrillas), it is precisely these "decorative" civilized tactics and paraphernalia that must be abandoned by the former if they are to defeat the latter.

In the eighteenth century, Islam had neither accepted nor been incorporated into the trinitarian Western world. The Muslim view of the world had formalized in the ninth century as the age of the initial conquests ended, and Muslims found themselves confront-ing their surviving infidel neighbors. They called the areas ruled by Muslim leaders and Islamic laws *dar al Islam* (the house or the abode of Islam). Beyond those borders lay the *dar al Harb* (the house or abode of war). Other "abodes"—for example, *dar al Sulh* and *dar al Ahd*—defined non-Islamic areas where the rulers were either in a state of truce or under some form of tributary status short of direct rule. Inherent in this worldview were several assumptions: the existence of non-Islamic abodes was temporary, the ultimate goal was to spread Islam to the entire world commu-nity, and, in the interim, Muslims' duties related to spreading their faith involved both preaching and force.

If conditions did not permit full-scale warfare against nonbe-lievers, Muslim rulers had a duty to raid the bordering regions of the dar al Harb. These raids, akin to those the Prophet launched against the Byzantines and Persians in the seventh century, served several purposes. They allowed a leader to gauge an enemy's strength before a larger attack and weakened the *harbis* (nonbe-lievers) along the frontier. The punishment—death, destruction, pillage, and slave taking—that accompanied these raids were of-ten sufficient to demonstrate the wisdom of accepting the protec-tion of Islam that came with subject, or dhimma, status.

Ghazis were the Muslim frontier warriors who conducted these raids. Their life was harsh, and they supported their opera-tions through taking booty and slaves. They occasionally gained great wealth and power, but they were more likely to die violently. Fellow Muslims, especially during the Ottoman age, accorded the ghazis a special status because of their willingness to risk their lives for their faith in combat with nonbelievers.

The activities of the ghazis were not restricted to the land frontiers; they operated on the seas as well. Ghazi bases generally developed along the fault lines between the Islamic and Christian worlds, initially in the Aegean basin.

In the mid-fifteenth century, when the Ottomans began to build up a naval force, they relied primarily on their Greek Christian millet for much of the shipbuilding expertise and manpower. For leadership the Turks turned to the ghazi captains of the Aegean.

At the end of the century, as Islamic rule drew toward a close on the Iberian Peninsula, the Spanish expanded their attacks to include the coastal regions of the Maghreb. The sea ghazis of the eastern Mediterranean migrated west and established themselves in what would become Algeria, Tunisia, and Libya.

Perhaps the best-known sea ghazi was Khair ad-Din, better known in the West as Barbarossa. He was one of four sea ghazi brothers born on the island of Lesbos of a *sipahi* (knight) or *devshirmeh* (conscripted soldier) father and the widow of a Greek priest. In 1505 Khair ad-Din's older brother, Aruj, set up a base in Djerba, an island off the coast of Tunisia. From there the sea ghazis attacked Christian commerce and smuggled Muslims from the Iberian Peninsula to the Maghreb. In 1516 they captured Algiers, driving out the local Muslim ruler. Following Aruj's death in 1518 in combat against the Christian Iberians and fearing that the Spanish were about to extend their rule into North Africa, Khair ad-Din sent appeals to the Ottoman sultan for help. In return for accepting Ottoman suzerainty (and agreeing to pay tribute), Barbarossa received the assistance of Turkish troops and the title *beylerbey,* or regent for the sultan in Algiers. The combination of Ottoman power ashore and Barbarossa's forces at sea checked the Spaniards' attempts to extend their power to the south.

The successes of the sea ghazis gained them notoriety and legitimacy within the Islamic world. In 1533 Sultan Suleiman "the Magnificent" named Khair ad-Din the commander of the Ottoman navy. Turks, Arabs, Spanish Muslims, Berbers, and even "renegade" Christians flocked to the "Barbary" coast to join the fray. Both Suleyman Reis (De Veenboer), an admiral in the Algerian fleet in the early seventeenth century, and Murad Reis (Jan Janszoon van Haarlem) were Dutch converts. While Islam may have motivated many of the sea ghazis, a desire for booty drove others, particularly the Christian "renegades."

In the later part of Suleiman's reign (1520–1566), the sultan's focus shifted to his campaigns in the Balkans. He left the sea ghazis to their own devices. The Barbary city-states, situated along the frontier between Christianity and Islam, had to compete not only with the galley fleets of the Mediterranean basin, but also with the Atlantic Europeans and round ships. The Barbary corsairs could not afford to remain wedded to the galley, as could the Ottoman navy to the east. The corsairs made the transition to the new European style of naval warfare, based on the evolving round ship. Nevertheless, they lacked the requisite infrastructure and remained heavily dependent on Western technicians (more renegades) and captured or purchased technology. Despite this dependency, the Barbary city-states—Algiers, Tunis, Tripoli—avoided destruction by exploiting existing European differences (e.g., between France and Spain) and adroitly playing the Europeans against each other. The sea ghazis raided as far afield as Ireland, where they seized the entire population of an unfortunate town in Cork; Iceland, where one raid netted 800 slaves; and the Newfoundland Banks.

The Barbary corsairs thus were not pirates, privateers, or state-sponsored terrorists. They were sea ghazis—a manifestation of the Islamic tradition of raiding as a prelude to, or in the temporary absence of, full-scale warfare.

The Americans had foreseen the possibility of having problems with the Barbary States as early as 1776. The draft "model treaty" drawn up by the Continental Congress to guide the negotiators in Paris had included a clause asking the French for help with Barbary to avoid attacks on American commerce. Article 8 of the 1778 Treaty of Amity and Commerce did provide for some French assistance but only with Morocco.

Morocco was a Barbary Coast state, but it was an independent kingdom and not a tributary to the Ottoman sultan. In the late eighteenth century, its ruler, Sultan Sidi Muhammad ibn Abdullah, sought to move his country's economic base from commerce raiding to trade. When he learned of the American colonies' revolt, he saw an opportunity and in December 1777 declared his ports open to American ships. His decree was the first formal recognition of the United States by a foreign power.

Understandably focused on issues closer at hand, the Americans failed to respond to his gestures, but the determined sultan continued his overtures for several years. Finally, following his strategic seizures of a few American merchant ships, he secured the requisite attention, and in 1787 the United States and Morocco signed their first trade treaty. The Americans and Moroccans have had a virtually continuous treaty relationship ever since.

Unfortunately for the Americans, the other Barbary States corsairs remained sea ghazis, interested in booty and forcing the non-Muslim United States into tributary status. In July 1785, Algiers declared war and began to attack American shipping.

After achieving independence, the Americans found themselves with limited economic opportunities. The mercantilist empires, especially Britain and France, continued to lock out many Yankee traders. The economies of the thirteen now-independent republics recovered but more slowly than expected. To find new markets, the Americans looked to areas not yet under mercantilist control: Russia, China, and the Mediterranean basin, including the Ottoman Empire.

The Barbary attacks presented the Americans with a dilemma. John Adams, the U.S. minister to Britain, thought the best course was to pay tribute, a response he expected would be much cheaper than fighting. Moreover, he doubted the willingness of Americans to shoulder the burdens of another war so soon after the Revolution. Thomas Jefferson, the minister to France, disliked the notion of paying tribute to "pirates" and thought the smallish Barbary States weak enough for even the fledgling United States to handle.

These debates were nevertheless moot. Under the terms of the Articles of Confederation, Congress lacked the power to raise either military forces needed to fight or taxes needed to pay tribute. The debt-ridden Congress relied on the states' contributions for its funding, and the states, short of funds, were themselves heavily in debt. In 1785 the Confederation Congress sold off the last of the Continental Navy's ships and lacked the means to respond with force. Congress did not have the money to pay the tribute demanded by the Algerians, and efforts to raise $50,000 from the states to ransom twenty-one Americans from Barbary captivity failed. The United States was powerless; the only hope was that the Barbary States would consider the Americans so weak and so poor that they would eventually judge the seizure of American vessels pointless.

That was not the Barbary response. Even without tributes or ransoms, they could still find money in seizing ships, cargoes, and Americans. As the years passed the number held in the Maghreb steadily rose. The seizures in the Mediterranean remained an embarrassment and evidence of the Confederation's weakness. This failure of government under the articles contributed to the growing sentiment in the states that the Confederation Congress was too weak and needed either enhanced power or to be replaced by some new form of national government.

Under the Constitution that went into effect in March 1789, the federal government possessed the power to tax, to regulate commerce, and to raise military forces. Nevertheless, during the republic's early years the administration of the first president, George Washington, lacked the resources to confront the Barbary States.

The situation changed dramatically in 1793, when Europe went to war against revolutionary France. Trade with a neutral United States increased, allowing the U.S. government to draw revenues from commercial duties.

Then in October 1793, the British struck an indirect blow against the Americans. London negotiated a truce between Portugal, Britain's ally in the Iberian Peninsula, and Algiers. Before, the Portuguese navy had contained the Algerians' depredations within the Mediterranean. Now the cork was out of the bottle, and the Barbary corsairs sailed into the Atlantic. The Algerians captured several U.S. merchant ships. In weeks the number of Americans held in Algiers reached about 150.

The Americans, especially in seaports, were well aware of these captives' fate. Popular plays and songs called attention to their plight. Organizations raised money for ransom and gathered petitions demanding government action. Most, though not all, Americans ignored the irony evident in Africans selling white Americans into slavery.

Late in 1793, Congress decided to act. It pursued what would become a familiar track, one rooted in the Roman Republic's policies: "if you want peace, prepare for war." In March 1794 Congress sent an emissary to Algiers to negotiate a treaty while it simultaneously passed a naval act to construct six powerful frigates that would form a new navy's core.

The resultant Algerian Treaty of 1796, and its 1797 revision, was a landmark event in American relations with the Middle East and the Islamic world. The treaty was the first American "arms-for-hostages" agreement, foreshadowing the Reagan administration's deal with Iran almost two centuries later. The U.S. government paid money; the Algerians released their hostages. Of the 150 sailors seized, about 112 eventually returned. The others had either died or disappeared. The treaties also marked the beginning of the U.S. arms trade with the Middle East. The United States agreed to construct, fully outfit as warships, and deliver to Algiers several schooners and a frigate.

The Algerian treaties set the standard for U.S. relations with the other Barbary States. American negotiators signed deals with Tripoli in 1796 and Tunis in 1797.

Shortly thereafter, the United States became embroiled in an undeclared naval war with France known as the Quasi-War (1798–1801). The six U.S. frigates constructed to fight Algiers soon were operating in the Caribbean against the French.

As the first foreign (and undeclared) war for the United States wound to a successful conclusion, the Barbary deys decided to get a better deal from the Americans. In 1800 when Capt. William Bainbridge of the U.S. Navy ship-of-war *George Washington* anchored in the harbor of Algiers, the dey threatened the Americans with destruction and forced Bainbridge to carry assorted human, animal, and material tribute to Istanbul for the sultan. Despite the embarrassment, Bainbridge's visit to the Ottoman capital established a new connection between the United States and the empire that would later prove valuable and lessened the immediate chances of an Algerine attack. To the east, relations between the Americans and the Tripolitans worsened, and in 1801 their dey sent a few soldiers to chop down the flagpole that stood in front of the U.S. mission. Tripoli had declared war.

When Thomas Jefferson became president in 1801, he remained as determined as ever to use military force against the

Barbary States. Although he did not ask Congress for a formal declaration, thus resulting in the second undeclared war fought under the new Constitution, in spring 1801 Jefferson dispatched a naval squadron to the Mediterranean and began to wage war against Tripoli. The president's strategy for the conflict evolved over the next several years as the Tripolitans refused to cut a deal with the United States. At first U.S. Navy warships escorted American ships and attacked those of Tripoli, be they commercial or military. When that failed, Jefferson directed the navy to blockade and bombard Tripoli, which it did with some difficulty. When that, too, failed, Jefferson undertook "regime change." His representatives located the deposed brother of the existing dey, promised him military and financial support, raised and trained an army of mercenaries in the Western Desert of Egypt, and launched this force, strengthened by a small detachment of eight U.S. Marines and supported by the U.S. Navy, into Cyrenaica. After a short siege the eastern outpost of the Tripolitan realm, Derna, fell.

The dey decided it was finally time to deal. In June 1805 the Americans and the Tripolitans negotiated a new treaty. Jefferson promptly jettisoned the dey's brother and his mercenary army in the desert. Nevertheless, he kept his naval squadron in the Mediterranean until 1807, when he withdrew it as relations between the United States and Great Britain began to deteriorate following the *Chesapeake-Leopard* affair.

In 1815 as the War of 1812 wound down, Algiers repeated the Tripolitans' mistake and attacked the Americans. President James Madison promptly dispatched Commodore Stephen Decatur with a naval squadron to bombard Algiers. Soon thereafter, the Americans signed a new treaty. This time the squadron remained in the Mediterranean until the outbreak of the American Civil War in 1861.

The Barbary wars were far more important than some forgotten early American military conflict. They represented the initial clash between two entirely different worldviews. The Americans, as children of the Enlightenment, sought the source of their laws not in revealed text but in concepts drawn from Jefferson's "the Laws of Nature and of Nature's God," which are exposed through the application of science and reason. The founders believed in the sanctity of reason, the people's sovereignty, and the laws they chose to create. Islam has always taken a very different view. Sayyid Qutb, in his *Milestones,* stressed the central idea that Allah's will, and not natural law, makes the world what it was and shall be: "This capability belongs solely to the Creator of the universe and of men, Who not only controls the universe but also human affairs, and Who implements a uniform law according to His will." Nor is such an approach limited to modern jihadists. The spring of "Wahabbism," Muhammad ibn Abd al-Wahhab al-Tamimi (1703–1792), in his *Kitab al Tawhid* (Book of Monotheism), wrote that the Qur'an warns Muslims "against worshipping those who are blessed with the power of thinking and logic."

In 1801, of course, neither Americans nor Muslims grasped the fundamental philosophical differences that divided them. Nevertheless, the Americans' interaction with the sea ghazis of the Maghreb in the late eighteenth and early nineteenth centuries marked an important, if not fully appreciated, asymmetrical moment in U.S. history. The Algerines' depredations in the 1780s served as a catalyst for creating a strong American federal republic, and the spoliations in the 1790s led directly to reestablishing a U.S. navy. When the Americans went to the Mediterranean interested solely in trade, the Tripolitan attacks in 1801 prompted the U.S. government to dispatch a naval force across the ocean and to maintain it in the Middle Sea. Of course, the non-trinitarian behavior of the sea ghazis did little to foster a positive view of Islam in the early Americans' minds.

The Tripolitan War also advanced the growth of American nationalism. The hostages and their supporters looked to the new federal government for salvation, not to the states or to their religion. The image of the U.S. government, so powerless under the

Confederation, became something very different under the federal Constitution.

In *The Cresent Obscured,* Robert Allison noted that Francis Scott Key's first set of lyrics penned to be sung to the tune of "To Anacreon in Heaven," the theme of London's *Anacreontic Society* (music best known today as "The Star Spangled Banner"), celebrated the American victory over Tripoli.

> Columbians! a band of your brothers behold,
> Who claim the reward of your hearts' warm emotion,
> When your cause, when your honor, urged onward the
>   bold,
> In vain frowned the desert, in vain raged the ocean:
> To a far distant shore, to the battle's wild roar,
> They rushed, your fair fame and your rights to secure:
> Then, mixed with the olive, the laurel shall wave,
> And form a bright wreath for the brows of the brave.
>
> In the conflict resistless, each toil they endured,
> 'Till their foes fled dismayed from the war's desolation:
> And pale beamed the Crescent, its splendor obscured
> By the light of the Star Spangled flag of our nation.
> Where each radiant star gleamed a meteor of war,
> And the turbaned heads bowed to its terrible glare,
> Now, mixed with the olive, the laurel shall wave,
> And form a bright wreath for the brows of the brave.

Had it not been for the War of 1812, perhaps the national anthem of the United States would have celebrated the nation's first clash with Islam. One can only wonder if Muslims would stand and listen to the lyrics with the same forbearance as our British friends and allies, or would the demands of "political correctness" force Americans to adopt a new anthem?

Nonetheless, the Americans' war against Tripoli and efforts to oust the dey reflected the novel nature of U.S. policy. Whereas the Europeans had learned to live with the Barbary sea ghazis' depredations, the Americans proved to be less accommodating. In that sense, the Americans, despite their military weakness and distance apart, set an example for the Old World. A few decades later, the European powers finally decided that enough was enough. In 1830 fifteen years after Commodore Stephen Decatur bombarded Algiers, the French invaded Algeria, colonized it, and ultimately made it part of metropolitan France.

The struggle with the sea ghazis was also the Americans' first foreign asymmetrical conflict. The Barbary States did not observe the Westphalian system. They did not differentiate between civilians and soldiers. They took slaves, not prisoners of war. They justified their actions within an Islamic context, namely, the need to force *harbis* along the maritime frontier into a tributary status. Ghazis fought for their faith or perhaps for booty, but certainly not for *raison d'état* (the national interest). More than two centuries ago, the Barbary States *forced* the United States to interact with the Islamic world on economic, political, and military terms. The young American republic demonstrated that it was capable of playing the game, of responding forcibly, and of engaging in an early form of asymmetrical warfare.

Despite their youth as a nation, Americans were no strangers to asymmetrical conflict. In fact even at this early stage in their history they were rather skilled practitioners of the art. Of course, they had yet to invent appropriate jargon or governmentese. In the new republic Americans called asymmetrical conflict something simpler—"Indian Wars."

Chapter 5
"The Sick Man of Europe"

As reported by Hafiz abu Y'ala, the Messenger of God—peace be upon Him—said: "Do not ask the People of the Book about anything. They will not guide you. In fact, they are themselves misguided. If you listen to them, you might end up accepting some falsehood or denying some truth. By God, if Moses had been alive among you, he would not be permitted (by God) anything except to follow me."

After this warning to the Muslims from God concerning the ultimate designs of the Jews and Christians, it would be extremely short-sighted of us to fall into the illusion that when the Jews and Christians discuss Islamic beliefs or Islamic history, or when they make proposals concerning Muslim society or Muslim politics or economics, they will be doing it with good intentions, or the welfare of the Muslims at heart, or in order to seek guidance and light. People who, after this clear statement from God, still think this way are deluded.

—*Sayyid Qutb*, Milestones

The Algerine "hijacking" of Commodore William Bainbridge's *George Washington* in late 1800 proved to be a fortuitous event for the United States. Bainbridge was well received in Istanbul and remained there for nearly two months, from November 9 until December 30, 1800. He had audiences with Sultan Selim III and

Grand Vizier Koca Yusuf Pasha. The Ottoman capudan pasha (Lord high admiral) Kucuk Huseyin feted Bainbridge and took the *George Washington* under his personal "protection." Bainbridge reported to Secretary of the Navy Benjamin Stoddert that the Turks hoped to establish a treaty relationship with the United States and had invited the Americans to send a minister to Istanbul.

Selim III was a reforming sultan, a man well aware of the problems facing his empire and the necessity, somewhat new for the Turks, to play an adroit diplomatic game to keep the Christian powers from unifying against and carving up the Ottoman domain. For a century the Turks had been losing territory in the Caucasus and the Balkans. When Bainbridge met the capudan pasha, the latter had just returned from the successful campaign to drive the French from Egypt, which had been invaded in 1798 by a young general named Napoleon Bonaparte. That the Ottomans had relied on British power to retake Egypt was symptomatic of the empire's deterioration.

The Ottoman Empire's decline was at first more apparent to the Turks than to outsiders. Ottoman prowess on the battlefield disguised the archaic system's shortcomings. Until the seventeenth century the long history of Ottoman victories deterred attacks along the frontier. When the Ottomans went to war, usually at times of their own choosing, their army triumphed with relatively quick, decisive victories. But as the Europeans' military proficiency increased, wars became more frequent and prolonged, taxing the Ottoman's still-feudal infrastructure.

As a result decay occurred gradually, the result of multiple causes. The empire's population grew but without the corresponding increases in agricultural and industrial output evident in the West. In fact the Western economies' growth exacerbated the problems within the Ottoman Empire. The West's less expensive manufactures and growing demand for raw materials disrupted the feudal and increasingly uncompetitive Ottoman economy. Prices rose, craftsmen lost out to foreign manufactures, and the imperial currency steadily lost value.

To remain competitive internationally, the Ottomans fell back on the usual method of increasing the tax burden on the land and their subjects. The sultan confiscated tax farms and auctioned them to the highest bidder. The administration eliminated and consolidated the smaller *timars*. Landless *sipahis* and overtaxed peasants turned to banditry and on occasion rebellion, even in the Turkish heartland of Anatolia.

To further complicate matters, at the very time the empire needed wise leadership, the caliber of the sultanate declined. With the death of Suleiman "the Magnificent" (1520–66), Selim II "the Sot" (1566–74) became sultan. There followed more than a century of damaging political infighting and intrigue among myriad factions. When Murat III (1574–95) followed his father, he immediately murdered his five brothers. Murat's son Mehmet III (1595–1603) killed his nineteen brothers and twenty sisters, all strangled by a loyal corps of deaf-mutes. During this period the Ottomans engaged in innumerable wars around the periphery of their empire and gained Cyprus but suffered a major naval defeat at Lepanto and failed to secure their northern frontier with Russia.

With Mehmet's passing in 1603, Anatolia erupted into revolt. Inflation, rising taxes, disaffection following fifty years of less-than-enlightened rule, and the expansion of the foreign-born devshirme faction's power base all contributed to the unrest.

Despite this turmoil, the Ottomans continued to field capable military forces. They quickly rebuilt their navy after Lepanto and made the transition to gunpowder both ashore and afloat. But the sultans found sustaining an increasingly modern army with a feudal economic base difficult. The shift on the battlefield from cavalry to infantry also posed peculiar problems for the Turks: in their *timar* system, the sipahi (knights) held title, albeit temporarily, to the land.

Osman II's short-lived reign (1618–22) witnessed the first comprehensive military reform effort. But his plans to build up a more national and Turkish force ran afoul of both the sipahis and the janissaries, whose 1622 revolt brought an end to the effort.

Murat IV (1623–40) reestablished a degree of central control, rooted out corruption, suppressed banditry, and reallocated many of the *timars*. But he also reestablished tax farms and, when faced with fiscal shortfalls, resorted to outright confiscation.

In 1625 Murat undertook a campaign to recapture Baghdad, which had been lost to the Persians in 1603. For the next seventy-seven years, the Ottoman Empire was in a constant state of warfare against, at various times, Persia, Venice, Poland, Austria, and Russia. In 1683 the Ottoman army reached the gates of Vienna for the final time. During the subsequent retreat the army routed, the Austrians captured Belgrade, the Venetians Athens, and the Russians Azov. For the first time in their history the Ottomans had to seek alliances, no longer for convenience, but for survival. They eventually regained Athens and Belgrade but not Azov.

By 1702 the Ottoman Empire had exhausted its supplies of men and money. With the Treaty of Karlowitz in 1699, the Turks lost Hungary to the Austrians and the Morea to the Venetians. A separate 1702 agreement with the Russians left them in possession of Azov.

Nevertheless, the significance of Karlowitz lay less in the territory lost than in the accord itself. For the first time, Ottoman diplomats actually had to negotiate rather than simply dictate terms. The Ottomans' weakness was now evident throughout Europe.

Reform was necessary for the empire's survival, but efforts remained tentative. One sultan would initiate reforms that his successor would halt or reverse. The most notable era, or the *Lâle Devri* (tulip period, 1718–30) saw modernization and Westernization. Istanbul witnessed dramatic changes in fashion, architecture, and city planning—all epitomized by a strange fascination with imported tulips. The empire underwent an intellectual renaissance, with a flowering of poetry, literature, history, science, and geography. For the first time in Islamic history, Muslims translated the works of contemporary Europeans, an effort aided by the establishment of Istanbul's first printing press in 1720.

Unfortunately for the Ottomans, the reform effort came too late. The period of peace — a much-needed breathing spell for an exhausted empire — was short lived. In the mid-1720s the wars began again, initially with Persia and then with Russia and Austria. A popular revolt, in part a reaction to both modernization and Westernization, brought the tulip period to an abrupt end in 1730.

Another six decades of political instability, insurrections, halting reforms, and continuous wars further wore down the empire. A Russian fleet, dispatched from the Baltic, entered the Mediterranean and defeated the Ottoman navy — its sailing men-of-war towed about by obsolete galleys — at Tchesma in July 1770. The July 1774 Treaty of Kucuk Kaynarca struck an especially egregious blow to Islamic pride. The loss of Muslim-controlled territory was painful enough, but the terms forced the Ottomans to pay tribute to the Russians and to grant them the right to oversee the condition of Orthodox Christians within the sultan's realm. By 1789 when Selim III (1789–1807) took the throne, successive wars against Austria and Russia had led to the loss of the Crimea and additional lands in the Balkans and Caucasus.

Selim III was determined to reform his empire. During his reign the Ottomans undertook military, naval, technical, administrative, economic, and social reforms. European advisers proliferated within the realm. Under their guidance, Selim formed the *Nizam-i-Cedit* (the army of the New Order). His internal reforms prompted several revolts, however, all of which he managed to suppress.

Reaction and events in Europe also hampered Selim's efforts. In 1793 in response to the French Revolution, a general war began in Europe. Of all the European countries, France had long had the best relationship with the Ottomans. But in July 1798 Napoleon Bonaparte's French army landed in Egypt and defeated the Mamluks, tributaries of the Ottomans. With British help, Selim checked the French at Acre, and then in August 1801 a predominantly British force landed in Egypt and defeated the French.

Already losing control within his empire, the sultan watched as his lieutenant in Egypt, the Albanian Mehmet Ali, seized effective control in Cairo. Selim named him viceroy and hoped for the best.

In 1807 the old order struck back, and rebellion erupted in Istanbul. The rebels secured a *fetva* (Arabic *fatwa*, or judgment) from the *ulema*, which declared the sultan's reforms violations of both Islamic and Ottoman tradition. Mustafa IV became sultan; Selim entered house arrest in the seraglio, where he met his end by strangulation. His successor ended most of the reforms and disbanded the *Nizam-i-Cedit*.

The unrest in Istanbul allowed Mehmet Ali, who considered himself the Ottoman answer to Napoleon, to secure his position in Egypt. He began to build up a Western-style military, ignoring the old order in Cairo. On March 1, 1811, he took a page from the history of the Abbasids, invited the surviving Mamluk lords to dinner, and killed them all.

Mehmet Ali's treachery in Egypt displeased the Ottomans, but the sultan found himself unable to challenge his viceroy and, on several occasions, actually had to turn to him for assistance. The sultan first sought Mehmet Ali's help to contain an internal Islamic conflagration on the Arabian Peninsula. A decade later, the Ottomans again called on the Egyptians for help in suppressing a Christian revolt in Greece.

Trouble had been brewing within Arabia throughout the eighteenth century. Muhammad ibn Abd al-Wahhab al-Tamimi (1703–1792) was a religious scholar from the peninsula's central Najd region. He sought to purify Islam and to remove the innumerable corruptions that, in his view, had accreted to Islam since the days of the early khalifas. Seeking a revival of Islam, he was what today would be termed a "fundamentalist," although he viewed himself as a reformer.

At some point in the mid-eighteenth century, Ibn Abd al-Wahhab joined forces with a Najd tribal leader—Muhammad ibn Saud—who helped spread the revived form of Islam as he extended his own control throughout the peninsula. In 1803 Saud's forces captured Mecca, threatening the sultan's legitimacy as the holy places' protector. In the east, the expansion of Saud's domain led to political instability and raiding, or piracy, in the Persian Gulf and Arabian Sea.

Powerless to contain the threat himself, the sultan turned to Mehmet Ali. In 1812 the new Egyptian army crossed the Red Sea, counterattacked, and retook the Hijaz (Mecca and Medina), reestablishing nominal Ottoman control. To contain piracy in the Persian Gulf, the British intervened and in the 1820s established the "Trucial States" (the present-day United Arab Emirates) to contain the attacks.

Egypt's conquest of the Hijaz dealt a blow to Ibn Saud, who retreated to the Arabian Peninsula's interior. Nevertheless, a century later his descendants would establish their own kingdom—Saudi Arabia.

Likewise Ibn Abd al-Wahhab's followers continued their efforts of purification. Generally, although inaccurately, termed "Wahhabis," these self-proclaimed "Salafists" (those who follow the examples established by the first three generations of Muslims) or "Muwahhidun" (monotheists, implying that those who do not agree with them are apostate "polytheists") would make their own comeback in the twentieth century.

As the situation in Arabia stabilized, that in the Balkans worsened. The French Revolution prompted a rise of nationalism within Europe, a powerful force that spelled trouble for multinational empires, be they Russian, Austrian, or Ottoman. Nationalism was a particular problem for the Ottomans because of the second-class status of its dhimmi population, a status hard-coded into Islam.

In 1804 the Serbs were the first of the ethnic groups to rebel. It took nine years for the Ottomans to suppress the revolt, only to have it erupt again in 1815. The second effort gained the Serbs a degree of political autonomy within the empire.

In 1821 unrest swept through the Greek communities.

Despite numerous handicaps, the Greeks had prospered as merchants within the Ottoman realm. But that prosperity and the window to the world that accompanied maritime commerce led to increasing disaffection. Outright revolt swept Ottoman control from the Morea, where the Greeks slaughtered local Muslims and seized power. The Turks struck back, perpetrating similar massacres, but they were unable to suppress the revolt. Well aware of the weakness in Istanbul, Mehmet Ali seized Crete in the sultan's name but had every intention of adding the island to his growing Egyptian mini-empire. Despite the threat posed by the Egyptian viceroy, the sultan felt compelled to turn to his vassal for further assistance.

Mehmet Ali dispatched his son, Ibrahim, with a contingent of troops and the bulk of the fleet to the Morea in 1824. The Egyptian army succeeded where the Ottomans had failed. But reports of the Egyptians' continued butchery and suppression of the revolt after three years moved the European powers to action. The British attempted to mediate, hoping to gain the Greeks' autonomy within the Ottoman Empire.

Amid the turmoil, Sultan Mahmut II decided to move against the janissaries, whose stock was at a low point because of their repeated failures against the Balkan rebels. The sultan first isolated the corps from its traditional sources of support. Mahmut neutralized the *ulema* by promoting some of its members, exiling others, launching a religious education program, and repairing old mosques and building new ones. In June 1826 he announced the formation of a new military corps and invited the janissaries to join. They recognized the trap and rose in revolt. But Mahmut was prepared. He moved quickly to eliminate their remaining power, massacring between 6,000 and 10,000 in what became known as "the Auspicious Event."

Meanwhile, the situation in the Morea deteriorated. On October 20, 1827, a combined British, French, and Russian armada destroyed the Egyptian fleet at Navarino. The Russians subsequently declared war against the Ottomans, and the British and

French convinced Mehmet Ali to withdraw. By 1829 the Russians were in Adrianople (Edirne), less than 125 miles from Istanbul.

Fortune saved the Ottomans. The British and French were reluctant to see the empire destroyed. Disease laid low the Russian army and forced the czar to negotiate rather than push the war to a military conclusion. The Turks lost more territory in the Balkans and the east, granted independence to a rump Greek state in the Morea, and agreed to pay another large indemnity.

The disasters of the 1820s led the Ottomans to redouble their efforts to reach an accord with the Americans. From the Turkish perspective, the United States was unaligned, uninterested in colonies or territory, and increasingly powerful.

When the War of 1812 ended, the Americans returned to the Mediterranean. Commodore Decatur bombarded Algiers in 1815. In 1821 the U.S. Navy established a base at Port Mahon to protect an ever-growing volume of trade.

Along with the commercial relations, missionary interests also revived. Americans established missions in Izmir (1819), Jerusalem (1821), Cairo (1823), and Beirut (1824). In Beirut they began to teach local children—starting out with six in 1824 and more than 300 a few years later—thus establishing the foundation for a network of colleges, or American universities, throughout the region.

The Greek revolt complicated U.S. policy. Many Americans sympathized with the Greeks as Christians and with Greece as the birthplace of democracy. The rebels recognized this connection and sought to enlist the United States in the struggle but with limited success. A handful of volunteers fought alongside the Greeks, some Americans contributed money, and a shipbuilder constructed a frigate for the rebel navy. But the U.S. government had no desire to get involved in a war in the eastern Mediterranean; nor did it wish to endanger expanded commercial opportunities with the Ottoman Empire.

In 1823 the Sublime Porte—that is, the Ottoman government as it was commonly known throughout Europe by the nineteenth century — countered the Greek efforts, offering the United States a treaty. But the American negotiators discovered that the Turks sought more than a mere commercial connection; they preferred an alliance and the right to build warships in U.S. ports. The Americans rejected this idea; they recognized that any alliance with the Ottoman Empire would inevitably drag the United States into distant and repeated wars.

Following the defeat at Navarino, the Porte renewed its approaches to the United States. By 1830 negotiators had reached an agreement that included establishing formal diplomatic relations, permitting American merchant ships to pass the Bosphorus Straits and enter the Black Sea, bestowing most-favored-nation status on both parties, and allowing a secret article that permitted the Turks to build warships and buy timber in the United States. The U.S. Senate rejected the secret clause when it ratified the treaty in 1831. Nevertheless, Henry Eckford, a shipbuilder best known for constructing Oliver Hazard Perry's flotilla on Lake Erie in 1812–13, sailed to Istanbul along with an American-built warship. By 1832 Eckford was overseeing the Ottoman navy's reconstruction, including its first steamship.

But the Ottoman Empire's troubles had not yet ended, nor would they ever. Thus Turkish reformers rarely had the time to undertake their work. As the Porte struggled to institute reforms, Mehmet Ali demanded control of Syria for his help in Arabia and the Balkans. The British attempted to arbitrate, offering the sultan's nominal viceroy hereditary rule in Egypt and Palestine. But Mehmet Ali sought more, much more, and the sultan's refusal to yield led to war with Egypt. In the winter of 1831–32, the Ottomans, who had recently survived the Russian advance to Adrianople, now seemed about to give way before Mehmet Ali's modern army.

Great Britain saved the Ottoman Empire by threatening intervention and dispatching the British fleet to Alexandria. In 1840 under pressure from the European powers, Mehmet Ali settled for hereditary rule in Egypt, yielding Syria, Palestine, and the Hijaz.

The British subsequently dominated the political scene in Istanbul, to the disadvantage of the United States. Nevertheless, American trade with the empire continued to expand.

Sultan Mahmut II died of tuberculosis in July 1839, as the crisis with Egypt came to a climax, and was succeeded by his sixteen-year-old son Abdulmecit I (1839–61). The new sultan was committed to continue his father's reforms, increasingly the handiwork of Mustafa Re°it Pa°a, the Ottoman foreign minister and later grand vizier. Re°it had witnessed the Ottoman defeats in the Morea as well as the more modern Egyptian army's successes. He had served for years as an ambassador in Europe and had a good understanding of European military technology and of the society that produced it. He had labored for years to strengthen and broaden Mahmut II's commitment to reform, and he found a willing partner in the new sultan.

Assisted by a core of supporters within the bureaucracy known as the *tanzimatçilar* (the reorganizers), Re°it oversaw the drafting and promulgation of the Imperial Rescript of Gülhane on November 3, 1839. The *Tanzimat* reforms were the broadest, deepest, and most comprehensive set of reforms yet attempted within the Islamic world. They included guarantees of life, honor (but not liberty), and property; a regular system to assess and collect taxes; procedures for conscripting and maintaining the Ottoman armed forces, including establishing reserve formations along European lines; the creation of a Western-type governing bureaucracy, including various executive branches; the first revamping of the empire's financial structure since 1500; the state assuming control of religion, education, and justice; and the formation of a proto-cabinet to advise the sultan. *Tanzimat* also called for extending centralized government from the core to the provinces, essentially ending feudalism in the mid-nineteenth century. To ensure central power, the reform package included plans for improved communications within the empire. While *Tanzimat* retained the system of millets, the members of each were no longer bound to select religious leaders to represent them. The non-Muslim millets gained a greater degree of religious protection but not full equality under the law. The major ethnic millets secured a degree of autonomy regarding the use of their languages and customs. The Ottoman government also established its own official printing house, nearly four centuries after Gutenberg unveiled his invention.

For the next several decades, Abdulmecit I served as a virtual figurehead. Power within the empire rested with the grand vizier and the *tanzimatçilar*. The reforms continued. An 1856 decree established full equality for all religions, a major departure from Islam and the Qur'an's strictures. An 1869 "nationality" law established Ottoman citizenship for all of the empire's people, whatever their ethnicity or religion. Finally, in 1876, Sultan Abdulhamid II. Abdulmecit's son, signed the first Ottoman constitution. The document incorporated the *Tanzimat* reforms, including equality for all, protection of private property from confiscation, and regularity in taxation. Islam became the empire's official religion, but the Qur'anic insistence that Christians and Jews be treated as *jizya*-paying dhimmis came to an end, at least on paper.

Unfortunately for the Ottomans, the reforms came too late to save "the sick man of Europe." The empire remained embroiled in near-constant warfare, with the most notable conflict being the Crimean War (1853–56). Ostensibly, the Ottomans emerged as the victors, alongside their British, French, and Sardinian allies. In the Treaty of Paris of March 1856, the Turks regained some of their lost lands, and the great powers guaranteed their territorial integrity. But the war further increased the Ottoman debt. By 1875 it had ballooned to about £200 million, bearing interest alone of nearly £12 million—a sum equal to the annual revenue of the entire Ottoman state! (The annual revenue of the U.S. federal government at the time was about £70 million.) Tax revenues remained inadequate. Hundreds of thousands of Muslim immigrants flooded into Anatolia from the Balkans as unrest and rebellions among the

Christian population increased. Moldavians, Walachians, Serbians, Bulgarians, Macedonians, and Montenegrins rose in revolt, providing Russia with continuous opportunities to intervene, alongside the Serbs and Montenegrins during the Russo-Turkish War of 1877. The Ottomans negotiated the Treaty of San Stefano in 1878 with the czar's army in the outskirts of Istanbul. The treaty secured additional territory for Serbia, independence for Montenegro and Romania, and autonomy for Bosnia and Herzegovina. The Porte granted Bulgaria status as a self-governing Ottoman principality. The Russians took Batum and Kars and a promissory note for a £30 million indemnity that the Turks could ill afford. Bureaucrats went unpaid; unpaid bureaucrats became corrupt.

To complicate matters, granting equality to ethnic and religious minorities failed to yield the expected dividends. On the one hand, after centuries of living as dhimmis, the Christian populations in the Balkans sought independence, not equality. On the other, the Muslim population and especially the Ottoman *ulema* did not universally favor granting legal equality to the dhimmis, who comprised a third to a quarter of the empire's population.

In 1878 Sultan Abdulhamid II (1876–1909) suspended the very constitution that he had signed two years earlier. The sultan ruled once again as an autocrat, although one committed to a degree of reform. But autocratic rule could not reverse the course of events. The continued loss of territory, the need to resettle a veritable flood of Muslim refugees in Anatolia, military defeats, and an ever-increasing debt undercut reforms.

What role did Islam play in the failures of the *tanzimatçilar*? The Ottoman *ulema* did challenge the *Tanzimat* reforms and supported Abdulhamid's suspension of the constitution; Islam provided a bulwark against the drive for ethnic and religious equality within the empire. Nevertheless, the primary cause of the reforms' failure was their inability to reverse the empire's steady course of decline. The same fate would befall Arab and other nationalists in the second half of the twentieth century.

The American Civil War and decades of turmoil within the Ottoman Empire handicapped U.S. expectations of an expanding relationship with the Porte as well as the latter's desire to use the United States as a counterweight to European influence. American commercial interests likewise suffered because of conflict, Ottoman indebtedness, and the growing influence of the British in Istanbul.

Nevertheless, American missionaries continued their outreach. Notable achievements included establishing printing presses and expanding their educational work. But the few conversions were rarely among Muslims and usually involved Roman or Eastern Catholics. Not surprising, the hierarchies of these churches did whatever they could to limit the inroads of the Protestant missions.

As Yankee prospects in the eastern Mediterranean darkened, those in the Indian Ocean basin beckoned. The Americans had been active east of the Cape of Good Hope since their independence. Sealers flew the Stars and Stripes from their bases on the nominally French islands of St. Paul and Amsterdam, and in 1800 the U.S. Navy dispatched the frigate *Essex* to the Sunda Strait. In the early nineteenth century, American merchants traded with those Arabs who dominated commerce within the Indian Ocean's western basin. While many Americans considered Muslims heathens, naval officers thought otherwise. "Mohammedan" ports were safe, if boring, venues for sailors anxious for shore leave so far from home. Alfred Thayer Mahan, who served as a young officer in the region, noted that when a party of men from his ship went ashore, he "had the unprecedented experience that they all came back on time and sober."

In this region the United States focused its attention on "Muscat and Oman." In the mid-nineteenth century, the sultanate was extensive, including much of the Arabian Peninsula's eastern and southern periphery, Africa's east coast, and the major entrepôt at Zanzibar. In 1833 Edmund Roberts, a Salem merchant, headed an American mission accompanied by the two-ship naval squadron of the sloop-of-war *Peacock* and the schooner *Boxer* that arrived in Muscat. On September 21, 1833, Roberts and the sultan signed a treaty of amity and commerce, establishing a diplomatic relationship that continues until the present day. Within a decade American trade flourished, and the Yankees held a near monopoly in Zanzibar. In 1841 a British diplomat discovered that the sultan had decorated his palace with prints of the U.S. Navy's victories over British frigates in the War of 1812.

As commerce increased in the region, the Americans sought a relationship with the Persian Empire. Representatives of the two countries met in Istanbul in 1851 and worked out an agreement. The Senate ratified the treaty, but British diplomats aborted the effort.

In the fall of 1854, with the British "occupied" in the Crimea, the Persians reopened negotiations with the United States in an effort designed to involve the latter in the region's affairs. The shah's expansive proposals surprised the Americans. He sought an agreement that would allow him "to buy or have constructed in the United States several vessels of war and to procure the services of American officers and seamen to navigate them." Other proposals included provisions for the United States to protect Persian ships, ports, and islands from attack; the right for the shah to re-flag his merchant vessels in times of crisis with the Stars and Stripes; and the dispatch of an American naval squadron to the Persian Gulf to support his own fleet. The Persians were doing their best to induce the United States to become a "player" in the south Asian "great game," but the Americans lacked the means as well as the desire to meet the Persians' demands. The shah's disappointed negotiators withdrew when the Americans refused to consider such extensive involvement.

Negotiations resumed in 1856, and by the end of the year the two parties had reached an agreement. The terms were purely commercial, although the American negotiator agreed to pass on the shah's request that the United States send an ambassador to

Tehran and a ship of war to the gulf as expeditiously as possible.

It took more than twenty years before that man-of-war arrived. In 1879 Commodore Robert Shufeldt in the steam-sloop USS *Ticonderoga* reached the gulf. He visited Muscat, in Oman, where he discovered that two-thirds of the sultanate's trade was with the United States. He called at the Persian ports of Bushire and Basra and steamed seventy miles up the Shatt-al-Arab, where the Tigris and Euphrates rivers joined.

After the American Civil War, the U.S. Navy likewise returned to the Mediterranean, from which it had withdrawn in 1861. The U.S. merchant fleet was in decline but not so the nation's trade. In fact the Yankees had a new export—kerosene, a petroleum product from the nation's oil wells. Then the United States was the world's largest oil producer and exporter and would remain so until 1948.

Missionary activity likewise revived after the Civil War. In 1866, 156 Maine Protestants arrived in Palestine to establish a settlement and await the Messiah's Second Coming. The effort of these "innocents abroad" quickly failed. But the mainstream missionaries met with somewhat better success, although mostly within existing Christian communities, such as those in the Balkans. Missionaries founded Roberts College in the Ottoman capital, Instanbul, and trained many of the Christian leaders who, in the late nineteenth and early twentieth centuries, helped to expel the Turks from the Balkans. T. E. Lawrence wrote of the American schools:

> Quite without intention they taught revolution, since it was impossible for an individual to be modern in Turkey and at the same time loyal, if he had been born of one of the subject races—Greeks, Arabs, Kurds, Armenians or Albanians—over whom the Turks were so long helped to keep dominion.

In the post–Civil War era, new opportunities beckoned in Egypt, now ruled by Mehmet Ali's reforming grandson, Ismail.

The khedive (viceroy) was intent on carrying out an aggressive plan of modernization and expansion. After a decade of construction, the Suez Canal opened on November 17, 1869, increasing Egypt's strategic and commercial importance. New industries sprang up along with a system of schools to educate some segments of the population. The khedive cooperated with the British in suppressing the east African slave trade and the institution of slavery itself. Ismail's efforts to expand and modernize his army provided a ready market for surplus and newly manufactured American weapons as well as for unemployed officers from both the Union and the Confederacy. Ismail contracted with Remington to provide the most modern rifles to his army. He employed American railroad men to develop an Egyptian rail system, although planning far exceeded construction. A former Union officer, Charles P. Stone, served as the chief of the newly established Egyptian General Staff. Stone reformed the military and pushed literacy among all the ranks, especially the officers. He also oversaw the first systematic mapping of Egypt and the surrounding region. A British national, Charles "Chinese" Gordon, directed the spread of Egyptian military power south to the Sudan and then to the Red Sea coast of what is now Eritrea.

Khedive Ismail's sixteen-year reign ended in disaster, and with it the American presence. A four-year-long war with Ethiopia (1875–79) ended in defeat. The decade-long attempt to create an industrial infrastructure, which the West had taken centuries to develop, collapsed. The Egyptian state debt, which was £3 million when Ismail took power in 1863, exploded to £100 million by 1879. To remain solvent, the khedive sold his shares in the Suez Canal to the British government, which became the largest single shareholder. Then ostensibly the Porte, but actually the European powers, forced the khedive to abdicate in favor of his son Tewfik. The Egyptian government's collapse and the subsequent European presence and control of the state's finances led to a series of nationalist uprisings and ultimately a full-scale revolt. In response to the unrest, the British bombarded Alexandria and landed a small army in Egypt. At the 1882 battle of Tel el-Kebir, they defeated Egyptian nationalist Col. Ahmad Urabi and his rebels and occupied Egypt. Mehmet Ali's dynasty, however, would continue to reign until King Farouk abdicated in 1952.

To the south, in the Sudan, the British confronted not nationalism but militant Islamic fundamentalism. In 1881 a thirty-seven-year-old holy man, Muhammad Ahmad ibn as Sayyid Abd Allah, declared himself *al Mahdi al Muntazar* ("the Expected One"), whose appearance heralded the approach of the final judgment day.

The Mahdi and his followers, the *Ansar,* represented a political reaction to Egyptian encroachment to the south and the disruption of Sudanese society, which the slave trade had dominated for several centuries. The Mahdi declared a jihad and drove north along the Nile. In January 1885 they captured Khartoum and beheaded Gordon, who commanded the Egyptian garrison.

The self-proclaimed Mahdi died in June well short of his goal of world conquest; however, he did form an Islamic government—the Mahdiya—committed to global jihad. In his modified interpretation of Islam, jihad replaced the hajj, or pilgrimage to Mecca, as one of the five pillars of the faith. But the Mahdiya could barely govern itself. Finally, in 1895, Field Marshal Horatio Kitchener and an Anglo-Egyptian army began a campaign to retake the Sudan. At Omdurman on September 2, 1898, Kitchener's force slaughtered the much larger Mahdist army. By the end of the following year, the war was over and the Mahdiya had collapsed. In less than twenty years, the Sudanese population had declined by 50 percent from the impact of war and Mahdist misrule.

The British occupation of Egypt in 1882, technically a tributary state to the Porte, further undercut the Ottomans' legitimacy. Nevertheless, autocratic Sultan Abdulhamid II struggled to move the empire forward through controlled modernization and a degree of secularization. But he faced the same problems that had undermined earlier efforts at reform: near-continuous warfare, internal discord, and a crushing debt burden.

Interest on the foreign debt consumed as much as 80 percent of state revenues. External pressures, or war, made it both difficult and dangerous to control, let alone reduce, spending. During the Islamic year that coincided with parts of the common era years 1877–78, the Porte collected 1,972 million kurus but spent 2,947 million kurus. By 1905–1906, revenues had increased by only 13 percent, or to 2,229 million kurus, while state expenditures actually declined.

The restricted revenue base left little money for implementing improvements to the communications infrastructure—railroads, roads, harbors, and telegraph—within the vast empire. Ottoman exports consisted overwhelmingly of agricultural products and raw materials and no longer included finished goods or manufactures. Imports were twice the level of exports. A nearly static tax base hindered efforts at educational and military reform.

The inability to markedly increase the realm's military strength posed grave dangers for the sultanate, since the diplomatic situation remained perilous. Russia, Austria, and even the smaller states in the Balkans threatened the empire. While Great Britain had sought to maintain the Ottoman Empire, the British had, on occasion, worked against the Porte's interests, most notably in Egypt. Prussian successes in wars against Austria (1866) and France (1870) raised the new German Empire's prestige and influence in Istanbul, and the Porte began to look more and more to Berlin for assistance. In 1898 Kaiser Wilhelm II became the first Christian monarch to make a state visit to Istanbul.

Internally, the sultan found limited support for modernization and reform. The Jews were most accommodating, because they were a small minority dispersed throughout the empire and stood to gain from any move toward equality, protection of life and property, and greater economic opportunity. Changes in property law also made it easier for Jews to purchase land, a change that permitted European Zionists to begin their first wave of immigration into Palestine. But for the other non-Muslim ethnic millets, reform arrived too late; moreover, these groups sought independence, not equality. One of the most aggressive millets was the Armenian. Frustrated by the reforms' failed implementation in the eastern provinces, they responded with a campaign of terror, including an attempt on the sultan's life while on his way to Friday prayer.

Abdulhamid II also had problems with the Muslim millets. Various strains of Arab nationalism developed in the south, primarily in Syria. In the Arabian Peninsula, the sultan faced a growing threat from tribesman bordering the Hijaz. Muslim Albanians sought independence in the Balkans, and even the Turks grew restless. Many sought more rapid, far-reaching reforms. Others saw the sultan as a threat to Islamic traditions.

Pan-Islamism—the idea that Islam was and ought to remain the bond uniting the empire—grew more determined after the *Tanzimat* reforms had given, on paper at least, equality to Christians and Jews and freed them from their *jizya* and dhimmi status. To placate the Islamists, the sultan increased state funding for *madrasas* (Islamic religious schools) and added religious education to the curricula of the heretofore secular state schools. Abdulhamid also stressed his role as khalifa to all Muslims, even those beyond the Ottoman borders.

Simultaneously, the sultan faced a national challenge from his fellow Turks, the realm's ethnic core. A sense of Turkish nationalism and Pan-Turanianism—the idea of uniting all Turks within and outside the empire—increased as a steady stream of refugees poured in from the Balkans and Central Asia and as those who remained behind often became oppressed minorities, suffering at the hands of Christian rulers. The most serious political threat came from an element known as the Young Turks, or secular nationalists committed to Turkish rather than Ottoman nationalism and to structural and social reforms. The Young Turks included unemployed and would-be bureaucrats, military officers, and Western-style liberals and intellectuals. They formed a European-wide political organization, the Committee of Union and Progress (CUP), in 1906. With many living as exiles and others operating in clandestine cells in fear of Abdulhamid's secret police, the Young Turks established networks throughout the empire and western Europe. While they differed in many of their goals and expectations, they all sought the constitution's restoration and the sultan's abdication.

Events came to a head in 1907. The empire suffered a poor harvest, tax yields declined, and soldiers and bureaucrats went unpaid. In Paris at the Second Young Turk Congress, the CUP and Armenian nationalists agreed to cooperate. When unrest broke out in Macedonia, the army proved unable or unwilling to suppress it. On July 24, 1908, Abdulhamid II responded to the pressure by restoring the Constitution of 1876. The Young Turks moved quickly and formed the Committee of Seven to advise the sultan, who agreed to abolish the secret police, relax censorship, allow freedom of the press, release political prisoners, and undertake additional reforms. The atmosphere throughout the empire was celebratory.

But the mood was short lived. The empire's neighbors viewed the situation in Istanbul as an opportunity. Austria annexed Bosnia-Herzegovina, Bulgaria declared its independence, and Greece annexed Crete. The loss of additional territory undermined the legitimacy of the Young Turks' leadership. And while they dominated the newly elected parliament, to the Greeks' and the Armenians' bitter disappointment, it soon became apparent that the Young Turks were also determined to rule the state.

The empire's Muslims were not solidly behind the Young Turks. Religious conservatives countered by forming their own political organizations, among them the Society of Islamic Unity. These groups railed against the *ulema*'s weakened role, the erosion of *Shari'ah,* and the civil, religious, and ethnic equality extended to Christians and Jews.

Abdulhamid recognized an opportunity to regain his lost

authority. In April 1909 he championed a conservative counter-revolution that swept the Young Turks from power.

The responses to the sultan's actions were swift. An Armenian uprising that began in Adana spread throughout the empire, ending with tens of thousands dead (figures vary from 20,000 to 100,000), mostly Christians. The Ottoman army in Macedonia marched to Istanbul and stormed the capital on April 24. Parliament met again three days later and deposed Abdulhamid II. His brother, Mehmet V, became the new figurehead sultan.

The situation continued to deteriorate, despite good intentions and further reforms. The state debt grew. Armenians and Greeks undertook terror campaigns to gain their freedom. A revolt broke out among the Muslims in Albania. Arab nationalism continued to foment, and unrest in Arabia threatened Ottoman control of the holy cities of Mecca and Medina. The empire's ethnic Turks had by this point developed a siege mentality. They realized they could not rely on the Greeks, Armenians, or the Arabs within the empire.

Amid internal political confusion, the diplomatic situation worsened. In 1911 Italy invaded Libya, a nominal Ottoman possession. In 1912 the First Balkan War began. By its end the empire had lost additional territory and granted the Albanians independence. When the Young Turks lost control of the parliament, they responded by staging a coup in Istanbul. Henceforth a dictatorial troika of the "Three Pashas"—Cemal, Enver, and Talat—ruled the empire.

When the Second Balkan war began in 1913, the Ottomans were, for once, spectators. They had little territory left to lose in the Balkans and thus faced fewer threats. They had shed many of their Christian subjects along the way, although large Armenian and Greek communities remained within the imperial borders. The Ottomans only joined the fray when it reached its climax, regaining Adrianople. On the surface, it appeared that the Young Turk coup had finally reversed a steady course of decline.

Nevertheless, several questions remained unanswered. The state still bore an enormous debt. How would it be paid? How would the smaller, but still multiethnic and multireligious Ottoman Empire define itself in the new century? And how would the Ottomans play the diplomatic game that was under way in Europe, with states aligning themselves into a pair of armed camps?

The Young Turk leadership drifted toward a closer relationship with Germany. The Kaiser's army was the most efficient military organization of the early twentieth century. Germany lacked a history of imperialism vis-à-vis the Ottoman Empire and appeared to have fewer colonial ambitions than Russia, France, or Britain. Alignment with Germany also served as a check against the Austro-Hungarian monarchy—Germany's junior partner.

In the summer of 1914, the Young Turks faced their most difficult challenge. On June 28, 1914, a Serbian terrorist assassinated the Austrian archduke Franz Ferdinand and his wife in Sarajevo. Europe geared for war. No alliance bound the Ottoman Empire to either camp. As in the Second Balkan War, the Turks had options: they could remain neutral, securing breathing space and time to recover from decades of internal discord and conflict; they could delay and then time their entry into the conflict as before; or they could sell their entrance to the conflict to the highest bidder or the alliance that appeared most likely to emerge victorious.

By 1914 the thirty-four-year-old, German-educated minister of defense, Enver Pasha, had become the dominant figure in the Young Turk dictatorship. He was a reformer but also an ardent Turkish nationalist and expansionist. He viewed the prospect of war as an opportunity for territorial expansion, not as a breathing spell for reform. On July 20, 1914, Enver informed the Austrians that the Porte had received offers to enter into an alliance with the Russians, Rumanians, and Greeks, when, in fact, Cemal Pasha had unsuccessfully approached the Entente. On July 22 Enver upped the ante, warning the Germans that if they refused his alliance offer, he would turn instead to Russia. The Germans, who had declared war on Russia the previous day, accepted and signed a treaty of alliance on August 2, 1914.

On August 3, 1914, Germany declared war against France. Britain seized a pair of modern battleships being built for the Ottomans. Although the British offered financial compensation, the move prompted public outrage in Istanbul. That same day, however, the Ottoman Empire declared its neutrality. Enver Pasha needed time to mobilize his army, a difficult task considering the miserable state of internal communications within the empire. On August 4, Britain declared war against Germany.

The Germans quickly capitalized on its treaty with Istanbul. Two German warships, the battlecruiser *Goeben* and the cruiser *Breslau,* were trapped in the Mediterranean. They raced for Istanbul and were turned over, complete with their crews, to the Turkish navy.

By the fall, despite the fact that the German offensive against Belgium and France — the Schlieffen Plan — had failed, as had the Austrian offensive against Serbia, Enver Pasha remained committed to joining the war alongside Germany and Austria-Hungary. Many among the Young Turk leadership had doubts about the policy, but Enver ordered the former German, now Turkish warships to strike Russian shipping in the Black Sea. These attacks provoked a Russian declaration of war on November 2, 1914. Subsequently, under the sultan's authority as khalifa, the Ottomans issued a *fetva* declaring jihad but only against non-Muslims occupying Muslim lands from North Africa to India.

While historians generally agree that the Ottoman *fetva* had little impact on the course of the conflict, it nonetheless demonstrates that the ideal of jihad as armed conflict had survived into the twentieth century. Nor can the fate of the wartime empire's Armenian population be entirely separated from the emotions the *fetva* unleashed. The jihad declaration called for various forms of struggle. The first was "war in secret," or an effort "to persecute and exterminate" unbelievers from the "face of the earth." There was also war "by word of mouth" that involved propaganda and incitement. Last, there was "physical war," divided into the "lesser" and "greater" modes. Physical jihad could take any number of forms: assassination, raids, or actual campaigns of outright conquest. In the absence of sufficient military forces, believers could wage war "secretly and deceitfully." The *fetva* noted: "This method is well known to every Muslim."

Whatever forces the jihad decree unleashed, they did not bring about an Ottoman victory. The Turkish army had benefited from modernization in the years before the war, but it was hardly prepared for a major European conflict. Further, communications within the expansive empire remained poor to nonexistent.

Nor was Enver's leadership up to the task. In January 1915, in the middle of winter, he directed the army to attack the Russians in the Caucasus. The offensive collapsed with 90 percent casualties. A February 1915 drive across the barren Sinai and against the British front along the Suez Canal likewise failed miserably.

But the Turks did win several victories of note. In March 1915 the British and French landed on the Gallipoli Peninsula, opening the ill-fated Dardanelles campaign. The Turks fought well, and in the fall of 1915 the Entente forces withdrew, defeated. A July 1915 British offensive from Basra toward Baghdad stalled at Kut al-Amara, where the besieged force surrendered ignominiously in April 1916. In October 1915 a German-Austrian force finally overran Serbia and drove south. A makeshift Allied contingent landed at Salonika, in Greece, where it remained, stationary, until the war's end.

Internally, however, the empire moved toward its final death throes. While most Arabs remained loyal, and far more served in the Ottoman army than ever rode with "Lawrence of Arabia," disaffection was on the rise. In the east the Turks viewed the large Armenian population, not without reason, as sympathetic toward the Russians. Enver decided to forcibly relocate these Christians in three provinces. Moving hundreds of thousands of people during wartime and in a region with a pitiful transportation infrastructure was destined to turn into a human tragedy. Historians continue to debate both the scale of that catastrophe and whether it was planned or an unfortunate by-product of the policies of resettlement and deportation. The number of Armenian civilians who died during the war ranges from 400,000 to 1 million. While many non-Armenian traditional scholars have given the Turks the benefit of a doubt, recent scholarship using German and Austrian archives suggests that the Turks were guilty of intentional mass murder—genocide.

By 1917 the external pressures on the Ottoman Empire were beginning to tell. Aided by the British and the flamboyant but effective T. E. Lawrence, an Arab revolt had driven the Turks from Mecca and Medina. A new British-Indian army drove toward Baghdad, which fell in March. That same month Sir Edmund Allenby commanded another British army that attacked at Gaza. Jerusalem fell in December. By October 1918, the British had entered Damascus, along with their Arab allies, and moved north toward the Anatolian plateau.

The sultan dismissed the discredited Young Turks and sought an armistice. On October 30, 1918, his representatives signed the Armistice at Mondros, under which the Turks were to repatriate all Entente prisoners of war, demobilize their armies, sever their relations with the Central Powers, open the straits to Entente shipping, and place the entire Ottoman territory at the victorious powers' disposal.

Thanks to secret documents the Bolsheviks released after they took Russia out of the war in March 1918, the sultan and his government knew that the Entente powers had plans to dismantle the Ottoman realm. Under the various treaties' terms, the most notorious of which was the Sykes-Picot Agreement, the Russians would have received control of the straits and Istanbul itself; the Italians, the Dodecanese Islands and the region around Antalya;

and the French and British, the area that now includes Syria, Lebanon, Palestine, Jordan, and Iraq. The British had already annexed Cyprus and Egypt when the Ottomans went to war in 1914.

Historians in both the Middle East and the West make much of the Entente powers' vulture-like nature and their eagerness to carve up the Ottoman Empire. All too often those accounts fail to address several contextual elements. First, the Entente powers did not force the Ottomans into the war. Enver Pasha and the other leading Young Turks gambled on a Central Power victory and lost. Second, the Ottoman Empire's fate in defeat had more to do with its multinational character than its Islamic past. The Entente powers also broke up the multinational and predominantly Christian Austro-Hungarian Empire. And with czarist Russia's collapse in 1917, even without Entente involvement, the multinational Romanov Empire fell apart. The Finns, Latvians, Lithuanians, Estonians, and Poles gained their independence, while other ethnic groups in the empire did so briefly before the Bolsheviks reconquered them. Third, had the Central Powers won the war, Enver Pasha had his own plans for Ottoman aggrandizement. He intended to regain Egypt, Cyprus, some territory in the Balkans, and additional land in the Caucasus, reaching north to the Volga and east beyond Persia to Afghanistan and central Asia—a Pan-Turanian fantasy. In fact when Russia collapsed in 1918, Turkish troops moved into the Caucasus and would have remained there had it not been for British victories in the Levant and Iraq.

In November 1918, Entente troops arrived in Istanbul. British forces already occupied Iraq and the Levant. Over the next few months the French moved into Cilicia and the Italians into Antalya. Sultan Mehmet VI and his government cooperated; the once-powerful Ottoman Empire had nearly reached the end of its long history.

But if the war had exhausted the empire's leaders, it had not done the same to its Turks. In May 1919 Greek forces landed in Izmir, a region with a substantial Greek population. The Greeks' arrival ignited a conflagration, with both sides committing atrocities. Unrest among the Turks spread throughout Anatolia; the British arrested the most prominent nationalists in Istanbul and exiled them to Malta. But in the countryside, beyond the Entente powers' reach, other nationalists, most notably Mustafa Kemal, began to reorganize the shattered Ottoman military.

Mustafa Kemal (1881–1938) was a Turk from Thessaloniki, in what is now Greece. One of his teachers bestowed upon him the name Kemal, or "perfection." He made his career in the army and participated in the counter-counterrevolution of 1908 as a commander of a Macedonian army unit that took Istanbul. He fought in Libya against the Italians and gained popular notoriety during the Gallipoli campaign of 1915. He also fought in the Caucasus against the Russians and in Palestine against the British. He accepted the Ottoman defeat and the loss of the empire's non-Turkish regions, but he refused to agree to the occupation or the loss of any Turkish areas in Anatolia. Kemal organized the army's remnants to resist the Entente.

The war-weary British soon recognized that they faced a rising tide of Turkish nationalism. At San Remo, Italy, in April 1920 they made new offers to the sultan's negotiators. Oil-rich Mosul would go to the newly formed state of Iraq. The straits would be internationalized. The Greeks would remain in Izmir for five years with the region's ultimate political fate to be decided by plebiscite. Armenia would become independent; Kurdistan, autonomous. The sultan would also guarantee people of various nationalities and religions equal rights. The Ottoman army would be restricted to a force of 50,000 men (while the Versailles Treaty reduced the once-mighty German army to 100,000). At Sevres in August 1920, the sultan agreed to these terms and recognized his empire's loss to Syria, Iraq, Arabia, Cyprus, and Egypt and the establishment of British and French protectorates.

But the sultan did not speak for the Turkish nationalists. In the spring of 1920, Mustafa Kemal commanded a force that drove the French southward, back into Syria. He then marched north and crushed the short-lived Armenian republic. He met with Bolshevik diplomats and, for the price of Batum, reached an accord that secured his northeastern frontier. In March 1921 the Italians, unwilling to fight to save their position in Antalya, agreed to withdraw in return for economic concessions.

The Greeks refused to deal. In the summer of 1921 against British advice, they launched their own offensive toward Ancyra, which had become Mustafa Kemal's de facto capital. By the fall the Greek advance had faltered. The following summer a Turkish offensive crushed and routed the Greek army. Mustafa Kemal's army captured Izmir in September 1922.

With the Greeks defeated, the Turks then marched on Istanbul. The British and French had no desire to fight and agreed to negotiate. In an October 1922 agreement formalized later at Lausanne, the Turks secured their old capital, an enclave in Europe that left them controlling both sides of the straits, and the Entente powers' total withdrawal. They also agreed to an exchange of populations, with 1 million Turks moving from the Balkans to Anatolia and a half million Greeks from Anatolia to Greece.

Mustafa Kemal's focus shifted to internal affairs. In November 1922 the Turkish Grand National Assembly deposed Sultan Mehmed VI. The Ottoman sultanate had met its end, although the ex-sultan's cousin, Abdul Mejid, became the new khalifa.

In October 1923 the Turks formed a secular republic. Their constitution, adopted in April 1924, placed sovereignty with the Turkish nation; granted equal rights to all citizens; provided for freedom of speech, thought, press, and travel; made Islam the official religion; and moved the capital formally to Ancyra.

Under the leadership of its first president, Mustafa Kemal (given the name Atatürk—father of the Turks—by the republic), Turkey underwent a forced and at times violent process of Westernization, modernization, and secularization. Atatürk insisted on adopting a Western style of dress, the Western calendar, and its alphabet. He even shifted the weekend to Saturday and Sunday. In 1934 women received the right to vote.

On March 3, 1924, Mustafa Kemal Atatürk and the Republic of Turkey eliminated the khalifate as an institution. To this day, the 1924 decision outrages Islamic fundamentalists. Many believe that only with the reestablishment of this institution and the identification of a new khalifa can the Muslim *ummah* hope to recover its past glory and demonstrate its faithfulness to Allah.

Chapter 6
War, Oil, and Israel

*Conditions change, the Muslim loses his physical power
and is conquered, yet the consciousness does not depart from
him that he is the most superior. If he remains a Believer, he
looks upon his conqueror from a superior position. He remains
certain that this is a temporary condition which will pass away
and that faith will turn the tide from which there is no escape.
Even if death is his portion, he will never bow his head. Death
comes to all, but for him there is martyrdom. He will proceed to
the Garden, while his conquerors go to the Fire. What a difference! And he hears the voice of his Generous Lord:*

*"Let it not deceive you that the unbelievers walk about in the
land. A little respite and their abode is Hell, and what an evil
place! But for those who fear their Lord are Gardens through
which rivers flow, to abide therein—a hospitality from God; and
that which is with God is best for the righteous." (3:196–98)*
                                            —*Sayyid Qutb,* Milestones

The disintegration of the Ottoman sultanate and the end of
the khalifate in 1924 closed a 1,300-year-old chapter of Islamic
history. For the first time since the seventh century no major Islamic political entity existed; no one had succeeded the Prophet.
Ibn Saud's still nascent kingdom was the only independent Arab
state.

Nevertheless, challenges to European domination remained. Arab, Persian, and Turkish nationalism represented rising forces, although they adopted modern, if not Western, orientations and secular instincts. While Islam remained vibrant, the era of political Islam—that is, the era in which Islam was a major political force—appeared to be over.

But several questions remained: could these nationalist forces meet the needs of the people for whom they claimed to speak? Could they throw off the colonial occupiers and establish states that were politically, economically, and socially viable? Could the nationalists and the modernizers provide sufficiently for their people's material welfare? And would that nationalism take a collective Arab form, or would it divide into myriad subsets—namely, Egyptian, Syrian, Iraqi, and so on? Could nationalists of whatever stripe find a means to separate the state and the mosque as Atatürk had in Turkey? After thirteen centuries of political domination, could Islam survive as a mere religion?

Despite the Entente powers' failure to occupy Anatolia, their position in the Middle East during the early 1920s appeared secure. The French held Syria and what is today Lebanon, and the British controlled Palestine, Iraq, and the Arabian coast of the Persian Gulf from Kuwait to Oman and then west to Yemen. But the region was hardly stable.

At the war's end the Arab desert army occupied Damascus, its leaders intent on establishing an independent state. In March 1920, the Syrian National Congress named king of Syria the Hashemite emir Faisal bin Husayn, son of the King Husayn ibn Ali of the Hijaz. Expecting to control the area as part of a series of accords going back to the Sykes-Picot Agreement, the French moved on the capital. When they faced opposition, they crushed it, occupied Damascus, and expelled Faisal. The Hashemite prince may not have been all that popular with the Syrians, but the French were less so, at least outside the regions inhabited by the Lebanese Maronite Christians. The French faced frequent unrest: a Druse rebellion and an uprising in Damascus in 1925, another Druse rebellion in 1927, and problems in the Kurdish regions in 1937. To placate the Syrians, the French agreed to the formation of an independent Syrian Republic; the Syrians, in turn, would be bound by treaty to France, which would retain certain rights of occupation until 1958.

The British faced similar problems in Iraq. They placed the short-lived king of Syria, the Emir Faisal, on the new Iraqi kingdom's throne. In 1926, with British support, Iraq gained the oil-rich Mosul district, which could just as easily have been assigned to Turkey. But throughout the occupation, the British faced unrest, especially along the new state's ill-defined frontiers. The Kurds in the north revolted in 1922, 1924, 1930, and 1932. When Great Britain withdrew in 1933, the Iraqis massacred at least 3,000 Assyrian Christians who had made the mistake of cooperating with the British.

To the south, King Ibn Saud continued his efforts to expand his domain. In May 1919 his forces defeated King Husayn's army in the Hijaz. In March 1924, after Mustafa Kemel Atatürk abolished the khalifate, Husayn declared himself khalifa. He hoped to secure his position as protector of the Holy Cities, but by 1925 Ibn Saud had captured both Mecca and Medina. Husayn fled to Trans-Jordan, where the British had set up his son, Abdullah, as emir (and became king in 1947). In the 1927 Treaty of Jeddah Great Britain formally recognized the kingdom of Hijaz and Nejd that in 1932 became Saudi Arabia.

Amid this political turmoil, the Middle East's importance steadily rose. The reason was simple—petroleum. The Industrial Revolution substituted power by men, animals, or natural forces with machine power. Industries had first consumed wood for fuel, then coal, and by the twentieth century petroleum. At the turn of the twentieth century the world's largest oil producer and oil exporter was the United States. American companies held no global monopoly, but they were the most powerful.

Great Britain was the first Western power to demonstrate an interest in the petroleum industry's potential in the Middle East. Unlike the Americans and Russians, who were also major oil producers, the British had no petroleum deposits of their own (until the development of North Sea oil in the late twentieth century). Moreover, they recognized that oil was a more efficient fuel for the Royal Navy's warships. This realization made gaining control of a secure source of petroleum a strategic imperative.

In 1901 a Briton, William Knox D'Arcy, gained a concession from the Persian shah that covered much of the empire's southwest. In 1909 the Anglo-Persian Oil Company (APOC), whose majority shareholder was the British government, struck oil and by 1913 was refining product at Abadan on the upper gulf.

On the eve of the Great War the British, along with other European powers, gained concessions from the Ottoman Empire covering the area that is now southeastern Iraq. The Americans made their own advances but without success. World War I began in 1914, bringing these projects to a temporary halt.

The war demonstrated petroleum products' growing importance. By 1918 the Abadan refinery had increased production by 400 percent. Nevertheless, the United States supplied 90 percent of the Western allies' petroleum needs during the war.

At the war's end, Great Britain's position in the Middle East appeared supreme. Germany had been defeated. Russia was torn by civil war. The Ottoman Empire had collapsed. The power posed by nascent Arab nationalism was not yet fully apparent.

The British moved quickly to maximize their advantage, especially regarding petroleum. They claimed that their prewar agreement with the Ottomans, involving the formation of the Turkish Petroleum Company (TPC) in what was now Iraq, remained in force. The British surrendered a 25 percent share to their French allies in the new company, Iraq Petroleum Company (IPC). Lest it compete with its international parent companies, the IPC was limited to refining and marketing for Iraq's internal needs. In compensation for allowing the other companies to participate in the IPC, APOC received a 10 percent royalty on all oil extracted. With the assistance of the Armenian C. S. Gulbenkian, better known as "Mr. 5 Percent," the IPC continued to operate within the prewar strictures established for the TPC—a nonprofit company, registered in Britain, that produced crude oil for a fee that was charged to the parent companies and based on their percentage of shares held. The IPC agreement remained an obstacle to American participation because it stipulated that any oil activity conducted in the Ottoman Empire by any shareholder would be shared by all partners. Gulbenkian had insisted on the clause to prevent his partners from cutting him out by establishing new companies. This clause, combined with America's lack of leverage because it had not declared war against the Ottoman Empire, left the Americans excluded, despite the best efforts of its oil interests and the U.S. State Department's protestations about the virtues of the "Open Door" Policy.

U.S. interest in Middle East oil remained purely commercial. American oil companies, being the largest and most powerful in the world, sought involvement in any corner of the globe where petroleum and its by-products could be discovered, extracted, refined, or sold. Nonetheless, Washington felt concerned about its future; in 1919 the Bureau of Mines reported that the United States only had a ten-year supply of oil left. A few years later, that estimate rose to twenty years, where it has remained for the past eighty years.

The Americans gained their first penetration into the Middle East oil market in 1928, although at the cost of abandoning its Open Door principle. On July 31, 1928, British, Dutch, French, and American oil companies signed the famous "Red Line Agreement," establishing a cartel controlling oil exploration and production in the region. The companies involved were APOC, the Dutch Shell Group, the Compagnie Française des Petroles (CFP), and the American Near East Development Corporation (NEDC). Each group held 23.7 percent of the shares, while Mr. 5 Percent, who had put the deal together, held the remaining but nonvoting 5 percent. In the early 1930s, NEDC—Sinclair, Texaco, Gulf, Indiana Standard Oil, and Atlantic—sold its shares to Standard Oil of New Jersey (later ESSO, then Exxon) and Socony-Vacuum Company (later Mobil, now Exxon-Mobil).

The original restrictions included in the 1914 TPC agreement remained in force after the 1928 reorganization. The revised deal gained the moniker "Red Line Agreement" because the participants were forbidden to operate independently within the boundaries set by a red line drawn on a map that included the Asiatic territories of the former Ottoman Empire and most of the Arabian Peninsula. The restrictive accord hamstrung the IPC partners from gaining concessions or developing oil in a large swath of the Middle East. Basically, the American companies could only expand their operations if their partners wished and had the resources to expand their own proportionately.

The United States would not be so easily contained in the world petroleum game. American oilmen constantly sought paths around the obstacles placed in their way. They were also, at least relatively speaking, flush with cash even during the Great Depression.

Despite their political dominance in the region, the British faced several problems. As royalties flowed into the Iraqi and Persian governments' coffers, cash-poor neighboring monarchs sought to develop their own resources. Unfortunately for the British, while they held extensive concessions throughout the Middle East, they lacked capital and markets. In 1929 Briton Frank Holmes, his concession covering Bahrain about to expire, found himself unable to interest any British concerns. As a result, he sold his rights to an American company, Gulf Oil, but at the time it was still a member of the Red Line cartel and could not act on the concession itself. Gulf Oil promptly resold the rights to Standard Oil of California (SOCAL), which was blocked by yet another British restriction that limited the rights of non-British firms to operate in Bahrain, the location of its British Persian Gulf command headquarters. SOCAL established the Bahrain Petroleum Company (BAPCO) as a wholly owned subsidiary incorporated in Canada. Drilling began in 1932 and soon struck oil. SOCAL sold half its BAPCO shares to Texaco, and then the two companies formed yet another corporation—CALTEX—to market the BAPCO product. Meanwhile after selling its rights in Bahrain, Gulf Oil purchased Holmes's concession in Kuwait, which was not covered by the Red Line Agreement. Alarmed by this latest American move, the British insisted on inclusion. APOC joined with Gulf Oil and formed yet another company—the Kuwaiti Oil Company (KOC).

The biggest prize remained to be won—that is, Saudi Arabia. At the end of the Great War, Britain held the dominant position vis-à-vis the Saudis. The Arab kingdom was a "protectorate"; Abdul Aziz could not grant mineral concessions to any country other than Britain, which paid Abdul Aziz a £5,000 annual subsidy. But in 1919 the British ended the subsidies, cutting the king loose. In 1927 after securing the Hijaz, Abdul Aziz signed the Treaty of Jeddah with Britain, ending the protectorate status and the economic restrictions binding the kingdom. The king, now fully independent, soon discovered that he needed money to maintain the tribal allegiances that held his monarchy together. The Saudis did not have much to sell other than oil, assuming that it could be found in their territory. In 1923 they had granted a concession to Frank Holmes, but no British firms were interested in exploring the possibilities of Saudi oil. That changed in 1932 when oil strikes in Bahrain suggested that oil could also be found in the adjacent Saudi Eastern Province. SOCAL, which was not bound by the restrictions of the Red Line Agreement, outbid a last-minute IPC blocking effort and gained a sixty-year concession for the new California Arabian Standard Oil Company (CASOC, later ARAMCO, and later yet Saudi-ARAMCO).

By the eve of the Second World War, much had changed in the Persian Gulf. Great Britain had retained its political-military primacy, but the United States was rapidly becoming the major economic player. Moreover, while the British imperial image was in decline, both as a result of its policies and its relative economic weakness, the Americans were gaining status. From 1920 to 1939 oil production had increased dramatically, by 900 percent, largely because of American involvement. Iraq, Saudi Arabia, and Bahrain had joined Persia as major producers. In 1920 the United States produced about 95 percent of the world's oil; by 1939 that number had fallen to about 86 percent, with an ever-increasing amount of the rest coming from the Persian Gulf. Nevertheless, the United States remained the world's largest petroleum exporter. And its interest in the Middle East and its oil remained commercial and private, not strategic or governmental.

When war began again in Europe in 1939, control of the Middle East's oil resources *was not* the belligerents' major goal, despite popular perceptions. The prospect of Axis forces reaching the Persian Gulf and transporting crude overland, across the Mediterranean, and to Germany's industrial centers was fanciful. Nor did the region's oil play a major role in Allied calculations, at least not until the conflict was virtually decided.

The war spread to the Middle East in June 1940, when Benito Mussolini's Fascist Italy declared war against France and Great Britain. In July Il Duce's forces struck from their Libyan colony against Egypt to reach the Suez Canal. In December the British routed the much larger Italian army. In February 1941 the German führer Adolf Hitler dispatched Erwin Rommel and the Afrika Korps to Cyrenaica to prevent the British from overrunning Libya.

The events of the spring and summer of 1941 stretched British resources to their limit. In April Rommel began his first offensive in the Western Desert, besieged Tobruk, and drove the Allies back to the Egyptian border. In May pro-Axis nationalist army officers staged a coup in Iraq, prompting a British invasion and reoccupation. That same month the British completed their successful campaign in East Africa, liberating Ethiopia from the Italians. In

June Commonwealth forces invaded Syria and Lebanon and wrested the area from Vichy French control. It was November before Britain could strike back in the desert, driving Rommel from Cyrenaica.

As the year ended, Great Britain faced yet another threat in Persia. The British there had encountered increasing challenges during the interwar period. In 1921 Reza Khan and other army strongmen staged a coup and seized effective control. The Persians signed a treaty with the Bolshevik regime in Moscow, giving the Russians the right to intervene should any foreign (most likely British) troops enter Persian territory. By 1925 Reza Khan gained dictatorial powers and shortly thereafter deposed the already exiled shah, declared himself Reza Shah Pahlavi, and established a new but rather short-lived dynasty. Instead of the British, the new shah turned to the Americans for financial advice and in 1932 insisted on renegotiating the APOC concession. In 1935 in a move generally considered a display of pro-Nazi sympathy, the shah changed the name of his country from Persia to Iran—Farsi for Aryan—to ensure that everyone, especially the Germans, understood that the Persians were an Indo-European people and not Semitic.

In January 1942 the shah's increasingly overt support for the Axis led Great Britain and the Soviet Union, which had been at war with Germany since June 1941, to jointly occupy his country. The Allies guaranteed Iranian territorial integrity, but they forced the shah to abdicate in favor of his twenty-two-year-old son, Mohammad Reza Shah Pahlavi. By 1943 Iran became the major conduit for U.S. Lend-Lease aid to the Soviet Union.

In the initial years of the war, the Persian Gulf's oil played a minor role for the Allies. Threats from the Axis, a lack of British capital, political instability, and a shortage of tankers after German U-boat attacks in the Battle of the Atlantic led to the capping of wells. Iraqi production declined from 32.6 million barrels in 1938 to 12.6 million in 1941 and only approached prewar production levels in 1945. Iranian production dropped from 78 million barrels in 1938 to 50.6 million in 1941, but it rose to more than 100 million by war's end. Declining production in this period also meant reduced royalties for local rulers. This circumstance further weakened the British position, since the rates of decline were lower where American companies operated—for example, in Bahrain and Saudi Arabia. The latter's production rose from 580,000 barrels in 1938, to 5 million in 1940, then fell to 4.3 million in 1941, but rose steadily to 21.3 million by 1945.

When the Americans entered the war in December 1941, they fully understood oil's importance to the global war effort. President Franklin Delano Roosevelt's administration established the Petroleum Administration for War (PAW) to manage this all-important resource. PAW recognized that the Allies would have to rely on Western Hemisphere and American sources for most of their petroleum-related needs. The Japanese had overrun the Dutch East Indies, and while the Persian Gulf remained secure, its distance from major refining centers and the tanker shortage posed major problems. Nevertheless, in its long-term planning PAW set goals to increase both production and refinery capacity in the Persian Gulf. As a result, between 1938 and 1945 refinery capacity nearly doubled. Moreover, Persian Gulf refineries began to produce specialized military-grade product for the U.S. Navy—aviation gasoline, diesel, and specialized fuel oil—at Abadan (Iran), Ras Tanura (Saudi Arabia), and Bahrain. As one PAW report noted, the Persian Gulf was rapidly becoming the "world oil center of gravity."

In late 1943 and early 1944, the Roosevelt administration developed the country's first national petroleum policy. Long-range trends indicated that the Western Hemisphere's resources would not meet expected postwar demands for petroleum. Nor did the planners believe it would be sound policy to expend every last barrel of crude in American fields. They wanted to hold those remaining resources as a strategic reserve for future use. In lieu of

American crude, the world would instead turn to the less than fully developed Persian Gulf fields. The United States would have to take the lead to expand the region's potential. Great Britain lacked the requisite capital, and given its colonial history PAW did not trust it to work in the best interests of the local states. PAW and Department of State planners believed that augmented production in the Middle East would take the pressure off American fields, provide countries in the Persian Gulf with increased revenues earned from greater royalties, raise the local standard of living, and lead "to consequent increased purchasing power and greater political and economic stability."

Essentially, Roosevelt administration policy makers *planned* to make the United States and the West *dependent* on the oil of the Persian Gulf. The alternative, as they saw it, was to exhaust in a decade or so the rest of America's oil reserves.

While their policy was sensible, it rested on several assumptions that proved to be naïve. First, the Roosevelt administration believed that the Grand Alliance between the Anglo-Americans and the Soviet Union would survive the end of the war. Second, the United States expected Great Britain to continue to provide for the region's defense, despite that its American ally was rapidly supplanting it economically *and* politically. No one asked whether the British would be so helpful in the postwar world. Third, American policy makers assumed that increased royalties and higher standards of living would lead to Western-style political development and greater stability in the Middle East.

The Lend-Lease program, in addition to petroleum, also led to an increased American involvement and presence in the Persian Gulf. The overwhelming majority of the matériel the western Allies shipped to the embattled Soviet Union moved by sea to Iran and then over the Caucasus mountains into southern Russia. Iran was occupied by the Russians and British, but the Americans were largely responsible for the requisite infrastructure advances to speed the flow of matériel north.

The Iranians noted the role played by the Americans in the gulf. The young shah and his advisers accordingly viewed cultivating the United States as a form of insurance against continued postwar occupation by the Russians and British. American advisers proliferated. Norman Schwarzkopf, Sr. — West Point graduate, Great War veteran, and former head of the New Jersey State Police — arrived in Tehran to reorganize the Iranian national police. The Americans extended Lend-Lease to Iran itself to strengthen the central government. The Iranians thanked the Americans by offering them oil concessions in the far north of the country, along the Soviet border. Accepting the offer would have all but ensured an American clash with the Russians at the war's end. The Roosevelt administration wisely turned down the offer.

The Americans also extended Lend-Lease to Saudi Arabia. In return the Americans received the rights to construct an air base at Dhahran in the Eastern Province. The United States expected the facility would play a critical role in transferring air units from the European to Pacific theaters after the defeat of Nazi Germany.

By the end of the war, despite its not having a formal role in the region, the local Arab and Iranian governments viewed the United States as the most important Western power. American oil companies had expanded production whereas British firms had had to reduce production. When cash-strapped Great Britain had refused to provide the Iranians and Saudis with assistance, the United States filled the gap with Lend-Lease aid. Moreover, the American Persian Gulf Service Command had grown to a force of 30,000 personnel by the war's end, with most of them stationed in Iran.

The Americans also played a larger role in the Mediterranean basin. In 1942 the United States moved elements of the U.S. Army Air Forces to Egypt to support the British in campaigns against the Axis. In November 1942 the United States participated in Operation Torch, the Allied landing in Vichy French–controlled northwest Africa. The Americans managed the landing and occupation of Morocco and participated in the occupation of Algeria and Tunisia.

Through the end of 1944, the pattern of expanding U.S. involvement within the Middle East followed that of the nineteenth century. The primary U.S. considerations remained commercial or directly related to the prosecution of the war. The local states welcomed American interest and frequently invited the United States to participate more broadly in their affairs. Arab and the Iranian leaders looked upon the United States as a useful counterweight to the far more dangerous imperial interests of Great Britain and the Soviet Union, implying greater American participation in the postwar period. Moreover, the Roosevelt administration's plans to shift the petroleum center of gravity from the Western Hemisphere to the Middle East made the gulf's security a strategic U.S. concern. Nevertheless, as late as 1945 the United States had no intention and no desire to maintain anything other than a commercial or perhaps advisory regional presence.

The American relationship with the Middle East states grew more complicated in the spring of 1945. On his return from the Yalta conference, President Roosevelt decided to meet with Saudi king Abdul Aziz. The two men and their entourages met on the U.S. Navy cruiser *Quincy* while anchored in the Great Bitter Lake of the Suez Canal. They discussed Arabian oil, the construction of the American air base at Dhahran, and the problem of Jewish immigration and Palestine's fate. The two leaders were largely in accord regarding the first two topics for the king preferred the Americans to the British. But the topic of Palestine proved to be far more difficult. Roosevelt had hoped to gain the king's support on settling Jews in Palestine; the king hoped to secure Roosevelt's promises that the United States would not support large-scale immigration or an independent Jewish state. The Palestinian problem was the first potentially dangerous political stumbling block the Americans had ever faced in the Middle East. In the end, both leaders left the meeting disappointed; however,

Roosevelt had agreed not to move forward on the issue without consulting the Saudis.

But it was not the Arab-Jewish problem or oil that first drew the United States more deeply into Middle East affairs in the post-war world. By the spring of 1946, the Middle East became strategically important in the larger struggle known as the Cold War.

In March 1946 Iran became the battleground for the first Cold War crisis. As part of the wartime agreement regarding Iran, the Soviet Union and Great Britain had agreed to withdraw their military forces six months after the war. The Soviets, much to their allies' chagrin, chose not VE day (May 8, 1945) nor VJ day (August 15, 1945) as their starting point but instead September 2, 1945—the day Japan formally surrendered to the Allies. According to that timetable, the Russians were bound to withdraw their forces from Iran by March 2, 1946.

As early as December 1945, the United States realized that the Soviets were instead reinforcing their positions in Iran and working through various nationalist and Communist organizations to undermine the Iranian government's control in the northern regions of the country. Simultaneously, the Russians pressured Iran's neighbor to the west, Turkey, for access to the straits and the border between eastern Anatolia and Soviet Georgia.

By late 1945 the Americans had concluded that their alliance with the Soviet Union was near an end. Nevertheless, in December 1945 the Department of State decided not to press the Russians on either Turkey or Iran. The following month the Joint Chiefs of Staff's (JCS) Joint Intelligence Committee issued a report that virtually wrote off Iran's northern provinces. In February the JCS approved a memorandum recommending that the United States adhere to its wartime plans and not undertake the defense of the Middle East. In all probability, the excellent Soviet espionage apparatus in Washington relayed these assessments to Moscow.

In early March the situation shifted both quickly and dramatically. On March 4, two days after the Soviets' withdrawal deadline, an American diplomat in northern Iran reported Russian armored forces moving south toward the capital, Tehran. The next day former British prime minister Winston S. Churchill delivered his famous "Iron Curtain" speech in Fulton, Missouri. On March 6 the State Department announced that the battleship *Missouri* would transport the remains of the late Turkish ambassador from the United States to Istanbul.

The shift in the American's approach was as much political as it was policy based. The seemingly constant drumbeat of Soviet aggressive actions in Manchuria, Eastern Europe, and the Near East caused a sea change in American politics. Republicans started attacking Democrats for being "soft" on communism, and the Truman administration had to find someplace to act tough. Moreover, the Soviets' moves seemed consistent with the behavior pattern that George F. Kennan—the father of containment and at the time an American diplomat stationed in Moscow—outlined in his famous February 1946 Long Telegram.

In the spring of 1946 the Truman administration took a fresh look at the Near East situation. The consequent policy changes and move toward containment were not based on the important petroleum resources of the Persian Gulf. The new strategy involved support for the defense of a northern tier of states—Greece, Turkey, and Iran—that lay athwart any possible Soviet southern advance. This geostrategic, as opposed to petro-strategic, focus is evident in the Truman Doctrine of March 1947, which extended formal protection to Greece and Turkey, the northern tier's left flank and center, but not to Iran, the right flank and the only country of the three with oil.

Whatever the roots of the new thinking, U.S. policy makers faced a problem: how best to ensure the region's defense. The Truman administration did not believe that the United States possessed the material or political wherewithal to directly assume the defense of the Middle East. Nor did Great Britain have sufficient power to protect the region. The Americans and the British thus favored a multinational solution, led by the British.

Unfortunately, two factors worked against this approach. The leaders of the strongest states in the Middle East—Iran, Iraq, Egypt, and Saudi Arabia—distrusted the British. The second complicating factor involved what American secretary of state Dean Acheson termed the "puzzle of Palestine."

The Palestinian question's roots—the Arab-Israeli dilemma— run deep in recorded history, to some as far back as the biblical history of the region and to others to Imperial Rome's dispersal of the Jews. Over the intervening centuries, the Ottoman Empire had often served as a haven for Jews fleeing persecution in Europe, and small numbers had occasionally chosen Palestine as their destination, joining those who had remained in the Holy Land. The more recent problem in Palestine began in the late nineteenth century. The rising sense of nationalism then prevalent in Europe led to the concept of a Jewish national identity that, as was true of other nationalist movements, sought its own homeland—in what became known as Zion. Simultaneously, the Ottoman *Tanzimat* reforms, which bestowed legal equality to religious and ethnic minorities, made migrating to Palestine more attractive and feasible. The first wave, or *aliya,* of Jewish settlers arrived in the late 1870s. In 1891 an Austrian Jew coined the term "Zionism" to describe the growing desire among European Jews to return to Palestine. Six years later Theodor Herzl, another Austrian Jew, formed the Zionist movement, which called for establishing a Jewish homeland and state. Herzl, however, was willing to consider locations other than Palestine.

By the eve of the Great War, about 75,000 Jews had reached Palestine, although about half found the going too difficult and left. During that war, when it became apparent the Ottoman Empire might not survive the conflict intact, the Zionists increasingly looked to Palestine as their potential homeland and approached the British government to secure that end. On November 2, 1917, British foreign secretary Arthur Balfour signed his famous, or infamous to some, declaration:

Dear Lord Rothschild,

I have much pleasure in conveying to you, on behalf of His Majesty's Government, the following declaration of sympathy with Jewish Zionist aspirations which has been submitted to, and approved by, the Cabinet.

"His Majesty's Government views with favour the establishment in Palestine of a national home for the Jewish people, and will use their best endeavours to facilitate the achievement of this object, it being clearly understood that nothing shall be done which may prejudice the civil and religious rights of existing non-Jewish communities in Palestine, or the rights and political status enjoyed by Jews in any other country."

I should be grateful if you would bring this declaration to the knowledge of the Zionist Federation.

Yours sincerely,

Arthur James Balfour

After the war, with the British controlling the region as part of their mandate, Jewish immigration resumed at a rate of about 10,000 new arrivals a year, and virtually all of them chose to remain. At this point, the 200,000 Arab residents heavily outnumbered the 80,000 to 100,000 immigrants and indigenous Jews. The arrival of the European newcomers, along with their technological and agricultural know-how, created an area of development within Palestine that benefited both Jews and Arabs. In fact, as quickly as Jews immigrated to the region, so, too, did Arabs from surrounding areas. Both populations continued to expand.

But as the population in Palestine grew, more problems developed. The Zionists had given little thought to the Arab inhabitants, assuming that they would be willing to share in the new prosperity under Jewish leadership. The scale of Arab immigration suggests that this notion was to an extent true. Unfortunately, Jewish purchases of land, while legal, often involved transactions with absentee owners of lands that were inhabited by Arab tenant farmers whose families had worked their farms for centuries. These families were often evicted to make way for Jewish settlers. Not surprisingly, the dislocated Arabs were irate. Nor were the Palestinian Muslims eager to live under the political control of Jews, whom they considered dhimmis. Tensions, evident in the late nineteenth century, turned violent as early as 1921 and took the form of anti-Jewish rioting.

Jewish immigration, however, continued. By the mid-1920s the rate reached almost 20,000 a year and increased after the Nazis assumed power in Germany in 1933. Jewish leaders pushed the British, without complete success, to loosen controls on immigration. Nevertheless, from 1929 to 1939 a quarter of a million Jews arrived in Palestine. Arab-Jewish tension worsened. In 1933 local Arab leaders demanded that the British use their authority in the mandate to halt land sales to Jews. When the British refused, the Arabs launched a boycott. In 1936 the Palestinians formed the Arab High Committee, a group committed to working against Jewish immigration and statehood. The committee's efforts led to large-scale violence aimed at Jews and to a general strike.

Throughout the 1930s, British policy makers issued several reports and white papers addressing the Palestinian problem, most of which involved severe limits on Jewish immigration. None of these proposals were acceptable to both sides. Finally, in 1937, the Peel Commission recommended, among other things, partitioning Palestine. The World Zionist Congress accepted the idea. In Syria the Arabs convened a Pan-Arab Congress, which opposed partition and countered with a proposal for forming an independent Arab state in which Jews could live as a protected minority. A new version of dhimmi status, however, was not what the Zionists had in mind.

By 1939 the situation had further deteriorated. The Arabs boycotted the next commission's work. In Tiberias an Arab mob massacred twenty Jews. The British deported the inflammatory

Grand Mufti of Jerusalem, but to no avail. Finally, the British produced yet another scheme, calling for a constitution within five years, an independent Palestine in ten, and shared governance by Arabs and Jews. Under this plan all Jewish immigration would stop after five years unless the Arabs agreed to allow it. The government would also have the power to prohibit the land transfers, a clause clearly aimed at restricting the Jews' rights to property. Neither side accepted the plan, and unrest continued.

During the Second World War the Jews, not surprisingly, supported the British, while many Arab leaders were, understandably, if not pro-Nazi, against the British. The exiled Grand Mufti even made propaganda appearances alongside Adolf Hitler. Unfortunately for the Arabs, much like the Turks in 1914, they had chosen the losing side in a desperate world war. By 1945 Great Britain had had its fill of Palestine.

By 1947 the British were looking for an exit strategy from Palestine. About 650,000 Jews lived in the mandate, or 200,000 more than had been present in 1939. But the Arab population, despite losing land to the Jews and the constant unrest, had also grown to 1.2 million, or double the number in 1922. The Jews sought an independent state within Palestine; the Arabs' preferred solution was to give the entire mandate to an existing state, such as Syria or Jordan. The newly established and big power–dominated United Nations (UN) assumed responsibility for finding a solution.

The "puzzle of Palestine" sent chills down American policy makers' spines. Many military leaders feared that if the Truman administration supported an Israeli state it would undermine U.S. policy in the Middle East, push Arab nationalists into the Soviet camp, and threaten Western access to the Persian Gulf's oil. If the United Nations established an independent Jewish state, American planners expected that it would quickly be threatened with extinction by its far more populous Arab neighbors and would call for a commitment of American and Russian military forces. Neither power would allow the other to send troops without sending them itself. This situation, the JCS declared, was a recipe for another world war. In October 1947 the chiefs recommended against committing U.S. forces to Palestine and against U.S. support for Israel's statehood.

On November 29, 1949, the United Nations, with U.S. support, adopted Resolution 181, calling for the partitioning of Palestine and the creation of both an Arab and a Jewish state. The Arab League rejected Resolution 181. Protests followed throughout the Arab world and, within Palestine, violence erupted against the Jews, who fought back. For the next several months the United Nations proved incapable of enforcing its will. Ultimately, the Jews declared their own independence on May 14, 1948; their Arab neighbors responded with a full-scale invasion. The exiled Grand Mufti summed up the effort: "I declare a holy war, my Muslim brothers! Murder the Jews! Murder them all!" The secretary general of the Arab League, Abdul Razek Azzam Pasha, avowed: "This will be a war of extermination and a momentous massacre which will be spoken of like the Mongolian massacres and the Crusades."

The Arab states staked their legitimacy, and not for the last time, on promises they could not keep. The nascent Israeli Defense Force (IDF) defeated the combined armies of Egypt, Jordan, Syria, and Iraq, along with troops from Lebanon and Saudi Arabia. When the fighting ended in early 1949, Israel had gained territory beyond that allocated to it in the original partition plan. Egypt and Jordan seized the remaining Palestinian lands—the Gaza Strip and the West Bank, respectively.

The Israeli victory, despite its shocking nature, failed to register fully with its neighbors. The embarrassed Arab states vowed to exterminate the Jewish state; raids and counterraids became the rule along Israel's still tenuous borders. Violence against Jews elsewhere in the Arab world led to a huge wave of refugees flowing into Israel. Between 1948 and 1950 over 500,000 Sephardic Jews from Arab countries and Iran resettled in Israel and over 175,000 in 1951, including 130,000 from Iraq alone, thus doubling the Israeli population in three years.

For Washington, the Israeli victory was problematic. Truman's support for partition outraged America's allies, especially King Abdul Aziz of Saudi Arabia, and for the first time made the Arabs reconsider their relationship with the United States. In the Pentagon, the same military planners who had predicted an Israeli defeat now saw cause for hope. Israel, they naively believed, could become the linchpin for Middle East defense, assuming, of course, that its defeated neighbors accepted the war's result and agreed to work alongside the Jews. In the interim American policy sought to stabilize the situation diplomatically, to work with the French and British to control the flow of arms to the region, and to move toward forming a multilateral defense organization.

American policy met with mixed success. In July 1951 assassins gunned down the two Arab leaders most likely to reach an accord with Israel—Lebanese prime minister Riad Bey al-Solh and King Abdullah of Jordan. The following July Gamal Abdel Nasser led a nationalist military coup in Egypt, overthrowing King Farouk. That same year nationalists gained power in Iran's parliament and began to nationalize the Anglo-Iranian Oil Company (formerly APOC). Despite having their own nationalized industries, the British resisted. The Americans were more concerned about the horribly managed nationalization effort that had plunged Iran into chaos than they were by nationalization's ramifications. When attempts to moderate between Britain and Iran failed, largely due to the intransigence of Iranian prime minister Mohammad Mossadegh, the British and Americans staged a coup in Tehran. They removed the prime minister and secured the power of Mohammad Reza Shah Pahlavi. Later that year the Americans finally secured a multilateral security accord, signing Turkey and Iraq to the "Baghdad Pact." The following year Britain, Iran, and Pakistan joined as well.

Any gains along the northern tier were offset by problems in Egypt, where Nasser turned to the Czechs—Soviet proxies—for an arms deal that threatened to upset the military balance in the region. Nasser next nationalized the Suez Canal, a move met in 1956 with an abortive Anglo-French invasion that was abetted by the Israelis, who destroyed Egyptian forces in the Sinai. President Dwight D. Eisenhower pressured the British, French, and Israelis to withdraw, which they did, but the American effort at evenhandedness only further legitimized Nasser. Recognizing the problem and the increasing incapacity of the British, the U.S. administration chose to play a larger role in the Middle East, expanded its military planning and intervention capabilities, and in March 1957 issued the Eisenhower Doctrine, declaring American willingness "to use armed forces to assist any such nation or group of nations [in the Middle East] requesting assistance against armed aggression from any country controlled by international communism." When a July 1958 nationalist coup in Iraq threatened to unhinge the region, the United States sent in the Marines after the Lebanese called for assistance. Shortly thereafter, British troops moved into Jordan. In 1959 with Baghdad torn from the Baghdad Pact, the Americans sponsored a new alliance— the Central Treaty Organization (CENTO).

By the mid-1960s, the American position along the Northern Tier seemed relatively secure, but the heart of the Middle East remained in turmoil because of Nasser's Arab nationalism and the continuing hostility between Israel and its neighbors. Earlier in the decade, when Nasser stoked troubles in the Arabian Peninsula, President John F. Kennedy stepped up military assistance to the Saudis, and they successfully battled the Nasserites in Yemen. By the middle of the decade, the situation between the Arabs and Israelis neared its crisis point. Unfortunately, the next U.S. administration, that of President Lyndon B. Johnson, focused on another crisis—its war in Indochina.

A short period of calm followed the 1956 Israeli victory in the Sinai. But soon the old pattern of border and retaliatory raids— some of which were rather large—resumed. On May 18 Nasser ordered the United Nations to remove its peacekeepers from the

Sinai, where they acted as a buffer between the Egyptians and the Israelis. On May 23 the Egyptians blockaded the Straits of Tiran, threatening all Israeli-flagged vessels. On May 30, Jordan's king Hussein, whom Nasser only a few days before had called an "imperialist lackey," signed a pact with the United Arab Republic of Egypt and Syria and declared, "Our basic objective will be the destruction of Israel. The Arab people want to fight."

While Nasser's moves were mostly bluster, the possibility that the Arab militaries might take a more threatening posture remained. The Israeli military depended heavily on reservists, and they could not be called up and kept under arms indefinitely without severe damage to the economy. Moreover, the Tiran blockade, as such, was technically an act of war. The Israeli cabinet met on May 23 and decided to launch an offensive in two days unless the blockade ended. The Israelis informed the Americans, who requested time to find a diplomatic solution. The Israelis agreed to wait ten days.

When the Johnson administration failed to act promptly, the IDF struck on June 5, 1967, catching the Egyptians by surprise. Flying mostly French-manufactured aircraft, the Israelis destroyed much of the Egyptian air force on the ground and proceeded to rout Nasser's army in the Sinai. When the Jordanians began shelling Israeli positions, the IDF captured the divided city of Jerusalem and drove King Hussein's army from the West Bank. Next the Israelis turned on the Syrians and captured the strategic Golan Heights. By June 10 the Six Day War was over.

In physical terms, the conflict was an incredible Israeli success. The Israelis lost 779 soldiers and airmen, while the Arab armies suffered 21,000 killed in action with twice as many wounded, missing, or captured. Egypt lost approximately 80 percent of the military equipment it had deployed to the Sinai. The Syrians lost half their tanks and almost all of their artillery on the Golan Heights.

The UN Security Council responded on November 22, 1967, and adopted Resolution 242, which called for the Israelis' withdrawal "from territories occupied" during the war in return for "the termination of all claims or states of belligerency" and the recognition of the right of "every state in the area to live in peace within secure and recognized boundaries free from threats or acts of force." Because of U.S. efforts, the resolution's English-language version purposefully avoided using the adjective "all" or the article "the" before the phrase "territories occupied."

Perceptions of the Six Day War's long-term impact have changed over the ensuing decades and will probably continue to vary in the future. The Israelis' occupation of the Gaza Strip and the West Bank with their large Arab populations proved to be a mixed blessing for Israeli security. But perhaps the most important, enduring effect of the Egyptian and Syrian militaries' inability to defeat tiny Israel yet again was to weaken the political legitimacy of Arab nationalists, secularists, reformers, and modernizers, including Nasser. Their failure combined with the shock, shame, and sheer frustration the Arabs felt in the wake of the 1967 war and left a gaping void.

The Second World War, the major petroleum-producing center's shift to the Persian Gulf during the early postwar period, the Cold War contest with the Soviet Union, and the decision to support Israel forced the United States to acknowledge that its commercial and strategic interests could not be left entirely to the British or any combination of regional states. During the second Eisenhower administration, the United States began to alter its command structure accordingly. In 1957 the military established the position of commander in chief, Middle East, and, in the following year, the Strategic Army Corps as a reserve force of those units, among them the 82nd Airborne Division, not already committed to other theaters of operation.

The Johnson administration's war in Indochina short-circuited these developments, nearly destroyed the U.S. postwar foreign policy consensus, undermined popular faith in the federal government, and tore apart the military. As a result, when the

American position in the Middle East came under pressure in the late 1960s and 1970s, the United States was not poised to respond effectively.

In the Six Day War's immediate aftermath, the United States faced the first of many challenges. The Arab nations of the Persian Gulf launched their first oil embargo. The producers' lack of solidarity and limited cash reserves minimized the effort's impact. Nevertheless, the gulf's Arabs learned important lessons they would put to good use in 1973.

In 1968 as the war in Indochina faltered, the Middle East situation deteriorated. In January Great Britain announced its intention to withdraw its military forces from "east of Suez." A few months later a Soviet naval squadron arrived for the first time in the Indian Ocean. In July Ba'athists staged a coup and seized power in Iraq. Richard M. Nixon, elected president in November, inherited difficult strategic problems in Southeast Asia and the Middle East.

Nixon shaped a policy that would avoid committing American forces, most especially ground troops. His Nixon Doctrine turned responsibility for regional defense to local states. In Indochina this policy became known as "Vietnamization"; in the Persian Gulf it took the form of the "Twin Pillars," or a reliance on Iran and Saudi Arabia.

The latter policy was, at best, a Hobson's choice for the United States. Iran was the more strategically placed vis-à-vis the Soviet Union and the stronger of the pillars, but it was also a non-Arab state frequently at odds with its neighbors, and its ruler was a pretentious monarch of questionable ability. Saudi Arabia was far better managed, but its population was at the time an eighth of that of Iran. As a result, the Twin Pillars policy, referred to in one 1973 State Department report as "the Odd Couple," required a massive buildup of the Iranian military.

This investment was fraught with difficulties and dangers. Expanding the shah's military to the degree necessary to blunt a

Soviet drive south inevitably upset the balance of power between Iran and its neighbor Iraq. In response, Moscow's arms transfers to Baghdad increased and posed a threat to the gulf's Arabs, especially Iraq's neighbors Kuwait and Saudi Arabia. The shah could not manage this massive arms buildup, marked by an almost 600 percent increase in military expenditures in ten years, the concomitant pressures of modernization, and the increased presence of Westerners in his country. Since the early 1950s, internal U.S. government reports reflected negatively on the shah. He suffered from delusions of grandeur, and a CIA report termed him "a dangerous megalomaniac." Nevertheless, the Nixon administration regarded the new shah as a first-class world leader and statesman.

Elsewhere in the Middle East the situation remained unstable. Between 1968 and 1970, Egypt and Israel waged the War of Attrition, a mostly artillery and aerial war over the Sinai and along the Suez Canal. The Egyptian Air Force fared poorly, and in the end Russian pilots flew at Nasser's request but to no avail. In early August 1970, the United States brokered a cease-fire. On September 28 Nasser, the wellspring of Arab nationalism, died of a heart attack. His vice president, Anwar al-Sadat, became president.

In Jordan a new threat to Israel began to take shape. Myriad Palestinian political organizations, most committed to terrorism, operated from Jordanian territory against Israel. In September 1970 after months of violent friction between King Hussein's government and Yassir Arafat's Palestinian Liberation Organization (PLO), terrorists attempted to assassinate the king and hijacked several European aircraft with passengers aboard on the ground in Amman. A civil war erupted in Jordan. When the fighting ended later that month, between 5,000 and 10,000 Palestinians were dead. Following Nasser's death, Arafat and his subordinate organizations lost their political position within Jordan and relocated to Lebanon. They did so with a sense of outrage at the Hashemite king and a bitter memory of what they termed "Black September."

The War of Attrition, however, had not been a complete debacle for the Egyptians. They had managed to move numerous Soviet-made surface-to-air missile (SAM) batteries closer to the Suez Canal. Under this defensive SAM umbrella the Egyptians launched a daring offensive across the canal on October 6, 1973, while the Syrians attacked Israel along the Golan Heights. Israeli intelligence had failed to uncover the attack until the day before it was launched. At American prompting, Prime Minister Golda Meir decided not to launch a preemptive strike.

The Yom Kippur War lasted until October 24. The Egyptians and Syrians performed better than expected, and in the early going Israel appeared to be tottering on the verge of defeat. The Israeli Air Force suffered heavy losses from Egyptian and Syrian SAMs. Israeli tanks incurred losses as well, fighting Egyptian units dug in along the canal's eastern bank. Rumors flew that Tel Aviv was readying its nuclear arsenal.

But the Israelis held their lines. By October 10 they had pushed the Syrians back to their start line, and by the fourteenth they were closing on Damascus. The next day they launched their counterattack in the Sinai. Ariel "Arik" Sharon commanded a division that penetrated Egyptian lines and made a surprise crossing of the Suez Canal. The Israelis fought off heavy Egyptian counterattacks against their expanding bridgehead. Another IDF division crossed the canal, then worked its way along the western bank, and isolated the Egyptian Third Army in the Sinai. At this point, amid Soviet and American global military and nuclear posturing, sufficient pressures mounted on the combatants that they agreed to a cease-fire and ended the conflict.

Once again, the Arabs had lost a war against Israel, although they had given the Israelis, and the Americans, a bit of a scare. Despite the Third Army's plight, the Egyptians had performed better than the West or Israel had expected, crossing the canal in the face of Israeli resistance and maintaining a secure northern bridgehead at the cease-fire. For the Egyptian military and President

Sadat, these successes led them to declare the war a victory for Egypt.

During the conflict, several major Persian Gulf oil producers employed their "oil weapon" against the West and especially the United States as it stepped up its support for Israel. The Oil Embargo, which began October 16, 1973, and ended March 17, 1974, saw petroleum prices in the West jump markedly. In the short term, Americans faced rationing and long lines to fill up their automobiles' gas tanks. The U.S. economy went into a slump, termed "stagflation," that was marked by inflated prices and high unemployment and that lasted into the early 1980s. But the embargo's long-term impact only became evident a decade later. Western economies used oil more efficiently. High-cost oil-producing areas began to compete with the Middle East, and increased exploration led to the discovery of new oil resources, for example, in the North Sea. By the end of the 1980s, competition began to hurt the Persian Gulf producers, and they lost market share. Moreover, as they accumulated their newfound wealth, termed "petrodollars," they had to find someplace to invest it, and they turned to Western financial markets. As their tens of billions of petrodollars went into Western markets, the oil-producing states faced a more difficult calculation when setting prices. A sharp rise in oil prices might well earn a producing state an extra dollar per barrel of oil, but if the jump sent Wall Street into a slump, lost investment dollars might more than offset the gains. In fact, by the late 1980s some of the Persian Gulf states were earning more on their investments than they were on oil production.

The embargo also made the United States think more clearly about the strategic importance of the region and its oil. But the U.S. did not reduce its commitment to Israel — quite the opposite. Instead, American military planners began to consider the eventual possibility of invading the region and seizing the oil fields. While it quickly became apparent that the United States lacked the capability to act, identifying the myriad shortcomings led to a changed command structure and set the tone for the next several decades of ever-deeper American involvement in the region.

In January 1977 Jimmy Carter became president of the United States. He faced a difficult situation on the domestic front, the aftermath of the Nixon administration's failed policy of détente with the Soviet Union, and a deteriorating American position in the Middle East. The new president did little to rally the nation with his talk of "malaise" and lower expectations. Nor was he wise, as he soon discovered, to dismiss what he thought was his predecessors' "inordinate" fear of communism. Nevertheless, Carter sensibly focused more attention on the Middle East.

Carter moved quickly. In mid-1977 Presidential Review Memorandum 10 identified the Persian Gulf as a "vulnerable and vital region." In August, Carter signed Presidential Directive 18, which called for establishing a mobile force capable of deployment either in Korea or the Persian Gulf—what became the Rapid Deployment Force (RDF). The administration also sought to enhance U.S. military capabilities throughout the Indian Ocean basin, initiated a ten-year plan to develop a network of bases and improved port facilities in the Arabian Peninsula, and explored the possibility of establishing a numbered naval fleet in the Indian Ocean.

In September 1978 Carter's focus on the Middle East began to pay dividends. Israeli prime minister Menachem Begin and Egyptian president Anwar Sadat signed the Camp David Accords. The Israelis agreed to allow the establishment of autonomous Palestinian authorities in the West Bank and Gaza Strip and to withdraw from the Sinai Peninsula. In turn the Egyptians agreed to establish normal diplomatic relations with Israel, to limit their forces in the Sinai, and to guarantee the Israelis freedom of maritime passage in the reopened Suez Canal and the Straits of Tiran.

Camp David was a major foreign policy success for the Carter administration. The agreement appeared to herald a new era for the Middle East. The head of a major frontline Arab state had sat at a table, negotiated with the Israelis, and reached and signed an agreement establishing peace between two nations that had been at war since 1948.

President Carter had little time to savor his Camp David triumph, however, before events in the Middle East went from bad to worse. On January 16, 1979, the shah of Iran abdicated and fled the country. Interim governments ruled Iran briefly before succumbing to an Islamic theocracy dominated by the Ayatollah Ruhollah Khomeini. On July 17 Saddam Hussein assumed the presidency of Iraq and within days began consolidating his power through intimidation. On November 4 Iranian students seized the American Embassy in Tehran and took sixty-six Americans hostages, who would be held for 444 days. On November 20, 500 Islamic militants in Saudi Arabia seized the Grand Mosque. When negotiations failed, Saudi troops launched an amateurish and bungled military assault against the holiest site in the Islamic world. On December 24, the Soviet Union began moving troops into Afghanistan in an effort to prop up a failing Communist regime.

Although Carter and his national security team had begun to focus greater attention on the Middle East in 1977, the scope of the 1979 crises went well beyond anything previous administrations had faced. The United States confronted simultaneous challenges from Arab nationalists (Hussein), Islamic fundamentalists (Khomeini), and the Soviet Union, which by invading Afghanistan had made its first cross-border move beyond Eastern Europe since 1945.

On January 23, 1980 Carter used his State of the Union address to annunciate what became known as the Carter Doctrine:

> Let our position be absolutely clear: an attempt by any outside force to gain control of the Persian Gulf region will be regarded as an assault on the vital interests of the United States of America, and such an assault will be repelled by any means necessary, including military force.

Throughout 1979 and 1980 the administration moved additional U.S. air and naval assets to the Persian Gulf. By the end of 1980 the U.S. Navy had increased its presence in the Indian Ocean basin by 300 percent. American aid flowed to the Afghan resistance fighters who were resisting the Soviet Union. In February 1980 reporters photographed Carter's national security adviser Zbigniew Brzezinski brandishing an automatic rifle in the Khyber Pass.

But the situation continued to deteriorate. In April, American Special Forces launched a botched attempt to rescue the Iranian hostages, which did little but embarrass the United States and the administration. On September 22 Iraq attacked Iran, initiating a futile and costly war that would last eight years and bankrupt both countries.

Carter faced the prospect of both Iran's and Iraq's oil being lost to the West and of this new war spilling into the Persian Gulf waters. He expanded his doctrine, which had been aimed at external—that is, Soviet—threats to the flow of oil. In a September 24 speech, Carter made it clear that the United States would not tolerate *any* infringement of shipping through the Persian Gulf. In October Secretary of State Edmund Muskie reinforced the same point: "We have pledged to do what is necessary to protect free shipping in the Strait of Hormuz from any interference."

The Carter administration was responsible for the most significant shift in American policy toward the Middle East since Truman. Carter was the first postwar president to place the region at the top of his foreign policy agenda; he was also the first American president to recognize that the United States had to take the lead, both politically *and* militarily, to defend it if necessary. Carter pledged that the United States would resist with armed force external or internal interference in the gulf's flow of oil to the West. The administration markedly increased the level of forces deployed to the region, including the Rapid Deployment Force, which would eventually grow into Central Command. And Carter and his team set in motion the infrastructure and basing developments that would allow the United States to fight the first Gulf War (1990–91).

Ronald W. Reagan's administration reaped the benefit of Carter's 1977–81 groundwork, although the new American president also inherited a continuing stream of troubles. In September 1981 Iranian aircraft bombed an oil facility in Kuwait. On October 1, faced at a press conference with a hypothetical scenario about Saudi Arabia going the way of Iran, Reagan replied, "There's no way that we could stand by and see [Saudi Arabia] taken over by anyone that would shut off that oil." The president's statement quickly became known as the "Reagan Corollary" to the Carter Doctrine. Then on October 6, 1981, militants from the Egyptian Islamic Jihad, an offshoot of the Muslim Brotherhood, assassinated President Anwar Sadat.

The situation to the west, in the Levant, also became more complicated. After Black September, the PLO had moved its locus of operations to Lebanon. There it became, as it had before in Jordan, a state within a state. The Palestinian presence undercut the delicate political balance between Lebanon's Christians and Muslims. In 1975 a vicious sectarian civil war broke out in Lebanon. The Christian president, with his fellow believers outnumbered and outgunned, feared a disaster and called for Syrian intervention. By the end of 1976, 40,000 Syrian troops patrolled Lebanon, operating under an Arab League mandate. But the disorder continued as week by week the violence destroyed Lebanon's infrastructure.

The turmoil in Lebanon posed a threat to the security of Israel's northern border. Attacks by Palestinian and other Islamic groups against northern Israeli settlements increased. In 1978 the Israeli army drove into southern Lebanon as far as the Litani River; they withdrew, but only after establishing a friendly Lebanese Christian militia south of the river.

The situation in Lebanon remained chaotic. Deploying a United Nations Interim Force in Lebanon (UNIFIL) did little to halt the violence. Fighting continued among the Lebanese factions and the Syrians, whose movement into the country was a major concern for Israel.

On June 6, 1982, the Israelis struck north again, but this time they drove past the Litani River and as far as Beirut. Their goals were twofold: clear the southern half of the country and destroy the Palestinian position in Lebanon. Six months later the Israelis faced international pressure to withdraw. They had destroyed much of the PLO infrastructure, the remainder of which Arafat planned to move to Tunisia.

Despite the seeming success, the Israelis had further scrambled Lebanese politics and set in motion a series of unforeseen events. Many Christian militias had sided with the Israelis and, while they had the temporary upper hand, tried to make the most of their opportunity. At two refugee camps—Sabra and Shatila—the Christians massacred as many as 800 Palestinians.

As the Israelis prepared to withdraw and the Palestinians prepared to relocate to Tunisia, the international community, led by the United States, decided to intervene. In August 1982 an American, British, French, and Italian multinational force deployed in western Lebanon. By the end of the month they were gone, as quickly as they had come.

Nevertheless, the situation in Lebanon remained one of disorder and violence. The Reagan administration formed a new multinational force with France and Italy and moved into the environs of Beirut in September 1982. The Western military presence did have a degree of success, bringing some stability to Lebanon. Unfortunately, the multinational force itself became the new target for Islamic militants. In April 1983 they bombed the U.S. Embassy in Beirut, killing more than sixty people. On October 23 Iranian-supported Hezbollah homicide truck bombers drove into the complexes housing American Marines and French paratroopers, killing 241 of the former and 58 of the latter. Despite tough talk from the American president, by the spring of 1984 all the Western troops were gone. The Syrians remained in Lebanon until 2005.

The Lebanese Civil War marked a transition in the history of the Middle East. Throughout the 1950s, 1960s, and the early 1970s

Lebanon had served as a model for those arguing that Arabs and Jews could live peacefully together in a secular Palestine, as did Christians and Muslims in Lebanon. After 1975 no one viewed Lebanon as a template for sectarian coexistence. The Lebanese experiences also marked the shift in the nature of terrorist acts—from those employed by a "national liberation front" organization, such as the PLO, to those employed by Islamic fundamentalists, or in this case Hezbollah (the Party of Allah). While it is true that a bombing is a bombing, determining the proper response to such an attack requires understanding its design. Moreover, the fundamentalists' goals were far more expansive, as will be seen, than those of the secular nationalists. Lebanon also demonstrated that terrorism worked. The Israelis destroyed the Palestinian infrastructure in Lebanon and retreated, only to find themselves later engaged with Islamic fundamentalists. Likewise the second multinational force left after the bombings of the U.S. Embassy and American and French barracks, setting a terrible precedent for the future.

At the time, that future was not readily apparent. The Reagan administration was understandably engaged in the endgame of the fifty year-long Cold War. The Iran-Iraq War took the form of a traditional, conventional struggle between two nations. Israel's neighbors, even the PLO, also operated within the state system so comfortably familiar to Americans.

In 1987 as the first Palestinian Intifada (shaking off) broke out in the West Bank and Gaza, the United States faced a new challenge in the Persian Gulf. When the Iran-Iraq War began in 1980, the Iraqis held the initiative but quickly lost it through poor decisions and an Iranian riposte. As the war dragged on it became an attritional struggle that left Iraq, with a third the population of Iran, at times on the ropes. Fearing the consequences of an Iranian victory for both the Arab gulf states and Israel, the Reagan administration began to tilt toward Iraq, and to supply Saddam Hussein with intelligence that allowed his army to fend off Iranian offensives. Hussein's air force struck Iranian oil exports to undercut Iranian finances. The Iranians could not respond in kind, because much of Iraq's oil moved via pipelines across Turkey or Saudi Arabia. The frustrated Iranian leadership chose to strike at Hussein's Arab allies, especially Kuwait. In December 1986 the Kuwaiti government asked the U.S. Coast Guard about the registration requirements to re-flag their ships with the Stars and Stripes. The request set off a political debate in Washington, but in the end the administration decided to re-flag eleven of Kuwait's larger tankers. On May 17, 1987, amid the political bickering that followed the decision, a French-built Iraqi fighter-bomber fired two antiship missiles into the U.S. Navy frigate *Stark,* killing thirty-seven Americans.

The administration nonetheless maintained its focus on Iran. What followed became known as "the Tanker War." U.S. military forces, aided by the British and several other European nations, worked hard to limit the Iranians' damage to international shipping. In April 1988, following the mining of the frigate *Samuel B. Roberts,* the U.S. Navy conducted Operation Praying Mantis, effectively destroying the better part of Iran's remaining sea-going naval force. But the more important blow to Iran came ashore, where the Iraqi army launched what became its final offensive of the war and regained the initiative along the front's southern sector. On July 2, 1988, the American cruiser *Vincennes* mistakenly downed an Iranian civilian airliner and killed 290 people. On July 18, with Khomeini's approval, the Iranian government accepted a United Nations cease-fire, ending the war.

The war's costs were enormous. Casualty figures remain uncertain, but as many as a million people — soldiers and civilians — may have perished on both sides. Collectively, Iran and Iraq had spent two dollars for every dollar they had earned in oil royalties since 1909. The conflict was not only one of the most expensive wars of the second half of the twentieth century, but the most futile as well: in the end the border had barely changed.

As the bloody Iran-Iraq War came to an end, the West hoped that the world was changing for the better. Soviet leader Mikhail Gorbachev had set in motion new polices—*perestroika* (restructuring) and *glasnost* (openness)—that both took the edge off the Cold War and unleashed forces within the Communist bloc that boded ill for its survival. By the summer of 1989 most analysts had concluded that the Cold War was either over or rapidly coming to an end. In November the Berlin Wall came down. Although the Soviet Union would not formally collapse until 1991, clearly a new age had dawned.

In the summer of 1989 political scientist Francis Fukuyama, who in the 1980s worked alternately for the RAND Corporation and the Policy Planning Staff of the Department of State, published "End of History" in the *National Interest*. The author's attempt to give some shape to the coming post–Cold War world gained immediate notoriety. Fukuyama's thesis, although by no means universally accepted (or understood), reflected the mood epitomized in a spring 1990 global review published by the *Economist*. Much of the globe, the editors noted, appeared to be on the verge of a new millennium of democracy and prosperity, whereas in the Arab world there was little but a "lack of euphoria."

As if on cue, in August 1990 Saddam Hussein, having narrowly survived his ill-fated attack on Iran ten years earlier, miscalculated once again. He ordered the Iraqi army into Kuwait and overran the emirate. For the first time since the UN was established a member-state had disappeared from the map. Moreover, Hussein had attacked the Arab gulf state whose threatened security had led to American intervention in the Tanker War of 1987.

Hussein grossly underestimated the Americans' capabilities to fight. His vaunted intelligence apparatus had apparently missed public congressional testimony in the spring of 1990 by the commander in chief, U.S. Central Command, Gen. H. Norman Schwarzkopf, Jr. After a decade of work begun during the Carter administration the preparations to defend the Arabian Peninsula were complete. Moreover, with the end of the Cold War in Europe, U.S. military assets were free to be deployed to the Persian Gulf. They would not have been available if Hussein had attacked a year earlier or if he had waited a few years until those forces had been demobilized.

Hussein also misjudged the Americans' willingness to fight. He informed the U.S. ambassador to Iraq, April Glaspie, that he expected the United States to strike "with aircraft and missiles" but not with ground forces. The United States, in his judgment, was "a society which cannot accept 10,000 dead in one battle."

President George H. W. Bush's administration responded in the summer and fall of 1990 by drawing a "line in the sand." He sent nearly a half million men and women to the peninsula, including Saudi Arabia; brought together a huge multinational coalition; and blockaded Iraq. Hussein refused to withdraw and instead foolishly sent forty divisions into the theater, where they had to be supplied over a single road in the face of overwhelming coalition aerial supremacy. The coalition forces began an extensive air campaign and followed it up with a hundred-hour ground war that drove the Iraqis from Kuwait.

The beneficial results of the first Iraq War were many. The coalition liberated Kuwait, freeing the Kuwaiti people and representing a major success for the United Nations as an institution. For the Americans, their military success appeared to put to rest the ghost of Vietnam. More significant, the United States became what commentator and historian Fouad Ajami termed the "guarantor of last resort," a role that had been long in coming but one that the Americans had nonetheless resisted for decades.

An unforeseen benefit of the conflict was its impact on the Palestinian issue. Arafat had supported Hussein and the invasion, and with the Iraqis' collapse the Palestinians were persona non grata in many of the gulf states, especially Kuwait. The first Intifada, which had begun in 1987, came to an abrupt end in 1991. Two years later the PLO signed the Oslo Accords, which set goals and timetables for solving the Arab-Israeli problem. The millennium did seem to be at hand.

But the first Iraq War accelerated or set in motion myriad negative forces. While deploying of American military forces in the Arabian Peninsula had not caused much of a stir in the much-touted Arab street, the presence had further inflamed the passions of many extreme fundamentalists. Despite expectations that Hussein would not survive his second major military debacle, he held tightly to power. When the Iraqi Shi'a rose in revolt in the south, he used the remnants of his military to crush them brutally, while American forces, strung along the border, took no action. Only when he moved to smash a Kurdish revolt in the north did the United States intervene and prevent comparable slaughters. Nor did Hussein cooperate fully with the UN's international inspectors to root out his stocks of and capabilities to produce chemical, biological, and nuclear weapons. As a result, the United States remained in a state of war with Iraq, continuing sanctions and a maritime blockade and overflying much of its territory with military aircraft.

On February 26, 1993, Muslim extremists struck once again at Americans, but this time in the United States: a truck bomb exploded in the parking garage under the North Tower of the World Trade Center complex in New York City, killing six and injuring over a thousand people. The attack was not a great success; the goal had been to topple the North Tower so that it would crash into and collapse the South Tower. The subsequent investigation uncovered a not-so-elaborate conspiracy, which included another plan to attack landmarks throughout the New York area. Among those implicated in the conspiracies were several radical Muslims, among them Ramzi Yousef and the charismatic Omar Abdel-Rahman, better known as the "Blind Sheik." Americans who paid attention to the investigation and trials read about the conspirators' links to a plethora of radical groups, such as the Egyptian "Islamic Group," Egyptian Islamic Jihad, and several organizations involved in the Afghan resistance against the Soviet Union. For the first time in history, violent jihad had come to American shores.

Chapter 7
"The Middle East Version of Teddy Roosevelt"

The foremost duty of Islam in this world is to depose Jahiliyyah from the leadership of man, and to take the leadership into its own hands and enforce the particular way of life which is its permanent feature. The purpose of this rightly guided leadership is the good and success of mankind, the good which proceeds from returning to the Creator and the success which comes from being in harmony with the rest of the universe. The intention is to raise human beings to that high position which God has chosen for them and to free them from the slavery of desires. This purpose is explained by Raba'i bin 'Amer, when he replied to the commander-in-chief of the Persian army, Rustum. Rustum asked, "For what purpose have you come?" Raba'i answered, "God has sent us to bring anyone who wishes from servitude to men into the service of God alone, from the narrowness of this world into the vastness of this world and the Hereafter, from the tyranny of religions into the justice of Islam."
—Sayyid Qutb, Milestones

Who were these Muslim extremists? What were their motivations? What were their goals? What was the force within Islam that they represented? The answers to these questions are by no means simple, nor are they comforting.

In a January 2003 interview with *Washington Post* reporter David Ignatius, then deputy secretary of defense Paul Wolfowitz stated, "We need an Islamic reformation and I think there is real hope for one." Many in the West and quite a few within the Muslim world long for such a reformation. The reasons are obvious: the by-products of the West's Protestant Reformation are generally viewed with favor. The Reformation changed the relationship between the church and the state and opened the path toward greater religious, political, and intellectual freedom as well as expanded economic opportunities. The Reformation led to greater secularism as well as economic and political pluralism. Likewise, an Islamic reformation, or so the argument goes, would generate long-overdue and comparable results within the Muslim world.

Unfortunately, those in the West waiting expectantly for an Islamic reformation are misreading history. They assume that an Islamic reformation would generate similar results to the Protestant Reformation in the West. Moreover, the focus on the end product misses the parallels between the forces unleashed by the Protestant Reformation and those of today's Islamic jihadists. Allow me to state it bluntly: there is no need to wait for an Islamic Reformation, because it has already arrived and its face is that of Osama bin Laden.

What was the Protestant Reformation? In its basic forms the Reformation was a sixteenth-century reaction to the Catholic Church's accretions of power and procedural abuses, a reaction that loosened the grip of that institution on the state and society. The reformers—men such as Martin Luther, John Calvin, Huldrych Zwingli, Philipp Melanchthon, and many others—sought to return Christianity to a more pristine form that predated what they felt the Catholic Church had become, a hierarchical organization that had more in common with the Roman Empire than a pure Christian faith.

The printing press, although not one of the Reformation's causes, most certainly fueled and sustained the effort. Printing the Bible, and later the Vulgate, in Latin broke the church's hold on the control of religious knowledge. As the holy book was translated and became more accessible, the church lost its monopoly on the interpretation of the word of God. And as the reform movement began, the printing press allowed the reformers to spread their own word widely and efficiently in a manner that would have been impossible a century earlier.

In the fifteenth century, the Ottomans consciously forbade the opportunities the printing press presented. When they finally allowed printing in the eighteenth century, they nevertheless sustained the ban on printing Islamic religious texts and continued to do so until the mid-nineteenth century. The widespread availability of the Qur'an and other primary Islamic texts, such as the hadiths, in the late nineteenth and early twentieth centuries is thus a rather recent event.

The availability of these texts, combined with existing yearnings for reform akin to those associated with the eighteenth-century Wahabi movement, synergized into what today is called "jihadism." Why? Just as Christian reformers sought to destroy the myriad accretions to their faith and return it to the more pristine form evident in early Christianity, Islamic reformers have always sought to do the same — to return to the early pristine form of Islam. In that sense, Osama bin Laden is to the Islamic Reformation what Martin Luther was to the Protestant Reformation.

I do not mean in any way to equate Luther with bin Laden, but rather I argue that they both epitomize the essence of reform within their respective and very different religions. The Protestant reformers sought to return to a form of Christianity that predated the Catholic Church's climb to worldly power, which began with its co-optation by the Roman Empire beginning in the fourth century. Of course, during their first two centuries Christians were a powerless sect of people who had no choice but to proselytize peacefully and separately from the state. The modern jihadists likewise seek to return to the early era of Islam before the less than righteous khalifas, sultans, kings, shahs, emirs, and presidents distorted and polluted their faith. However, the early Muslim era to which they wish to return is markedly different from that of the Christians': Islam under the early khalifas, or successors to the Prophet, controlled a united *ummah* and combined religious, political, and military responsibilities in an effort to spread Allah's word throughout the known world, if necessary by the sword. And just as the printing press accelerated the process of Christian reform, modern communications advances—radio, audio tapes, satellite television, and the Internet—have amplified the force of the Islamic reformers' or jihadists' message.

The trail of political jihadism is complex but deeply rooted. As shown in this book, jihad through fighting and Islam have always gone hand in hand. If Islam was not spread by the sword, it certainly spread along with it. In the fourteenth century, Ibn Khaldun wrote: "In the Muslim community, the holy war is a religious duty." "Islam grew with blood," the Ayatollah Khomeini told an audience of Iranian theology students in an August 1979 speech. "The great prophet of Islam," Khomeini stressed, "in one hand carried the Koran and in the other the sword." From the seventh through the seventeenth centuries, when the Islamic world held the upper hand, Muslims regularly raided or invaded neighboring territories. Only in the nineteenth century, when the Ottomans were clearly on the defensive, did attacks cease for fear they would prompt an overwhelming Western reaction. But even then, wars continued between the Ottomans and their neighbors until the empire's final demise in the early 1920s. A quiet of a sort existed during the sixty years that followed Atatürk's elimination of the khalifate, although to an extent Islam was still a root cause of the modern-day conflicts between Pakistan and India and Israel and its neighbors. But the period of general peace between the West and Islam was short lived. *It has now come to an end.*

If jihadism's distant roots can be traced to Islam's origins, its intermediate roots can be found on the Arabian Peninsula of the eighteenth century. The alliance between the followers of the eighteenth-century Arabian religious leaders Muhammad ibn Abd al-Wahhab al-Tamimi and Muhammad ibn Saud sought the political purification of Islam.

While Mehmet Ali checked the spread of this strain of fundamentalist Islam, the ideal remained, both on the peninsula and elsewhere, as salafism. Salafis were, and remain, proponents of an Islam modeled after that practiced (or believed to have been practiced) during the era of the "righteously guided" khalifas of the mid-seventh century.

The 1924 demise of the khalifate was a shock to pious Muslims throughout the world. Islam, for the first time, lacked a successor to the Prophet Muhammad.

The first political noteworthy reaction came in Egypt, the most populous Arab country. Between 1798 and the end of the Great War, Egyptian Muslims more so than their Arab brothers faced the challenges of modernization and Westernization begun by Mehmet Ali and European occupiers—initially the French but later the British. In 1928 twenty-two-year-old Hassan al-Banna founded the Jama'at al-Ikhwan al-Muslimin (the Society of the Muslim Brotherhood).

Al-Banna's personal ideology is difficult to categorize. Like the Salafis, he sought a return to Islamic fundamentals. Initially, the Muslim Brotherhood served as a private educational and welfare organization. But perhaps because he was a Sufi (mystic) initiate, al-Banna remained tolerant of Islam's various strains. Nor did he reject modernity: al-Banna sought to combine Islam, modernization, and constitutionalism.

Al-Banna himself was not an ideological stepping-stone along the road toward developing political jihad, but his success at building an Islamic political force in Egypt laid the groundwork for future actions. By the 1940s more militant members of the Ikhwan had established the secret apparatus committed to terrorism against the British and those members of the Egyptian government guilty of cooperating with the occupiers. Likewise, as friction developed in Palestine in the 1930s and 1940s, some members undertook violent actions against Jews in Egypt.

By the late 1940s the Brotherhood had grown to almost a million Egyptian members, with branches in several Arab countries. Despite or perhaps because of these successes, a long period of radicalization of the Ikhwan began. The involvement of some members in terrorism and assassinations in Egypt led to a wave of repression, the torture of imprisoned members, and, in February 1949, al-Banna's assassination by the Egyptian police. The Brotherhood supported the national revolution that brought Nasser to power in 1952, only to discover that the army had no intention of sharing power. More violence led to additional repression, and so it went, decade after decade. Whereas al-Banna had preached against violence, by the 1950s it had become the group's second nature. The new debate became one of degree and focus, and along the way the Ikhwan inspired various offshoots, such as the Islamic Group and Egyptian Islamic Jihad.

Increasingly violent forms of jihad were by no means limited to Egypt. During the interwar years in British India, Sayyid Abul A'la Maududi, a Muslim scholar-journalist, was a proponent of an Islamic revival that offered India's Muslims an alternative to nationalism and communism. His sense of Islam, the dilemmas it faced, and its need for reform had their roots in the Deobandi school of the subcontinent, a nineteenth-century Indian equivalent of Wahhabism. In the late 1920s Maududi published a series of articles that later became one of his most important works, *Jihad in Islam*.

In many ways the tone of his work is reminiscent of Communist tracts of the early twentieth century. Maududi wrote:

> The truth is that Islam is a revolutionary ideology which seeks to alter the social order of the entire world and rebuild it in conformity with its own tenets and ideals. "Muslims" is the title of that "International Revolutionary

Party" organized by Islam to carry out its revolutionary programme. "Jihad" refers to that revolutionary struggle and utmost exertion which the Islamic Nation/Party brings into play in order to achieve this objective. Like all revolutionary ideologies, Islam shuns the use of current vocabulary and adopts a terminology of its own, so that its own ideals may be clearly distinguished from common ideals.

Maududi did not believe that Muslims could live as believers under non-Muslim governments. In his view it was

impossible for a Muslim to succeed in his aim of observing the Islamic pattern of life under the authority of a non-Islamic system of government. All rules which he considers wrong, all taxes which he deems unlawful, all matters which he believes to be evil, the civilization and way of life which he regards as wicked, the education system which he views as fatal . . . all these will be so relentlessly imposed on him, his home and his family, that it will be impossible to avoid them.

The logical force of his line of argument called for revolution in those Muslim areas under non-Muslim, mostly European rule. In that sense, Maududi's philosophy can be deemed anticolonial.

But Maududi went a step further. He considered Islam an eternal and universal message, requiring that "all of mankind should be devoted to the worship of one God." As such, Islam was not simply another religion; the world's other faiths in his view were "nothing more than a hotch-potch of beliefs, prayers, and rituals."

Islam is not merely a religious creed or a name for a collection of a few acts of worship. It is a comprehensive system which seeks to annihilate all evil and tyrannical systems in the world, and enforce its own programme of reform, which it deems best for the well-being of mankind.

Islam, Maududi argued, was

the call for a universal and complete revolution. It proclaimed loudly: "Sovereignty belongs to no one except Allah." No one has the right to appoint himself ruler of men, to issue orders and prohibitions on his own authority. To acknowledge the personal authority of a human being as the source of commands and prohibitions is tantamount to admitting him as a partner in the Power and Authority of Allah [*shirk,* or polytheism]. This is the root of all evils in the universe. Allah has instilled the correct spirit in man, and has shown him the right way of life.

Those who affirm their faith in this ideology become members of the party of Islam and enjoy equal status and equal rights, without distinctions of class, race, ethnicity or nationality. In this manner, an International Revolutionary Party is born, to which the Qur'an gives the title of Hizb-Allah [alternately Hizbollah], otherwise known as the Ummah [Nation] of Islam. As soon as this party is formed, it launches the struggle to attain the purpose for which it exists. The rationale for its existence is that it should endeavour to destroy the hegemony of an un-Islamic system, and establish in its place the rule of that social and cultural order which regulates life with balanced and humane laws, referred to by the Qur'an by the comprehensive term "the Word of Allah." If this party fails to strive to effect a change in the government and establish the Islamic system of government, then it loses its very raison d'être, for this party exists for no other purpose. There is no other purpose for this party but to strive for the cause of Allah. The Holy Qur'an states only one purpose for the existence of this Ummah: "You are the best of Peoples, evolved for mankind, enjoining what is right, forbidding what is wrong, and believing in Allah."

Unlike earlier Islamic revivalists such as Abd al-Wahhab and al-Banna, Maududi's vision of Islam was more ambitious.

> The aim of Islam is to bring about a universal revolution. Although in the initial stages, it is incumbent upon members of the Party of Islam to carry out a revolution in the state system of the countries to which they belong, *their ultimate objective is none other than a world revolution* [emphasis added].

In Maududi's interpretation of Islam, the Prophet and his immediate successors had provided the template: Islamic leaders should extend an "invitation" to non-Muslims to convert, and if they failed to do so, when the "Muslim Party" possessed sufficient strength, it would "eliminate un-Islamic governments and establish the power of Islamic government in their place."

Maududi considered jihad a requirement and a responsibility for Muslims, given the world situation. He preferred the term "jihad" to "war" for two reasons. The latter referred to conflicts between states or nations, whereas the purpose of jihad was "the benefit of mankind." Moreover, jihad involved a broader range of activities than warfare. He explained:

> The purpose of Islam is to set up a state on the basis of this ideology and programme, regardless of which nation assumes the role of standard-bearer of Islam, and regardless of the rule of which nation is undermined in the process of the establishment of an ideological Islamic state. Islam requires the earth—not just a portion, but the entire planet—not because the sovereignty over the

earth should be wrested from one nation or group of nations and vested in any one particular nation, but because the whole of mankind should benefit from Islam, and its ideology and welfare programme.

It is to serve this end that Islam seeks to press into service all the forces which can bring about such a revolution. The term which covers the use of all these forces is "Jihad." To alter people's outlook and spark a mental and intellectual revolution through the medium of speech and the written word is a form of Jihad. To change the old tyrannical system and establish a just new order by the power of the sword is also Jihad, as is spending wealth and undergoing physical exertion for this cause.

But what of the non-Muslim populations that would come under Islamic control as a result of this jihad? Would they be forced to convert?

Islamic Jihad does not seek to interfere with the faith, ideology, rituals of worship and social customs of the people. It allows them complete freedom of religious belief, and permits them to act according to their creed. However, Islamic Jihad does not recognize their right to administer affairs of the state according to a system which, in the view of Islam, is evil. Furthermore, Islamic Jihad also forbids them to continue with such practices under an Islamic government if those practices are detrimental to the public interest according to Islam.

For example, as soon as the Ummah of Islam seizes state power, it will outlaw all forms of business transacted on the basis of usury or interest; it will not permit gambling; it will curb all forms of business and financial dealings which contravene Islamic Law; it will shut down all brothels and other dens of vice; it will make it obligatory for non-Muslim women to observe the minimum standards of modesty in dress as required by Islamic Law, and forbid them to go about displaying their beauty as in the Days of Ignorance; it will impose censorship on the film industry. With a view to ensuring the general welfare of the public and for reasons of self defence, the Islamic government will not permit such cultural activities as may be permissible in non-Muslim systems but which Islam regards as detrimental and even fatal to moral fibre.

If a person feels inclined, on hearing this, to level charges of intolerance against Islam, he should consider the fact that no creed in the world has shown more tolerance to the devotees of other faiths than has Islam. In other places, the followers of other faiths are so repressed that, finding existence unbearable, they have no other choice but to emigrate. Islam, however, provides full opportunities for self-advancement to the people of other faiths, under conditions of peace and tranquility. It displays such magnanimity towards them that the world has yet to come up with a parallel example of tolerance.

Maududi was one of the most important figures in political Islam's rise during the twentieth century. He helped to establish Jamaat-e-Islami (the Party of Islam) in Lahore in August 1941. Jamaat-e-Islami remains a powerful force in Pakistani politics to the present day. His Islamic education combined with his training and experience as a journalist allowed him to bridge the gap between traditional Islamic ways of thinking and a more modern, political, and actually Western approach. To a degree he evoked the jargon of the Left, viewing his party as the vanguard of a larger, universal, utopian, revolutionary movement. One could substitute the word "Communist" for "Islam" in many sections quoted above without losing the statements' coherence. And undoubtedly Maududi's brand of Islam was totalitarian in its outlook. His Islamic state would control every aspect of life for both its Muslim and non-Muslim subjects. Moreover, his movement's goals were global and violent jihad an acceptable option.

Maududi's influence was not restricted to his contemporaries in the subcontinent. During the 1930s his books were translated into Arabic and influenced successive generations of Salafis and continue to do so. In fact, any Internet search will reveal innumerable English-language Islamic sites where one can find attestations about his importance, downloadable excerpts from his writings, and links to booksellers.

One significant Arab writer Maududi influenced was the Egyptian Sayyid Qutb. For most of his life Qutb appears to have been a bit of a lost soul, looking for something to which he could commit himself. His reflexes were from the start Islamic and conservative. For example, he opposed the modern "sick" music often played on Egyptian radio and complained of female bathers' licentiousness on Alexandria's beaches.

In 1948 the forty-two-year-old Egyptian came to the United States to continue his education as a teacher. The following year he earned his master's degree at what was then Colorado State Teachers College in the small town of Greeley, a "dry" town founded in 1869 as a Utopian experiment. Nevertheless, even such a conservative backwater town was too decadent for the middle-aged Egyptian. Qutb left the United States with a profound sense of disgust and a rather garbled understanding of U.S. history. He wrote, for example, of colonial Americans clashing in the seventeenth century not only with the native population but also with Latin Americans.

On Qutb's return to Egypt he joined the Muslim Brotherhood. By 1952 he was the head of the Ikhwan's propaganda department. During the 1950s and 1960s he shared the fate of his organization — periodically legalized and banned, its members freed from prison and rearrested. Qutb spent years in and out of prison and suffered at the hands of Nasser's torturers. Despite imprisonment, Qutb published extensively during the 1950s and 1960s. For the purposes of this study his most important book was his last, *Milestones,* which was published in 1965, the year before his execution.

Qutb opened *Milestones* with a warning:

> Mankind today is on the brink of a precipice, not because of the danger of complete [nuclear] annihilation which is hanging over its head—this being just a symptom and not the real disease—but because humanity is devoid of those vital values which are necessary not only for its healthy development but also for its real progress. Even the Western world realizes that Western civilization is unable to present any healthy values for the guidance of mankind. It knows that it does not possess anything which will satisfy its own conscience and justify its existence.

To define the problem, he expanded on a concept Maududi developed: the world, including the nominally Muslim states such as Egypt, suffered from *jahiliyyah,* or an ignorance of Allah.

> The *jahili* society is any society other than the Muslim society; and if we want a more specific definition, we may say that any society is a *jahili* society which does not dedicate itself to submission to God alone, in its beliefs and ideas in its observances of worship, and in its legal regulations. According to this definition, all the societies existing in the world today are *jahili.*

To Qutb, adhering to a fundamental Islam and establishing an Islamic state were the only solutions to the world's problems for both Muslims and non-Muslims.

As had been true of Maududi, the Egyptian conceived of an expansive, politicized, and militant version of Islam. Moreover,

Qutb argued that the ultimate goal—a global Islamic polity—could not exist without fighting, or what he termed *jihad bis saif* (striving through fighting).

> This movement uses the methods of preaching and persuasion for reforming ideas and beliefs and it uses physical power and Jihad for abolishing the organizations and authorities of the *Jahili* system which prevents people from reforming their ideas and beliefs but forces them to obey their erroneous ways and make them serve human lords instead of the Almighty Lord. This movement does not confine itself to mere preaching to confront physical power, as it also does not use compulsion for changing the ideas of people. These two principles are equally important in the method of this religion. Its purpose is to free those people who wish to be freed from enslavement to men so that they may serve God alone.

In *Milestones* Qutb provided a rationale both for creating an Islamic polity and for its global expansion by force if necessary. He argued against forcible conversion to Islam; instead he offered a rather disingenuous line of argument about creating an environment within which a non-Muslim could make a truly free decision regarding religion. While it would be wrong to use force to expand Islam as a religion, it was proper and in fact a responsibility to expand Islamic political control to remove the *jahili* roadblocks, be they institutional or behavioral, to Islam's reach and acceptance. In short, while everyone did not have to become a Muslim, everyone *did* have to live under Islamic political control. Nor did Qutb have patience for those writers, be they Muslim or Western, who sought to soften or redefine the term "jihad" into an internal thought process or who argued that it was a military option undertaken only as a defense against external aggression.

When writers with defeatist and apologetic mentalities write about "Jihad in Islam," trying to remove this "blot" from Islam, then they are mixing up two things: first, that this religion forbids the imposition of its belief by force, as is clear from the verse, "There is no compulsion in religion" (2:256), while on the other hand it tries to annihilate all those political and material powers which stand between people and Islam, which force one people to bow before another people and prevent them from accepting the sovereignty of God. These two principles have no relation to one another nor is there room to mix them. In spite of this, these defeatist-type people try to mix the two aspects and want to confine Jihad to what today is called "defensive war." The Islamic Jihad has no relationship to modern warfare, either in its causes or in the way in which it is conducted. The causes of Islamic Jihad should be sought in the very nature of Islam and its role in the world, in its high principles, which have been given to it by God and for the implementation of which God appointed the Prophet— peace be on Him—as His Messenger and declared him to be the last of all prophets and messengers. . . .

Those who say that Islamic Jihad was merely for the defense of the "homeland of Islam" diminish the greatness of the Islamic way of life and consider it less important than their "homeland." This is not the Islamic point of view, and their view is a creation of the modern age and is completely alien to Islamic consciousness.

In short, for Qutb, jihad was not a defensive strategy; it was a Muslim's obligation.

The establishing of the dominion of God on earth, the abolishing of the dominion of man, the taking away of sovereignty from the usurper to revert it to God, and the

bringing about of the enforcement of the Divine Law
[*Shari'ah*] and the abolition of man-made laws cannot
be achieved only through preaching. Those who have
usurped the authority of God and are oppressing God's
creatures are not going to give up their power merely
through preaching; if it had been so, the task of establishing God's religion in the world would have been very easy
for the Prophets of God! This is contrary to the evidence
from the history of the Prophets and the story of the
struggle of the true religion, spread over generations.

Despite the title, *Milestones* did not provide Muslims with a
road map to follow. Qutb planned to write additional volumes, but
the authorities executed him first. Thus, only the initial step was
described, namely, reviving the spirit of the initial righteous khalifas'
era and establishing a "vanguard" to lead the subsequent revolution. Beyond that, *Milestones* was replete with a call to sacrifice
and, if necessary, martyrdom in the Lord's service. And Qutb ended
his book with a warning, the themes of which should resonate with
anyone familiar with the language of today's jihadists.

We see an example of this today in the attempts of
Christendom to try to deceive us by distorting history and
saying that the Crusades were a form of imperialism.
The truth of the matter is that the latter-day imperialism
is but a mask for the crusading spirit, since it is not possible for it to appear in its true form, as it was possible in
the Middle Ages. The unveiled crusading spirit was
smashed against the rock of the faith of Muslim leadership which came from various elements, including
Salahuddin the Kurd and Turan Shah the Mamluk, who
forgot the differences of nationalities and remembered
their belief, and were victorious under the banner of Islam. "They were angered with the Believers only because

they believed in God, the All-Powerful, the All-Praisewor-
thy." Almighty God spoke the truth, and these treacherous
deceivers are liars!

For Qutb, the clash between the West and Islam was a struggle
that had begun in the seventh century and could end only with the
triumph of Islam, because that is what God had willed. He saw at
its root the *jahili* world's opposition to the will of God on earth
and mission to destroy Islam. Imperialism, colonialism, or any of
the "isms" were but western concoctions meant to camouflage the
"crusading" anti-Muslim spirit of the West.

Sayyid Qutb's *Milestones* is often considered the *Communist Manifesto* of the jihadist movement. Some analysts go so far
as to attribute to him a peculiar version of radical Islam, or Qutbism.
Whereas Maududi laid the foundation for political Islam, Qutb
spelled out with greater clarity the ultimate goal—a global Islamic
polity—and the means by which that goal would have to be
achieved, or jihad. He left a marked impact on the more radical
members of the Muslim Brotherhood, especially on Ayman al-
Zawahiri, who is now Qaeda al-Jihad's number-two man. Zawahiri
wrote in 2001: "Sayyid Qutb's call for loyalty to God's oneness
and to acknowledge God's sole authority and sovereignty was the
spark that ignited the Islamic revolution against the enemies of Islam at home and abroad. The bloody chapters of this revolution
continue to unfold day after day." Qutb's brother, Mohammad,
fled Egypt and later taught at a Saudi university, where one of his
students was Osama bin Laden. *Milestones* also remains in print
and readily available in English in several Internet editions in the
United States, Canada, and the United Kingdom.

Because Nasser executed Qutb, the more detailed approach
that the jihadists should follow remained uncertain. Subsequently,
a debate developed among the various jihadi factions between those
who favored a concentration on the "near" enemy—that is, the *jahili*
Muslim states—and those who focused on the "far enemy," most

notably the United States. But for anyone who accepted the fundamentals of Qutb's philosophy, such distinctions represented nothing more than alternative strategies, all of which sought the same ultimate goal. Nothing in Qutb's or Maududi's writings would permit, to use the Communist analogy, an interpretation of Islam comparable to Joseph Stalin's concept of "socialism in one country" or "peaceful coexistence" between the Communist and capitalist worlds. Qutb made this clear, writing:

> It may happen that the enemies of Islam may consider it expedient not to take any action against Islam, if Islam leaves them alone in their geographical boundaries to continue the lordship of some men over others and does not extend its message and its declaration of universal freedom within their domain. But Islam cannot agree to this unless they submit to its authority by paying *Jizyah,* which will be a guarantee that they have opened their doors for the preaching of Islam and will not put any obstacle in its way through the power of the state. . . .
>
> Islam provides a legal basis for the relationship of the Muslim community with other groups. . . . This legal formulation is based on the principle that Islam—that is, submission to God—is a universal Message which the whole of mankind should accept or make peace with. No political system or material power should put hindrances in the way of preaching Islam. It should leave every individual free to accept or reject it, and if someone wants to accept it, it should not prevent him or fight against him. If someone does this, then it is the duty of Islam to fight him until either he is killed or until he declares his submission.

During the 1960s, while Qutb wrote in Egypt, pressures were building in Iran, in the core of Shi'a Islam. There, too, Islam had long struggled with the currents of modernization, especially those undertaken by Mohammad Reza Shah Pahlavi during the 1960s. The shah's well-intentioned 1963 "White Revolution" was poorly executed. The costs of rapid modernization grossly outweighed its benefits. Moreover, the monarchy's readily apparent ineptitude and corruption provided the religious establishment, who stood to be the biggest losers had the effort succeeded, with a rallying cry against the government.

In Iran a religious cleric, an ayatollah, provided much of the philosophy and the leadership for the 1978 revolution that forced the shah's flight the following year. Ruhollah Khomeini was born in 1902. As early as the 1930s he was speaking out against the regime of Reza Shah Pahlavi. The British and Russian occupation of Iran in 1942 further enraged the cleric who was rapidly making a name for himself as a religious leader. In a short piece from 1942, attributed to Khomeini, he noted that those who studied jihad would "understand why Islam wants to conquer the whole world. . . . Those who know nothing of Islam pretend that Islam counsels against war. Those [who say this] are witless. Islam says: Kill all the unbelievers just as they would kill you all!"

The intervening decades between the Second World War and the Iranian Revolution did not soften Khomeini's views. In a 1970 series of lectures, later compiled into a book titled *Hukumat-i Islami* (Islamic government), the ayatollah spelled out his views on the subject. Several themes emerge in the work: Islam is a way of life and not a religion akin to Christianity, there could be no separation of the mosque and the state, the ideal ruler would be someone well versed as an Islamic jurist, and no one should trust the implacable enemies of Islam, namely, the crusaders and the Jews. Khomeini wrote:

> Do not allow the true nature of Islam to remain hidden,
> or people will imagine that Islam is like Christianity (nomi-
> nal, not true Christianity), a collection of injunctions

pertaining to man's relation to God, and the mosque will be equated with the church. . . .

The Commander of the Faithful [in the seventh century] was also a ruler; he ruled over all the Muslims and the whole of the broad Islamic realm. Were you more zealous than he in promoting the glory of Islam, the Muslims, and the lands of Islam! Was your realm more extensive than his! The country over which you ruled was but a part of his realm; Iraq, Egypt, and the Hijaz all belonged to his realm, as well as Iran. Despite this, his seat of command was the mosque: the bench of the judge was situated in one corner of the mosque, while in another, the army would prepare to set out for battle. That army was composed of people who offered their prayers regularly, were firm believers in Islam; you know well how swiftly it advanced and what results it obtained!

Perhaps because of his advanced age or perhaps because the Shi'a were a minority among Muslims, Khomeini focused his efforts primarily on establishing Islamist rule in Iran. In his writings and in the logic of his sense of his faith are implications of the ultimate requirement to spread Islam globally. But for the rest of the twentieth century, while the state supported external Islamic groups, Iranians were not in the forefront of the Islamic movement.

Thus it was in Egypt that the theme of a global Islamic revolution continued to evolve. Myriad Egyptian groups struggled to identify the practical steps along the path to realizing the Islamist goals Maududi and Qutb outlined.

One such group was Jama'at al-Muslimin, a 1970s' offshoot of the Muslim Brotherhood. As were so many other jihadists, Shukri Mustafa, perhaps the group's best-known member, was at least partially radicalized while in an Egyptian prison. Jama'at al-Muslimin became more popularly known as al-Takfir w'al-Hijra, a name derived from their advocacy of two concepts. The first (*takfir*) involved the excommunication of those infidels (*kufr*) who retained an allegiance to any of the nominally Muslim governments that Qutb had defined as *jahili*. The term "hijra" referred to the Prophet Muhammad's tactical retreat from Mecca to Medina until his movement was strong enough to make its return. Shukri Mustafa argued that Egyptian Muslims should have nothing to do with the government, but they should also avoid a direct clash with its security organs until they had sufficient strength to defeat them. As they had with Qutb, the government arrested Shukri Mustafa and tried and executed him in 1978.

With that execution the already limited attraction of the Jama'at al-Muslimin's approach dissipated. Nevertheless, retaining legitimacy in jihadist thinking were its concepts of *takfir*—that is, excommunicating one's political opponents as a prelude to violent action against them—and of a tactical retreat, if not into the caves of the Egyptian desert then to Islam's frontiers in the mountains of Afghanistan.

In 1981 Muhammad Abd al-Salam Faraj penned one of the most important jihadist tracts of the late twentieth century, *Al-Faridah al-Gha'ibah* (The neglected duty). This call to jihad led to his arrest and execution following Anwar Sadat's excommunication and assassination that same year.

Faraj coined the terms "near enemy"—that is, the apostate nominally Muslim states, such as his native Egypt—and the "far enemy," or the non-Muslim states, such as the United States. He maintained both enemies could only be overcome through violence. "There is no doubt," Faraj wrote, "that the idols of this world can only be made to disappear through the power of the sword." In their place, Faraj sought for all Muslims the obligatory "establishment of an Islamic State and the reintroduction of the Caliphate."

In a sense, Faraj attempted to complete the detailed outline that Qutb's execution had left undelineated. Faraj spelled out those proposals that he considered useless, if not dangerous: political parties, working within the existing system, emigration, study, and peaceful proselytization. All such behaviors were, in his mind, counterproductive in that they offered individuals alternatives to the "neglected duty" of jihad.

Faraj admitted the course's difficulty. Like Maududi and Qutb he recognized that, at least initially, the jihadists would be a distinct minority, or a vanguard. But he believed that a base of jihadists, through their willingness to sacrifice themselves, could gain successes and thus legitimacy for their efforts and broader support. He quoted the Qu'ran: "When comes the victory of God, and the Conquest, thou seest the people entering into the religion of God in crowds." (Qu'ran 110:1-2)

Faraj argued that the most important threat facing the jihadists was the near enemy. "To fight an enemy who is near," he argued, "is more important than to fight an enemy who is far." Such regimes' existence permitted Western influences to penetrate into Muslim lands. And it was jihad's neglect that caused of "the lowness, humiliation, division and fragmentation in which the Muslims live today."

Again following Maududi's and Qutb's lines, Faraj did not regard jihad as a defensive concept. "This is a false view," he told his readers, however often it was repeated. Faraj's preference for engaging the "near enemy" first was purely a question of sequencing. "Islam spread by the sword," he reminded his readers, "and under the very eyes of these Leaders of Unbelief who conceal it from mankind." After assuring the "base"—al-qaeda—within Islam's realm, the proper course was to call the remaining unbelievers to the faith and, if they refused to heed the call, to unleash jihad against them.

Akin to many Western critics of Islam, Faraj spent a great deal of time discussing myriad commentaries on the Qur'an's sura 9:5, often termed the "verse of the sword": "Then when the sacred months have slipped away, slay the polytheists wherever ye find them, seize them, beset them, lie in ambush for them everywhere."

For Faraj, the message was clear: jihad was every able Muslim's individual duty. Rationales for avoiding jihad were mere excuses and a neglect of religious duty. He even dismissed "the fear of failure," namely, the view rooted in history that even if somehow the jihadists were able to resurrect the khaliphate, "after one or two days a reaction will occur and put to an end everything we have accomplished." He wrote:

> The refutation of this (view) is that the establishment of an Islamic State is the execution of a divine command. We are not responsible for its results. Someone who is so stupid as to hold this view — which has no use except to hinder Muslims from the execution of their religious duty by establishing the Rule of God — forgets that when the Rule of the Infidel has fallen everything will be in the hands of Muslims, whereupon (*bi-ma*) the downfall of the Islamic state will become inconceivable. Furthermore, the Laws of Islam are not too weak to be able to subject everyone who spreads corruption in the land and rebels against the command of God. Moreover, the Laws of God are all justice and will be welcomed by everyone, even by people who do not know Islam.

Faraj also outlined the methods by which the jihadists could wage their struggle. Among the tactics enumerated were deception, flexibility, lying, infiltration into the enemy's ranks, surprise attacks, night attacks, and what he termed "Islamic Planning" — primarily myriad stratagems used by the Prophet or his companions for assassination and murder. Faraj also argued that what would normally be described as suicidal attacks were not, in fact, suicide: "it is permissible for a Muslim to penetrate into the ranks of the infidel army even though this will lead to his death."

Faraj's execution demonstrated that the Egyptian regime was too powerful to tackle directly, as al-Takfir w'al-Hijra had argued in the late 1970s. For many jihadists, the next step appeared to be a migration to the frontier—to Afghanistan—to fight against the Soviet infidels, who in 1979 had invaded the country in an effort to prop up their Communist Afghan puppets.

This shift's leading proponent was Abdullah Azzam, born on the Jordan's West Bank near Jenin in 1941. As a youth he joined the Muslim Brotherhood. In 1973 Azzam obtained his doctorate in *fiqh* (Islamic jurisprudence) at Al-Azhar University in Egypt. While in Egypt Azzam developed ties to the Qutb brothers, the "Blind Sheik" Omar Abdel-Rahman, and Ayman al-Zawahiri, ten years Azzam's junior. He began his academic career at Amman University but lost that position because of his radical views. He fled Jordan and taught next at Abdulaziz University in Saudi Arabia, where he may (sources vary) have first met Osama bin Laden.

Azzam made no secret that he considered himself a disciple of Sayyid Qutb's, whose family befriended him during his stay in Egypt. In his 1984 book *Defence of Muslim Lands: The First Obligation After Iman*, he argued, much like Faraj, that after *iman* (faith) one "of the most important lost obligations is the forgotten obligation of fighting. Because it is absent from the present condition of the Muslims, they have become as rubbish of the flood waters."

Azzam further argued that the obligation for fighting in jihad was *fard ayn*—that is, an individual responsibility of "every Muslim on the earth"—and not *fard kifaya,* or a collective responsibility that did not demand everyone's response. He considered it forbidden, for example, to save money "while the jihad is in need" and warned, "Neglecting the jihad is like abandoning fasting and praying." To support his ideas, he cited ibn Rushd, a scholar famed in both the Christian and the Islamic worlds: "It is agreed that when jihad becomes Fard Ayn it takes precedence over the Fard of the Hajj" (the fifth required pillar of faith for all Muslims).

Azzam had no doubts that jihad, if properly supported by the *ummah,* would succeed, despite the seeming disparity of forces between the West and Islam.

> If only the Muslims would apply their Allah's command and implement the laws of their Shariah concerning the General March [mass response to the call for jihad] for just one week in Palestine, Palestine would be completely purified of Jews. Similarly, the situation in Afghanistan would not last long if only the Ummah would march forward. . . . Instead, in every instance, we wait and we weep. We watch the Islamic region as it falls under the domination of the Kuffar, until it is swallowed whole.

In 1988 Azzam published *Join the Caravan,* yet another call to the *ummah* to join the jihad. The pathetic state of the Islamic world, he argued, resulted from the lack of widespread support for violent struggle, which he termed the "highest peak of Islam."

> Anybody who looks into the state of the Muslims today will find that their greatest misfortune is their abandonment of Jihad (due to love of this world and abhorrence of death). Because of that, the tyrants have gained dominance over the Muslims in every aspect and in every land. The reason for this is that the Disbelievers only stand in awe of fighting.

As for numbers and state power, Azzam showed no fear or hesitancy about using violent jihad tactics against the West.

> It will be like the small spark which ignites a large keg of explosives, for the Islamic movement brings about an eruption of the hidden capabilities of the Ummah, and a gushing forth of the springs of Good stored up in its depth. The Companions of the Prophet were exceedingly few

in number compared to the troops who toppled the throne
of the Persian Kisra and overthrew the Caesar of Rome.

Azzam played a critical role in amalgamating the universal
and utopian philosophies of Maududi and Qutb with the practical
problems and opportunities of an actual jihad campaign. It was
also Azzam who served as the key operational leader in the struggle
the Arab contingent waged in Afghanistan against the Soviet Union
in the 1980s. During that conflict, Azzam relied on Osama bin Laden
as the effort's financier. It was Azzam who came up with the concept that jihad had to be waged from a "solid foundation," which
he termed "al Qaeda al-Sulbah."

As the prospect of success in Afghanistan looked more certain in the late 1980s, a debate began in jihadist circles about their
future. Documentation of their inner debates is sketchy at best.
Despite his rhetoric, Azzam appears to have been the pragmatist
among the leadership, perhaps because he had witnessed first-
hand the actual price of the "victory" in Afghanistan. Nevertheless,
he agreed with those who favored establishing an elite corps of
jihadists who could respond to threats against Muslim communities in such locales as Bosnia, Kosovo, Chechnya, and Palestine.
But in a departure from Qutb's philosophy, Azzam was apparently
reluctant to turn the jihadists loose against Muslim regimes. This
stance was understandable, given that the Saudis had bankrolled
his organization in Afghanistan. Nor, reportedly, was Azzam a proponent of unleashing jihad against the "far enemy," that is, the West.
The focus of his writings, evident in the title *Defence of Muslim
Lands: The First Obligation after Iman*, could easily be considered a doctrine of defensive jihad.

Whatever the actual nature of the jihadists' internal debates
during the late 1980s and early 1990s, several important facts are
known. In 1988 in Afghanistan Osama bin Laden established
the organization now generally known as al-Qaeda. In November 1989 a car in which Abdullah Azzam and his two sons

were driving exploded in Peshawar, Pakistan. His assassins have never been identified. Responsibility for the car bombing has been placed variously on the CIA, the Soviets, Israel, bin Laden, and the man who benefited most from Azzam's death—the Egyptian Ayman al-Zawahiri. Some speculate that many in the al-Qaeda camp had come to believe that Azzam was in the pay of the CIA. Whether those reports were accurate or not, they may well have led to the man's assassination. The impact of his death on the jihadist movement's future direction will never, of course, be known.

Nevertheless, given the clear positions on jihad evident in the writings of Maududi, Qutb, and Faraj, it appears whimsical to suppose that the jihadists would not have moved sooner or later against the far enemy. The differences among the jihadist philosophers mentioned thus far were primarily tactical rather than strategic. They all believed that Islam's ultimate goal was to establish Allah's sovereignty globally. The question as to method was one of sequencing. With the collapse of the Soviet Union between 1989 and 1991, the jihadists believed they had not only saved Afghanistan for Islam but had also brought low the world's second-strongest power.

To the Americans, the Soviet defeat at the hands of the Afghan and Arab mujahedeen was by no means miraculous. The same sort of debacle had befallen the United States in Indochina at the hands of well-motivated Vietnamese Communists, who had no God on their side. Nor in the late twentieth century was communism's inability to compete with the West a complete shock, except to those on the far left fringe.

But to Osama bin Laden and the Arab mujahedeen, their victory in Afghanistan and the Soviet Union's subsequent fate were linked and represented a clear example of God's power to bestow victory on those willing to fight and die and his willingness to punish those who opposed his *ummah*. Thus the prospect of a victory against the United States was no more of a forlorn hope than had been in the war with the Soviets. A successful conclusion depended on a test of faithfulness, not on some measure of the correlation of forces. Moreover, as Egyptian jihadists such as al-Zawahiri could attest, the near enemy of the Arab world's dictatorial regimes and Israel had thus far successfully resisted the jihadists' efforts to topple them primarily because of American support. If the United States could be forced to withdraw that support, at a stroke the far enemy would be chastised and the near enemy left vulnerable.

Some scholars who study the jihadist movement—for example, Gilles Kepel and Fawaz Gerges—view the shift in focus from the near to the far enemy almost as a desperate act. Internal division and a degree of weakness, epitomized by the failures of the mujahedeen in Algeria and Egypt, plagued the movement. The struggle against the apostate Arab regimes *did not* develop along expected lines during the early to mid-1990s. And there were, and remain, schisms among the jihadists. Nevertheless, their decision, though by no means unanimous, to strike the United States did not necessarily reflect desperation or poor strategy. Conventional military strategists prefer to attack the source of the problem. And if major attacks against the United States would convince the Americans to withdraw from the Middle East, the local states that constituted the near enemy would most likely collapse in quick succession. Moreover, the impact of a victory over the United States would be enormous in terms of the shift in regional power and the popular legitimacy to be gained by jihadists and Islamists.

The movement's principal aim was to reestablish a khalifate on the model of the early "righteous" khalifas. Realizing this goal rested on two prerequisites. First, the jihadists had to secure an area large enough to be termed a khalifate—an area larger than a single country and ideally inhabited by Arabs. Second, any khalifate would have to be ruled by a khalifa.

Legitimate leadership has been an issue throughout Islam's history. Even the "righteous" khalifas, who are so important to the jihadists, were often assassinated by rivals. The Sunni-Shi'a split resulted from a disagreement over khalifal succession. The jihadists viewed hereditary succession, prevalent for khalifas, sultans, and kings from the ninth through the nineteenth centuries, as aberrant and rejected it. The same was true for Western-style democratic elections. So from where would a legitimate khalifa emerge?

While leading jihadists could model themselves as emirs, or princes—no one could declare himself khalifa. The "righteous" khalifas of the seventh century were selected from among the Islamic leadership by the acclamation of their peers. Anyone who presumed to become the new Islamic khalifa would have to achieve some heroic and near-miraculous victory in the service of the *ummah*, preferably while staking out the new khalifate's domain.

The Islamic world's periodic rejuvenation historically had followed certain patterns. When the Umayyads faltered, the Abbasids, who had proven themselves on the central Asian frontier, seized power and ushered in the final age of Arab greatness. When the Abbasids weakened, Turkic peoples, most notably the Seljuks and Mamluks, likewise moved from the frontier to the core and defeated the crusaders and the Mongols. In the west, when the Christians threatened the residue of the Umayyad khalifate in al-Andalus, the Almoravids, after proving themselves on the Saharan frontier, moved into Morocco and then the Iberian Peninsula and checked the Christians' advance. When the Almoravids likewise weakened, the Almohads followed the same pattern. In the east, after the destruction caused by Tamerlane, the Ottomans moved from the Anatolian frontier into the Islamic world's core, which they controlled for the next five centuries. The historic pattern is clear: gain political, religious, and military legitimacy along the frontier battling the infidels, shift to one of Islam's core areas, and trade that legitimacy for the khalifa mantle.

Within this historic context after the Soviets' defeat in Afghanistan the jihadists had to decide what to do. They had legitimacy to spend, but they had to earn a great deal more before they could hope to proclaim the establishment of a new khalifate. They ultimately split. Some remained focused on the near enemy, while others, most notably the Osama bin Laden's faction, chose instead to strike the far enemy.

Bin Laden played the critical role in shaping this new strategy. Osama bin Muhammad bin 'Awad bin Laden was born on March 10, 1957, in Riyadh, Saudi Arabia. His father was a wealthy construction and management executive whose family originated in Yemen. The details of bin Laden's childhood are sketchy. His father had ten wives, the last of which was bin Laden's mother. He was one of over fifty children sired by Muhammad 'Awad bin Laden and perhaps his seventeenth son. There are questionable reports that as a youth bin Laden traveled to the United Kingdom, the United States, and Sweden. Bin Laden studied engineering, economics, business, and public administration between 1979 and 1980 at King Abdulaziz University in Jeddah. During these university years bin Laden attended courses on Islam taught by Sayyid Qutb's brother, Muhammad, and Abdullah Azzam. Accounts vary as to whether bin Laden actually earned a degree.

After a short stint working for the family business, the twenty-three-year-old bin Laden traveled to Peshawar, Pakistan, where he became involved in the Arab component of the resistance effort against the Soviet invasion. Bin Laden quickly became a major player, organizing the administrative and financial base in Pakistan and the Tora Bora region of Afghanistan.

In 1990, during the internal debate among jihadists about which path to take, Saddam Hussein's Iraqi army rolled into Kuwait. Bin Laden approached the Saudi monarchy and proposed to shift jihadist forces from Afghanistan to the Arabian Peninsula. The Islamists were no friends of Hussein or of his ruling secular, nationalist Ba'ath party. The Saudis, no doubt not eager to see their kingdom become another Afghanistan even if in "victory," turned instead to the United States and allowed the West to send a huge military force to the peninsula. Although Western units did not deploy to the sacred Hijaz, home of the holy cites of Mecca and

Medina, bin Laden considered the Saudis' move as a violation of the sacred Koran, which had forbidden the presence of Jews and Christians anywhere on the peninsula. At this point bin Laden turned on his own country. He also shifted his focus from the near to the far enemy.

Osama bin Laden grossly underestimated the Americans' willingness to wage a war against al-Qaeda. His August 1996 *fatwa*—"Declaration of War Against the Americans Occupying the Land of the Two Holy Places"—clearly demonstrated the al-Qaeda leader's assumptions about Americans' reluctance to fight back. Referring to Clinton administration secretary of defense William J. Perry's June 1996 statement that was issued following the Khobar Towers attacks on U.S. military personnel in Saudi Arabia, bin Laden replied:

> We say to the Defence Secretary that his talk can induce a grieving mother to laughter! and shows the fears that had enshrined you all. Where was this false courage of yours when the explosion in Beirut took place on 1983 AD (1403 A.H)? You were turned into scattered pits and pieces at that time; 241 mainly marines solders were killed. And where was this courage of yours when two explosions made you to leave Aden in less than twenty-four hours!
>
> But your most disgraceful case was in Somalia; where—after vigorous propaganda about the power of the USA and its post cold war leadership of the new world order—you moved tens of thousands of international force, including twenty-eight thousands American soldiers into Somalia. However, when tens of your solders were killed in minor battles and one American Pilot was dragged in the streets of Mogadishu you left the area carrying disappointment, humiliation, defeat and your dead with you. [President William J.] Clinton appeared in front of the

whole world threatening and promising revenge, but these threats were merely a preparation for withdrawal. You have been disgraced by Allah and you withdrew; the extent of your impotence and weaknesses became very clear. It was a pleasure for the "heart" of every Muslim and a remedy to the "chests" of believing nations to see you defeated in the three Islamic cities of Beirut, Aden and Mogadishu.

Available evidence suggests that bin Laden was not involved in the Khobar Towers attacks. Nevertheless, he viewed the lack of an American response, comparable to that following the 1993 debacle in Mogadishu, Somalia, and that same year the World Trade Center bombing, as evidence that "the American soldier was just a paper tiger." From bin Laden's perspective, he had every reason to assume that the Americans lacked the resilience and will necessary to combat a global jihad.

In February 1998 Osama bin Laden announced the formation of the World Islamic Front and issued his infamous *fatwa*—"Declaration of War Against Jews and Crusaders." Bin Laden argued that the United States, in concert with Israel, had unleashed a veritable war against Islam. That being the case, every Muslim had the duty to respond to his call to jihad. "[T]o kill Americans and their allies—civilians and military," bin Laden declared, was "an individual duty incumbent [*fard ayn*] upon every Muslim in all countries, in order to liberate the al-Aqsa Mosque [in Jerusalem] and the Holy Mosque [in Mecca] from their grip, so that their armies leave all the territory of Islam, defeated, broken, and unable to threaten any Muslim."

Six months later powerful bombs ripped through the American embassies in Kenya and Tanzania, killing over two hundred people, mostly Africans. These August 1998 attacks were the first that can be definitively attributed to bin Laden. In an Aljazeera interview bin Laden did not claim responsibility for the attacks, although he welcomed them and noted the great "joy" they had spread throughout the Islamic world. In response to questions concerning his *fatwa* against Jews and crusaders, bin Laden again pronounced his low opinion of the United States.

> We believe that America is much weaker than Russia, and we have learned from our brothers who fought in the *jihad* in Somalia of the incredible weakness and cowardice of the American soldier. Not even eighty of them had been killed and they fled in total darkness in the middle of the night, unable to see a thing. After this, great commotion filled the globe about the new world order. People can, if they fear God—who knows that it is in His power—wage *jihad*, and who knows the situation now still needs the right conditions. God knows best.

On May 26, 1988, bin Laden sat for an interview with ABC reporter John Miller. During the interview, which aired on *Nightline* on June 6, bin Laden returned to his theme of American weakness. His response to a question concerning events in Somalia is worth quoting in full.

> After our victory in Afghanistan and the defeat of the oppressors who had killed millions of Muslims, the legend about the invincibility of the superpowers vanished. Our boys no longer viewed America as a superpower. So, when they left Afghanistan, they went to Somalia and prepared themselves carefully for a long war. They had thought that the Americans were like the Russians, so they trained and prepared. They were stunned when they discovered how low was the morale of the American soldier. America had entered with 30,000 soldiers in addition to thousands of soldiers from different countries in the world. . . . As I said, our boys were shocked by the

low morale of the American soldier, and they realized that the American soldier was just a paper tiger. He was unable to endure the strikes that were dealt to his army, so he fled, and America had to stop all its bragging and all that noise it was making in the press after the Gulf War in which it destroyed the infrastructure and the milk and dairy industry that was vital for the infants and the children and the civilians and blew up dams which were necessary for the crops people grew to feed their families. Proud of this destruction, America assumed the titles of world leader and master of the new world order. After a few blows, it forgot all about those titles and rushed out of Somalia in shame and disgrace, dragging the bodies of its soldiers. America stopped calling itself world leader and master of the new world order, and its politicians realized that those titles were too big for them and that they were unworthy of them. I was in Sudan when this happened. I was very happy to learn of that great defeat that America suffered, so was every Muslim.

An enthusiastic Miller, no doubt aware that he was pulling off a journalistic coup, ended what was an otherwise informative interview with some rather vapid questions. His next to last query demonstrated his awareness that the interview would ensure that both his own name and bin Laden's would soon be newsworthy back in the United States. Miller asked, "The American people, by and large, do not know the name bin Laden, but they soon likely will. Do you have a message for the American people?" Unfortunately, bin Laden spoiled the spirit of the moment with a brutal, threatening, anti-Semitic rant.

I say to them that they have put themselves at the mercy of a disloyal government, and this is most evident in Clinton's administration. . . .We believe that this administration represents Israel inside America. Take the sensitive ministries such as the Ministry of Exterior [State Department] and the Ministry of Defense and the CIA, you will find that the Jews have the upper hand in them. They make use of America to further their plans for the world, especially the Islamic world. American presence in the Gulf provides support to the Jews and protects their rear. And while millions of Americans are homeless and destitute and live in abject poverty, their government is busy occupying our land and building new settlements and helping Israel build new settlements in the point of departure for our Prophet's midnight journey to the seven heavens. America throws her own sons in the land of the two Holy Mosques for the sake of protecting Jewish interests.

The American government is leading the country toward hell. . . . We say to the Americans as people and to American mothers, if they cherish their lives and if they cherish their sons, they must elect an American patriotic government that caters to their interests not the interests of the Jews. If the present injustice continues with the wave of national consciousness, it will inevitably move the battle to American soil, just as Ramzi Yousef [of the 1993 strike against the Twin Towers] and others have done. This is my message to the American people. I urge them to find a serious administration that acts in their interest and does not attack people and violate their honor and pilfer their wealth.

Not batting an eye after bin Laden's outburst about Jews controlling the U.S. government, Miller closed the interview with perhaps the most inane question ever asked of bin Laden: "In America, we have a figure from history from 1897 named Teddy Roosevelt. He was a wealthy man, who grew up in a privileged situation and who fought on the front lines. He put together his own men—hand chose them—and went to battle. You are like the Middle East version of Teddy Roosevelt."

One can doubt that bin Laden had a clue as to who Teddy Roosevelt and his Rough Riders were. As Miller had, bin Laden stuck to his script.

> I am one of the servants of Allah. We do our duty of fighting for the sake of the religion of Allah. It is also our duty to send a call to all the people of the world to enjoy this great light and to embrace Islam and experience the happiness in Islam. Our primary mission is nothing but the furthering of this religion. . . . Let not the West be taken in by those who say that Muslims choose nothing but slaughtering. Their brothers in East Europe, in Turkey, and in Albania have been guided by Allah to submit to Islam and to experience the bliss of Islam. Unlike those, the European and the American people and some of the Arabs are under the influence of Jewish media.

If bin Laden subsequently learned who Teddy Roosevelt was, his opinion of Miller's intelligence probably sank as low as his opinion of the American soldier's courage.

Chapter 8
The American Crusade

*Jahiliyyah is evil and corrupt, whether it be of the ancient or
modern variety. Its outward manifestations may be different
during different epochs, yet its roots are the same. Its roots are
human desires, which do not let people come out of their ignorance and self-importance, desires which are used in the interests of some persons or some classes or some nations or some
races, which interests prevail over the demand for justice, truth
and goodness. But the pure law of God cuts through these roots
and provides a system of laws which has no human interference,
and it is not influenced by human ignorance or human desire or
for the interests of a particular group of people.*
— Sayyid Qutb, Milestones

After September 11, 2001, John Miller probably would not
compare Osama bin Laden to Theodore Roosevelt. But that he
did in 1998 even after the U.S. embassy bombings in East Africa
demonstrates the difficulty Americans had, and continue to have,
coming to grips with the real threat al-Qaeda poses.

Terrorism originating in the Middle East was not a new
problem for the United States. Since Richard Nixon's presidency,
administrations had talked tough about the issue but approached
the problem as if it were the international equivalent of the common cold—an inconvenience that was nearly impossible to cure

but, fortunately, not life threatening. In January 1996 when James B. Steinberg, then director of policy planning at the Department of State, outlined the American foreign policy's scope, he barely mentioned the terrorist threat. He tossed it into the hopper of the Clinton administration's desire to create "a world safe from destabilizing conflicts and threats from crime, terrorism, and environmental decay." A year later, little had changed. Outgoing secretary of state Warren Christopher spoke collectively of the threats posed by "proliferation, terrorism and international crime, drug trafficking, and damage to the environment."

But by late 1998, after bin Laden's fatwa and the embassy bombings, the administration began to shift its policy regarding the bin Laden threat and its connection to other regional problems. In a December 8, 1998, speech at Stanford University, Sandy Berger, Clinton's national security adviser, focused on American policy toward Saddam Hussein's Iraq from a broad regional perspective. He described two competing forces in the Middle East: those who supported political and economic pluralism and development and those opposed who sought instead to isolate Islam from the modern world by resisting "liberalizing forces." While Berger was cautious about the ability of the United States to influence the course of events in the region, he noted the positive and constructive forces that had resulted from the coalition's military victory over Saddam Hussein in 1991. He told the audience:

> The [Arab-Israeli] peace process has moved forward in part because, ever since the Gulf War, the immediate military threat Saddam poses has been contained—albeit at a substantial price. But even a contained Saddam is harmful to the stability and to positive change in the region. Conversely, a constructive Iraq would help change the equation in the region.

Years before the advent of the George W. Bush administration and the neoconservatives, Berger continued by coupling the dangers posed by Saddam Hussein's Iraq and al-Qaeda.

> Fundamentalists like Osama bin Laden may be utterly different from Saddam, yet they can still take advantage of his conflict with the world to win recruits for their cause.
>
> As long as Saddam remains in power and in confrontation with the world, the positive evolution we and so many would like to see in the Middle East is less likely to occur. His Iraq remains a source of potential conflict in the region, a source of inspiration for those who equate violence with power and compromise with surrender, a source of uncertainty for those who would like to see a stable region in which to invest.
>
> Change in Iraq is necessary not least because it would help free the Middle East from its preoccupation with security and struggle, and make it easier for its people to focus their energies on commerce and cooperation.

Berger acknowledged the containment policy pursued since the war's end had worked, but it had been costly, Hussein had manipulated the system, and the Iraqi people had suffered more than their leader. "[W]e cannot tolerate it endlessly," the national security adviser warned. Ultimately, the optimal outcome would involve a change of regime in Baghdad, a realization that led the Clinton administration to adopt a policy that aimed to "delegitimize" and destabilize Saddam's government. "The sooner the situation in Iraq is normalized," Berger explained, "the sooner the people of the Middle East can get on with the business of building a more stable region, and the more likely we are to realize our goal of seeing the region integrated, with the consent of its people, into the international system."

By late 1998 the Clinton administration had connected the Hussein regime's continued existence with the larger issues of regional instability, which included the emerging al-Qaeda threat. Berger did not claim that Hussein was physically supporting Osama bin Laden's actions. The national security adviser's argument was that Hussein's continued disdain for the West and its UN-led embargo, the burdens of which fell on the long-suffering Iraqi people, exacerbated regional tensions, hindered progressive developments, and thereby helped al-Qaeda and other groups thrive.

Historians will long debate the question of the Clinton administration's ability, or lack thereof, to take strong action against bin Laden. Nevertheless, linking the jihadist and Hussein threats predated the U.S. election of 2000 and the Bush administration. I do not mean to suggest that had the Democrats retained the presidency in 2000 they would have invaded Iraq in March 2003. The policy options Berger outlined in his speech did not involve an invasion but focused instead on exerting international political and economic pressure, continuing UN sanctions, promoting regime change from within, and weapons inspections. Nevertheless, the question remained, what if these options failed to achieve the desired results? As Berger warned his audience, the administration's policies were not necessarily "sustainable over the long run." But how long was that run? And how would it change on September 12, 2001?

On October 12, 2000, al-Qaeda struck again. A small boat loaded with explosives sped into the side of the American destroyer USS *Cole* while it was refueling in the harbor of Aden, Yemen. It blew a forty-by-forty-foot hole in its port side, killing seventeen sailors and wounding thirty-nine. The Clinton administration weighed the options for retaliation but took no action because of less than perfect (meaning incomplete) intelligence (intelligence is always less than perfect) and fears that any counterstrike would inflame Muslim passions. Even the Department of Defense proved reluctant to strike. The U.S. government's 9/11 report notes that a frustrated Michael Sheehan, the State Department's counterterrorism coordinator, asked presciently, "Does al-Qaeda have to attack the Pentagon to get their attention?"

Uncertainty about who was responsible for the attack and later the prospect that the Republicans would control the White House in January 2001 did little to move Clinton toward a military response to the *Cole* attack. By the time the national security team of the new president, George W. Bush, was in place — a process held up by the confusion surrounding the electoral result and by congressional hearings that delayed some appointees' confirmations until July 2001 — the *Cole* issue had become, in the words of the new deputy secretary of defense, Paul Wolfowitz, "stale."

The new Republican administration did not have long before it faced its own challenge from Osama bin Laden. In June 2001, bin Laden's al-Qaeda merged with Dr. Ayman al-Zawahiri's Egyptian Islamic Jihad, since 1998 a member of the World Islamic Front, to form a new jihadist association — Qaeda al-Jihad. The new organization shortly thereafter conducted the largest terrorist attack against a U.S. target and did it on American soil. On the morning of September 11, 2001, nineteen Muslim men hijacked four civilian airliners. They flew one each into the North and South Towers of the World Trade Center in New York City. A third commandeered jet struck the Pentagon. On the fourth flight — United 93 — cell phone–connected passengers learned what had happened on the other aircraft and fought back. They died when they caused their plane to crash in a field near Shanksville, Pennsylvania, and thus prevented the hijackers from flying the Boeing 757 into either of its chosen targets: the Capitol or the White House. More than three thousand people, mostly Americans, lost their lives that day.

Bin Laden initially denied responsibility for the attack. But there could be no doubt about his joy at what he saw as a great Islamist accomplishment. He rejoiced in an October 7, 2001, statement:

> God Almighty hit the United States at its most vulnerable spot. He destroyed its greatest buildings. Praise be to God. Here is the United States. It was filled with terror from its north to its south and from its east to its west.

Praise be to God. . . .

As for the United States, I tell it and its people these few words: I swear by Almighty God who raised the heavens without pillars [towers] that neither the United States nor he who lives in the United States will enjoy security before we can see it as a reality in Palestine and before all the infidel armies leave the land of Mohammed, may God's peace and blessing be upon him. God is great and glory to Islam. May God's peace, mercy, and blessings be upon you.

Two weeks later, on October 21, 2001, bin Laden granted an interview to Taysir Alluni, head of Aljazeera's Kabul bureau. Alluni asked the jihadist leader about the wisdom of taking on the United States. Bin Laden's response followed his usual line of argument: it was not a battle between al-Qaeda and the United States, but between the world's Muslims and the "global crusaders." He recalled that people used to ask him in Afghanistan:

"How will you defeat the Soviet Empire?" The Soviet Empire has become—with God's grace—a figment of the imagination. Today, there is no more Soviet Empire; it split into smaller states and only Russia is left. So the One God, who sustained us with one of His helping Hands and stabilized us to defeat the Soviet Union, is capable of sustaining us again and of allowing us to defeat America on the same land, and with the same [Qur'anic] sayings. So we believe that the defeat of America is something achievable—with the permission of God—and it is easier for us—with the permission of God—than the defeat of the Soviet Empire previously.

Later in the interview, Alluni asked bin Laden if he thought his struggle was part of a "clash of civilizations." Alluni was referring to an article entitled "The Clash of Civilizations," which Samuel P. Huntington, director of the John M. Olin Institute for Strategic Studies at Harvard University, published in the summer 1993 issue of *Foreign Affairs*. Huntington argued that the eras of war among monarchs, states, and ideologies had ended. The next round of clashes would pit opposing cultures against each other, and one of civilization's main fault lines ran between the West and Islam. From bin Laden's response it was not evident that he had read or was aware of Huntington's work in any detailed sense, but bin Laden accepted his thesis. "I say," he replied to Alluni, "that there is no doubt about this." The Qur'an had foreseen it all: the ultimate clash between the believers and the nonbelievers, between the Muslims and the crusaders and the Jews. Bin Laden then recited by memory a passage from the Hadith of al-Bukhari. According to the account, the Prophet spoke to his companions of the final victory of Islam:

> The Hour will not come until the Muslims fight the Jews and kill them. When a Jew hides behind a rock or a tree, it will say: "O Muslim, O servant of God! There is a Jew behind me, come and kill him!" All the trees will do this except the boxthorn, because it is the tree of the Jews.

There could never be a permanent peace between Muslims and the Jews, bin Laden stressed, nor with the American government, which was nothing more than the "agent of Israel."

Despite his harsh language, Osama bin Laden is not a fool. He knows how to play to Islamic and Western audiences and how to drive wedges into the political divisions within the West. He uses the victim narrative exceedingly well to portray his jihad as a purely defensive struggle Western actions forced upon the Muslim world.

We are only defending ourselves against the United

States. This is a defensive jihad to protect our land and people. That's why I have said that if we don't have security, neither will the Americans. It's a very simple equation that any child could understand: live and let others live.

Many in the West eagerly embrace that line, because it fits their own view of Western history and allows them to ignore the jihadists' larger goals, just as many in Europe in 1938–39 were eager to yield the Sudetenland and then the rest of Czechoslovakia to Hitler in the pursuit of peace. In a March 21, 2006, speech British prime minister Tony Blair referred to this phenomenon as "the painful irony of what is happening." The jihadists, he noted:

> have so much clearer a sense of what is at stake. They play our own media with a shrewdness that would be the envy of many a political party. Every act of carnage adds to the death toll. But somehow it serves to indicate our responsibility for disorder, rather than the act of wickedness that causes it. For us, so much of our opinion believes that what was done in Iraq in 2003 was so wrong, that it is reluctant to accept what is plainly right now.

Bin Laden has also worked diligently to peel away American allies. In a November 12, 2002, message he vowed not to strike those countries that refused to support the United States. These efforts have been partially successful. Following the March 11, 2004, train bombings in Madrid, which killed 198 people, Spain withdrew its troops from Iraq.

Nevertheless, bin Laden's jihadist pedigree dictates that, despite what he often spouts for Western audiences, his quest is for a restored and global khalifate. Not that bin Laden is all that close-mouthed about his intentions. He began a detailed October 2002 address to Americans with a litany of the usual outrages the West committed against Muslims going back for almost a century and including Israel's establishment. If the Americans want to have peace, he warned, they would have to desist in such endeavors and stop interfering in the Islamic world's affairs. Further, in the second part of his message, often ignored by the media, he revealed the jihadist movement's broader goals. To end the jihad the Americans had to meet additional demands: stop confusing immorality with personal freedom and reject "fornication, homosexuality, intoxicants, gambling, and usury"; end racism; sign the Kyoto Treaty; stop the practice of electing men and women to legislate (i.e., to make laws); and agree to live under *Shari'ah*. "You separate religion from your policies," bin Laden warned, which contradicts the Islamic ideal that reserves "absolute authority to the Lord and your Creator." Americans also had to rid their country of the Jews. (Bin Laden mistakenly believes Benjamin Franklin had warned his fellow countrymen about the Jews, but that "Franklin prophecy" was manufactured in 1934 by William Dudley Pelley, an American Nazi from North Carolina.) Bin Laden also labeled AIDS "a Satanic American invention." "If you fail to respond to all these conditions," he warned, "then prepare to fight with the umma, the Nation of Monotheism, which puts complete trust on God and fears none other than him." Islam, he informed his American audiences, was a "Nation of Martyrdom; the Nation that desires death more that you desire life." And if the United States did not heed his warnings, "then your fate will be that of the Soviets who fled Afghanistan to deal with their military defeat, political breakup, ideological downfall, and economic bankruptcy."

The Bush administration understood that totally withdrawing from the Middle East and abandoning the state of Israel would not end the Islamist threat. It would have quite the opposite effect: such successes would only further bin Laden's legitimacy within the Islamic world and exacerbate the existing problem. Thus the administration adopted a four-part strategy in what it would eventually call the Global War on Terrorism (GWOT):

- deny Qaeda al-Jihad its base of operations in Afghanistan
- harden the United States as a target
- pursue regime change in Iraq
- assail the jihadists wherever they were to be found, by whatever means were available

On October 7, 2001, the United States and its principal ally, Great Britain, began Operation Enduring Freedom—the campaign to destroy bin Laden's infrastructure in Afghanistan and to remove the Islamist Taliban from power. The American-led operation was well thought out. The small footprint of the invading force, heavily reliant on precise strikes from the air and on special operations units, drew heavily on the lessons learned from the Soviet Union's 1979 invasion and sought to avoid a wide-scale and negative reaction throughout the Islamic world. The operation was successful in that the Taliban were driven from power, there was no widespread response on "the Arab street," and the jihadists' training camps were destroyed. If bin Laden had envisioned an overbearing, Soviet-like U.S. military response that would spark a popular uprising among the Afghan people, he was disappointed. Nevertheless, the attack's measured nature all but ensured that the Taliban and Qaeda al-Jihad, though defeated, avoided destruction.

To make the United States more secure the administration sponsored a bundle of legislation termed the "Uniting and Strengthening America by Providing Appropriate Tools Required to Intercept and Obstruct Terrorism" Act—better known by its acronym USA PATRIOT—which became law on October 24, 2001. Prompted in part by the Democrats, the following year the Bush administration proposed a new federal executive department, the Department of Homeland Security. Its basic mission is to "prevent terrorist attacks within the United States; reduce the vulnerability of the United States to terrorism; and minimize the damage, and assist in the recovery, from terrorist attacks that do occur within the United States." Passing the PATRIOT Act and establishing the new department re-sparked an age-old and legitimate debate among Americans about the proper balance between security and domestic freedoms, the details and importance of which are beyond the scope of this book.

The administration recognized that passing legislation, setting up a new bureaucracy, or fighting in Afghanistan would not bring the GWOT to a successful conclusion. All were primarily defensive measures designed either to protect the United States or to limit the jihadists' capabilities. To defeat Qaeda al-Jihad and other jihadist groups required an entirely different and long-term approach.

The administration outlined this plan in its September 2002 publication, *The National Security Strategy of the United States of America*. Most public discussion about the document focused on the bold statement that the United States would use military force to preempt a possible terrorist attack. The new strategy admitted deterrence had worked during the Cold War but only because both the Russians and Americans were reasonable and deterrable. The jihadists were not. The new policy acknowledged

> new deadly challenges have emerged from rogue states and terrorists. None of these contemporary threats rival the sheer destructive power that was arrayed against us by the Soviet Union. However, the nature and motivations of these new adversaries, their determination to obtain destructive powers hitherto available only to the world's strongest states, and the greater likelihood that they will use weapons of mass destruction against us, make today's security environment more complex and dangerous.

Lost amid the media furor over the administration's public adoption of preemption was a far more important pronouncement: Bush and his national security team had embraced the view that there was only a single road to the future. In a passage that harkened back to Francis Fukuyama's "End of History," the administration argued that the

> great struggles of the twentieth century between liberty and totalitarianism ended with a decisive victory for the forces of freedom—and a single sustainable model for national success: freedom, democracy, and free enterprise. In the twenty-first century, only nations that share a commitment to protecting basic human rights and guaranteeing political and economic freedom will be able to unleash the potential of their people and assure their future prosperity. People everywhere want to be able to speak freely; choose who will govern them; worship as they please; educate their children—male and female; own property; and enjoy the benefits of their labor. These values of freedom are right and true for every person, in every society—and the duty of protecting these values against their enemies is the common calling of freedom-loving people across the globe and across the ages.

Bush and his advisers believed the jihadists not only posed a threat but also provided the United States with a "moment of opportunity to extend the benefits of freedom across the globe."

> For most of the twentieth century, the world was divided by a great struggle over ideas: destructive totalitarian visions versus freedom and equality. That great struggle is over. The militant visions of class, nation, and race which promised utopia and delivered misery have been defeated

and discredited. America is now threatened less by conquering states than we are by failing ones. We are menaced less by fleets and armies than by catastrophic technologies in the hands of the embittered few. We must defeat these threats to our Nation, allies, and friends. This is also a time of opportunity for America.

The administration recognized that problems in the Islamic world were related more to a poverty of ideas than to a poverty of riches. Saudi Arabia had had access to billions of petrodollars and to the Western world's education systems for more than fifty years, but it had hardly become a modernized, Western-style, democratic republic. Most of the 9/11 hijackers were, like bin Laden himself, Saudis.

The September 2002 document declared the United States was about to embark on an aggressive policy—a politically focused crusade—to modernize the Middle East. Until 9/11, the West and the Americans had been willing to allow modernization to run its own faltering course in the Islamic world. But after the 2001 attack the Bush administration and its "coalition of the willing" undertook to jump-start the historical process and hasten the development that they believed would eventually undercut those whom the writer Christopher Hitchens labeled "Islamo-fascists."

But why did Iraq become the focus of the new policy? Saddam Hussein was no Islamist, and his regime would not long survive a jihadist triumph in the Middle East. Despite his mouthing of Islamic slogans and his adding Qur'anic passages on the Iraqi flag in 1990, Hussein was at heart a secular Arab nationalist and a thug. The link between the Hussein regime and terrorists was tentative, though not necessarily nonexistent. And although for more than a decade, assorted Westerners and many in the Middle East had good reason to believe Hussein had developed WMDs, his alleged possession of such weapons was not the primary cause of the U.S.-led invasion, despite what was said at the time.

Myriad factors led the Bush administration to link Saddam to the GWOT and to invade. Iraq's location, demography, and history all helped the United States focus its sights on Baghdad.

First there was the notion of unfinished business from the first Gulf War (1990–91). After his defeat, Hussein had managed the one feat that no one had thought he would be able to achieve — he had survived!

Maintaining the ideal of the triumph of Western values at the end of the twentieth century also shaped Bush policy. This view reflected Fukuyama's assertion in "End of History," namely, the concept of "the universalization of Western liberal democracy as the final form of human government."

Virtually unnoticed at the time and since was the link the Clinton administration made in late 1998 between Hussein and the jihadist threat in the wake of the embassy bombings. As Sandy Berger had remarked in his Stanford speech: "As long as Saddam remains in power and in confrontation with the world, the positive evolution we and so many would like to see in the Middle East is less likely to occur."

Secretary of State Condoleezza Rice shared the Bush administration's perspective during an interview with members of the *New York Times* Publisher's Group on September 12, 2005:

> If you believe that, in fact, what we encountered on that day [9/11] was the violent awakening . . . a wake-up call, that what we faced was a global extremist ideology that had found its footing and was networked worldwide and was going to do more of this time and time again, then you had to ask whether or not what you wanted to deal with is the root cause of that extremist ideology. And it goes right to the heart of the Middle East. That extremist ideology of hatred comes out of a Middle East where there is such a freedom deficit that the people have lost hope, that you have, you know, in 2003 22 of the economies

of the region with the combined GDP of Spain, where authoritative governments have choked off any legitimate channel for opposition and so the only manifestation of political activity has become extremism. And if you believe that you've got to change the nature of the Middle East, then you've got also to change Iraq . . . when you have the opportunity to build a different kind of state in the core of the Middle East, take it and make your goals for an Iraq actually goals that are consistent with a different kind of Middle East

The Bush administration had concluded that the policy of containing Iraq had run its course and was, as Sandy Berger had warned in 1998, no longer "sustainable."

The nature of Iraq and its people also played a role in the adminstration's decision to invade. Modernization requires four indispensable categories of capital: intellect, water, natural resources, and finances. Iraq is the only state in the Arab Middle East where one can find all four. Iraq has one of the best-educated, secularized populations in the Middle East. Iraq has two major rivers—the Tigris and Euphrates—and innumerable natural resources, including some of the world's largest petroleum reserves. That petroleum can be converted into the financial capital that a modernization effort requires. The region's other nations lack at least one of these four basic resources. Egypt, for example, has a talented population and a river but few natural resources and little oil. Saudi Arabia has the oil and the capital but far from a secularized population and little water.

Iraq's demography—its distinct Shi'a, Sunni, and Kurdish communities—also was important. Any opposition the coalition would face, most likely from Sunni Arabs, would either be limited, because they were a small percentage of the overall population, or be counterbalanced by the likely positive reception from the Kurds and the Shi'a. A comparable undertaking in any other

Arab country—Egypt, for example—risked encountering more opposition from a much larger and more homogeneous population. While the United States might find enemies in Iraq, at least it also faced the prospect of finding internal and highly motivated allies who would fight to the death to prevent the Sunnis from regaining power.

Iraq was historically one of the core regions of Islam and of the Arab world. Baghdad had been one of the khalifate's capitals and, until its destruction by the Mongols, one of Islam's intellectual centers.

If the Bush administration could not jump-start modernization in Iraq, then it believed it could not be done anywhere. The alternative was to accept the likelihood of decades, and possibly centuries, of fighting "the war on terror." Such a prediction might sound far-fetched, but the often-bitter struggle in the Iberian Peninsula between Christians and Muslims lasted more than seven hundred years!

That is not to say that there were not dangers inherent in the Bush administration's policy, or that it was destined to succeed. The lesson drawn from Afghanistan of using an invasion force with as small a footprint as possible ensured planners would deploy a lean invasion force to Iraq, but perhaps one that would be too lean for the jobs of occupation and reconstruction. Since the first Gulf War, Osama bin Laden had been preaching that at the end of the Cold War the Jews and the Americans had embarked on a crusade against Islam. The Bush administration's response to bin Laden's jihad operations did, in fact, lead to an American-led crusade—not a religious crusade to destroy Islam, but a political one intent on modernizing the region. Nevertheless, after the March 2003 American invasion of Iraq, Muslims were more likely to be swayed by bin Laden's arguments. Most important, by carrying the GWOT to Baghdad, the Bush administration all but ensured that the focus of the jihadist campaign would be drawn into an all-important core area of the Islamic world. Such a move might deflect jihadist attacks against the United States, but once the struggle was joined in Iraq, the political stakes grew exponentially for both the West and Qaeda al-Jihad.

Operation Iraqi Freedom reflected the long traditions of American strategy, as outlined by the late Russell F. Weigley in his 1973 classic *The American Way of War: A History of United States Military Strategy and Policy*. The United States consciously chose to carry the fight to heart of the Middle East rather than dicker about in some prolonged and most likely inconclusive peripheral struggle in Afghanistan, along the the Islamic world's frontier. The Bush strategy took certain high risks, because if it failed, the costs would be enormous for the United States, its Arab allies, Israel, and the entire West. Conversely, its success would carry devastating ramifications for the legitimacy of Osama bin Laden and the jihadists.

Whether people in the West like it or not, the Bush administration has embarked on a campaign that, now joined, *cannot be lost*. As Tony Blair stressed in his March 2006 speech, the war against the jihadists "is one we must win."

> What happens in Iraq or Afghanistan today is not just crucial for the people in those countries or even in those regions; but for our security here and round the world. . . .
>
> Naturally, the debate over the wisdom of the original decisions, especially in respect of Iraq will continue. Opponents will say Iraq was never a threat; there were no WMD. . . .
>
> But whatever the conclusion to this debate, if there ever is one, the fact is that now, whatever the rights and wrongs of how and why Saddam and the Taliban were removed, there is an obvious, clear and overwhelming reason for supporting the people of those countries in their desire for democracy.

An American failure in Iraq—a victory for the jihadists—would be an unmitigated disaster. The Islamists might not reestablish their khalifate and go on to overrun the rest of the world, for the West has sufficient firepower, and hopefully the will, to prevent such an outcome. The human and ethical costs of defeating the jihadists down the road, if Qaeda al-Jihad is successful in Iraq, however, would be enormous—akin to the price of defeating Nazi Germany in 1945 instead of stopping Hitler in the Rhineland in 1936. People in the West and their Arab allies need to recall that when the war clouds gathered over Europe in the 1930s, many made excuses for Hitler and argued that their choice was one between peace or another Verdun, the longest battle of World War I. Unfortunately, as the Frenchman Jean Dutourd wrote in *The Taxis of the Marne* (1957), the options were far more constricted— "between Verdun and Dachau."

Conclusion
"The Will to Live . . . The Will to Die"

There is only one place on earth which can be called the home
of Islam (Dar-ul-Islam), and it is that place where the Islamic
state [is] established and the Shari'ah is the authority and God's
limits observed, and where all the Muslims administer the affairs
of the state with mutual consultation. The rest of the world is the
home of hostility (Dar-ul-Harb). A Muslim can have only two
possible relations with Dar-ul-Harb: peace with a contractual
agreement, or war. A country [with] which there is a treaty will
not be considered the home of Islam.
—Sayyid Qutb, Milestones

From the start the paths of civilization in the ancient Near
East and the West diverged. Initially, the differences were small,
seemingly inconsequential. But as the centuries passed, small fis-
sures became consequential, and by the late twentieth century the
consequential had generated a veritable chasm. No particular outcome was predetermined, however. Throughout history both the
Near East and the West had options to take one road or the other.
On the whole, over time, the West chose better, although not because of any collective or cultural acumen. For most of recorded
history, progress remained glacial, occurring as a steady arithmetical
progression—2, 3, 4, 5, 6, 7, 8, and so on. In the ancient world,
when civilizations realized that they had taken the wrong path, they
could change course and draw level with others. But in the eras to

231

follow, when advances took on a more exponential progression—2, 4, 8, 16, 32, 64, 128, and so forth—falling behind became far more dangerous. And that is what happened to Islam in the fourteenth century. That stagnation is why in the early twenty-first century such a divergence exists between the Occidental and the Near Eastern worlds. Thus Western imperialism was not the cause of the Islamic world's problems. It was the latter's refusal to modernize that is the root cause of the frictions between the Near East and the West today.

While Western intellectuals avoid concepts that smack of Manichaeism the way housecats avoid water, the clash between the Islamists and the West (at present represented by a not all-together lonely United States) *is* Manichaean in nature. And it is worth remembering that it was bin Laden and his World Islamic Front who declared open season on "crusaders and Jews."

Some in the West view bin Laden as an Arab Robin Hood (or a Teddy Roosevelt?), but bin Laden and his fellow jihadists are utopian, totalitarian, and anti-Semitic. The jihadists want the world for Islam, even if they can get only one slice at a time. Why? Because their god told them in the Qur'an that it is theirs and that they are the best people on Earth. The jihadists believe their sacred duty is to secure the world for their faith and for their God. And once they have, everyone—both Muslim and non-Muslim—will live within the behavioral boundaries established by *Shari'ah* in a global khalifate. Jihadists view the Christians and Jews—most especially the latter—as committed enemies hell-bent on thwarting the attainment of this Muslim millennium and, in the service of Satan himself, on destroying Islam. Bin Laden and his followers believe that on the Final Day of Judgment even the trees and rocks will reveal their anti-Semitism and point the Jews out to the Muslims so that the last of the Hebrews may be slaughtered. The totalitarian and anti-Semitic aspects of Islamism and the jihadists are so glaring that white supremacists in the United States have embraced Islam and jihad. In the fall of 2005 David Duke toured and spoke in Syria, and in March 2006, when John Mearsheimer and Stephen Walt published their controversial paper "The Israel Lobby," the former Klansman's website proudly proclaimed: "Harvard Researchers Adopt David Duke's View of Iraq War." The website for Aryan Nations now includes a slogan in Arabic beneath its banner, and its members speak openly of "Aryan jihad." The organization also has a "Minister of Islamic Liaison," who explained the reasons for the budding alliance.

> [W]e both share the same enemies—such as Zionism, Democracy, Globalization, Capitalism, Communism, Freemasonry, Liberalism, Feminism and all the other jew bastard creeds—and this makes it even more necessary that we see each other as allies so as to defeat our common enemies. The benefits to such an alliance between Muslims upholding the authentic Salafi Jihadi creed and the Aryans upholding National Socialism are too numerous to mention here, but let it be stated that there already exists a strong historical precedence for such an alliance in history.
>
> We Muslims who uphold the ideals of the Salafi da'wah, Islamic revivalism, Jihad in the Cause of Allah and the rebuilding of Khilafah have the same spiritual ancestors who show us the path towards success in both this world and the Hereafter. These include Imam Hasan al-Banna Shaheed (d. 1949), founder of the Ikhwaan al-Muslimeen (Muslim Brotherhood), and Mohammad Amin al-Husseini (d. 1974), the Grand Mufti of Al-Quds (Jerusalem). . . . These two great men already showed us the way from their alliance with the honorable warriors of National Socialism in Germany and Europe.

Jay Farber, the "pastor" of Aryan Nations, dismissed on his website (www.agentofchaos.invisionzone.com) those who questioned the group's "alliance with Islam" as "Biblically Illiterate itiots [*sic*] with the IQ of the roving bands of savage negro beasts shooting their own rescuers in New Orleans." "Our alliance is Biblically accept-able," he explained, "as well as acceptable from the Querran [*sic*]. Death to the jew, [*sic*] peace be upon the Islamic Jihadeen [*sic*]."

Americanism, like Islam, does have a universal streak. Since its inception its adherents have assumed that it shall ultimately domi-nate the planet—not in a direct sense of political rule but as a philosophical construct, or a civic religion that combines political and economic pluralism, secularism, and the expansion of human liberties. To Americanists—that is, those who embrace the con-cepts of Americanism—Muslims and assorted traditionalists around the globe do not stand in the way of American or Western power, progress, or control; they obstruct their own advancement into the modern age. Americanists understand that traditional societies can-not enjoy the material benefits of modernity without first letting go of the traditional. That is the price of material wealth, and it is one the West still pays. And in a sense, the bin Ladens of the world have it right: the West has sold its traditional soul for the wealth and pleasures of modern materialism.

Islamists and other traditionalists have the right to refuse such a bargain. Many groups within the United States—the Amish, for example—refuse to yield fully to modernity in an effort to retain their traditions and faith. But the Amish do not blame nonbelievers for their lack of electricity. Despite the societal pressures on their young, they do not demand that everyone become Amish or live under Amish rule or sport dynamite vests in pizza parlors in nearby towns. Merely rejecting modernity, however, is insufficient for the jihadists. Unlike the Amish, the jihadists seek to square the circle— they want the prosperity of the modern world without modernity. Moreover, they know, rightly, that the modern world's tempta-tions will inevitably entice the spiritually minded toward the mate-rial, lead the sacred toward the profane, and tempt the believer to doubt. To survive, the jihadists are convinced that Islam must rid the world of modernity as defined by "crusaders and Jews" and secure the world for a new modernity circumscribed by Allah and his *Shari'ah*. Modernity, to paraphrase the words of Father Jacques Jomier, must be Islamized, lest Islam be modernized.

What are the implications of this clash for the United States and, more broadly, for the West? To answer that question we must accept certain fundamental, albeit uncomfortable, truths.

The Arab and the Islamic worlds are not products of Western colonialism and imperialism. While the West did exploit the Middle East and other areas of the globe, as history shows, the Islamic world fell behind the West because of its own problems, problems inherent *within* Islam. Western scholars are reluctant to say that Islam *is* the problem. It is much easier to blame "history" or "the West." But unfortunately Islam lies at the root of the Muslim world's failure to keep pace with the West as the latter modernized.

When trying to understand the clash of cultures, too many people in the West focus on the wrong question: Why do they hate us? But that's not the proper query if we wish to understand what is happening. People around the world and even within the American body politic hate the United States and Americans. The question to ask instead is, Why is it that of the myriad peoples about the planet who have a grudge against the United States, only Muslims are intent on killing us and often themselves? There are people in all our lives whom we grow to dislike and even hate. That's the way life is. But few of us murder the objects of our hatred or their loved ones.

So what can we find in Islam to help us answer the question? Any Muslim or Western specialist will say the same thing: Islam is not a mere religion; it is a comprehensive, God-centered way of life. It is that very comprehensiveness that gives Islam its internal strength. But that same breadth also became its Achilles' heel.

There are two ways to think about Islam. If you read the Qur'an and believe that it is the literal, timeless, and universal word of God Almighty, then you are a Muslim. If you are not, then you should become one posthaste, repair immediately to the nearest mosque, and prove your faith by reciting the shahada: "There is no God but Allah; Muhammad is the Messenger of Allah." But if you do not accept Islam as your religion, then Islam is a philosophy of life conceived by a man who recorded inspirational passages and led a group of followers in the Arabian Peninsula during the seventh century AD. It is, in short, an all-embracing prescription for a medieval way of life that, not surprisingly, continues to yield medieval results.

Imagine that tomorrow something happens that demonstrates conclusively that Jesus Christ was not the Son of God nor the Bible the revealed word of God. What would the impact be in the West? Obviously, attendance at Christian churches and schools would drop off markedly, priests and ministers might feel as if they had wasted their lives, and the archbishop of Canterbury might not crown the next British monarch. But beyond those peculiarly religious aspects of life, how much would actually change? In the United States would we throw out the federal Constitution, the Bill of Rights, or the Declaration of Independence?

Conversely, imagine that tomorrow something happens that demonstrates conclusively that Muhammad was not the Prophet he claimed to be and that the Qur'an is not the Word of Allah. What would the impact be on the Islamic world? The shock would be far, far greater. Why? Islam is a continued central and comprehensive presence in the everyday lives of its faithful, an aspect of the religion that since the Middle Ages Christianity in the West could not match.

In its first few hundred years Islam was, relatively speaking, progressive. Yes, daughters received a half share of the inheritance bequeathed to sons, but that was a better deal than women had in the West. Yes, Christians and Jews were second-class citizens, or dhimmis, but their status as minorities was much better than that shared by comparable minority groups in the West. Jews, as it is so often rightly said, were usually better off in the Islamic realms than they were in Christendom until recently. Some verses of the Qur'an do seem harsh, but they were written down and honestly stated. In the West even worse things were done, often under the guise of religion, because there were few written or accepted universal rules. In that sense Islam, because of its comprehensive nature, offered a superior way of life *at the time*. That is one of the major reasons that it spread so quickly.

So what went wrong? Several fundamental internal problems exist within Islam—not as a religious creed—as a way of life. First, unlike Christianity, Islam was hard-wired. As I have discussed elsewhere in this book, Islam allows far less flexibility than there is in Christianity. Thus as the West modernized, Christianity adjusted in a way that Islam has not. As Father Richard John Neuhaus noted of the West, Christianity was gradually squeezed from the "public square," or the state, leaving it "naked" but free to adapt to a changing world. But in the Islamic world the mosque, in a literal sense, has long been the "public square." Richard Bulliet wrote in his *The Camel and the Wheel* that after the Islamic conquests mosques often replaced the open agoras and forums of the older Greco-Roman Near East towns.

The clearest example of Islam's relative inflexibility came in the late fifteenth century, when news of the printing press reached Istanbul. The sultan showed interest in the new development; the *ulema* rejected it. Only the empire's Christians and Jews were permitted to use it. Considering the immense historical impact of printing in the West, the Ottoman *ulema*'s decision marked the greatest self-inflicted wound suffered by the Islamic world. It may seem harsh for a Western scholar to castigate Islam for its failure to adopt the printing press, but imagine what Western historians would say if the Catholic Church had done the same *and* sustained that ban in southern Europe for the better part of four centuries. Any Western scholar would call such a decision "backward."

Not surprising, while al-Qaeda rails against the evil West, it relies on cell phones and the Internet for communications, audio and videotapes for propaganda, music videos for recruitment, and Western-designed and manufactured weapons for its fight. Without modern Western technology Osama bin Laden would have virtually no reach beyond his most recent refuge.

Why is it that bin Laden and his jihadists have to rely so heavily on the West? In part, at least, the answer goes back to the story of the printing press. For example, the United Nation's *Arab Human Development Report, 2002,* painted a bleak picture of the state of the Arab world. The report concluded:

> Arab countries need to embark on rebuilding their societies on the basis of:
> • Full respect for human rights and human freedoms as the cornerstones of good governance, leading to human development.
> • The complete empowerment of Arab women, taking advantage of all opportunities to build their capabilities and to enable them to exercise those capabilities to the full.
> • The consolidation of knowledge acquisition and its effective utilisation. As a key driver of progress, knowledge must be brought to bear efficiently and productively in all aspects of society, with the goal of enhancing human well being across the region.

The report cited supporting statistics that highlighted the abject failure of the Arab world's modernization. For instance, the "Arab world translates about 330 books annually, one fifth of the number that Greece translates. The cumulative total of translated books since the Khaliph Maa'moun's time (the ninth century) is about 100,000, almost the average that Spain translates in one year." This statistic is incredible, considering the tradition of Islamic scholarship and learning so evident in the faith's early centuries, but understandable after Islamic leaders' ban on printing for almost four centuries. And the result?

Economic productivity, despite the region's oil wealth, is low. The GDP of all Arab countries (with a population of approximately 270 million) was "$531.2 billion in 1999 — less than that of a single European country, [the 40 million people of] Spain ($595.5 billion)." In a review of the report, the *Economist* identified the unaddressed question: "The most delicate issue of all, again carefully skirted by the authors of the report, is the part that Islam plays in delaying and impeding the Arab world's advance towards the ever-receding renaissance that its intellectuals crave."

The dhimmi system was yet another self-inflicted wound on the Islamic world. The *dhimma* was either decreed by God or based on a scheme worked out by Muhammad so that Muslims could dominate nonbelievers on the Arabian Peninsula. In the communities with which the Prophet was familiar, Christians were almost nonexistent and Jews but a small minority. Decreeing that these groups had to live as second-class citizens was of little practical importance to the society as a whole. But as the Muslim realm expanded and the khalifate incorporated huge numbers of nonbelievers, a system that made sense on the Arabian Peninsula became nonsensical. Setting aside questions of inequality and human rights and focusing simply on the material, this system was counterproductive. The conversion process for a Christian area overrun by Muslims lasted about five centuries. After 250 years or so, about half the population of a given area would have converted. In Egypt as late as the mid-twentieth century, about 20 percent of the population was still Christian. In practical terms, then, adhering to the dhimmi system caused several problems. First, the khaliphate or empire denied itself the full use of a substantial portion of, and at times majority of, its population for military service. Second, the disgruntled population represented a potential fifth-column during times of conflict. Third and especially true of the Ottoman Empire, the dhimmis were often concentrated in those very sectors of the economy — banking, commerce, shipping — that in the West led the way from the feudal to the modern system; thus these sectors did not modernize fully, letting the Islamic world fall more behind.

Another brake on Islamic development was the Ottoman Empire's adoption of the feudal *timar*. The Ottomans embraced the system just as the West was breaking free from the confines of feudalism. Moreover, while the nonhereditary nature of the *timar* system avoided the political challenge to centralized control that was inherent in Western feudalism, it did so at the expense of internal economic development.

The *timar* and *dhimma* systems combined with centuries of restrictions on printing are alone sufficient to explain why the Islamic world fell so far behind the West. *All were self-inflicted wounds.* No one in the West forced the *timar* or *dhimma* systems on the Muslim world; no Westerner prevented the Ottomans from adopting the printing press. Bernard Lewis titled one of his more recent books about the Middle East *What Went Wrong?* The answer is fairly simple: *Islam placed a gun to its head and pulled the trigger not once, not twice, but three times.*

Another uncomfortable fact that Westerners have to accept is that despite claims by many, including George Bush and Tony Blair, Osama bin Laden did not "hijack" Islam. Bin Laden represents a legitimate line of Islamic interpretation. His understanding of Islam does not represent the faith's only explanation, but it is one of several perfectly legitimate interpretations. Until we understand this fact, we cannot begin to comprehend why bin Laden plays so well to so many Muslims. He knows his sacred texts and, although not as well as some clerics, can cite them in a sacerdotal enough manner to engage and convince the average believer. As a non-Muslim, I can attest that if I were a practicing Muslim and had read through the writings of Maududi, Qutb, bin Laden, and others, I would have a hard time not accepting the bulk of what they have to say. They write well, they write persuasively, and they cite scripture with an ability that would be the envy of any Christian televangelist.

This leads to another concept that is difficult to accept. If we assume that Islam serves as a brake on development in the Middle East, that Islam is inflexible, and that many Muslims are increasingly disenchanted because they do not share in the wealth and progress evident in the West, what does that imply? There are three possibilities. First, Muslims can continue to watch and see which way, and how strongly, the wind blows. Second, they can join bin Laden and the jihadists and Islamize the West. Third, Muslims can embrace modernization and face the prospect that the process will erode, if it does not destroy, the faith that heretofore has been the core of their way of life.

Such remarks may well appear insensitive, but some Muslim intellectuals and reformers take an even harsher line. For example, Libyan reformer Dr. Muhammad al-Houni wrote,

> Arab societies have only one of two options: either to sever their ties with Western civilization and its cultural institutions and to continue to [harm] themselves . . . or to irrevocably sever their ties with the religious legacy of the Middle Ages, in order for their philosophy to be a philosophy of life and freedom, and not one of death and hatred.

Islam is in trouble. It *is* under siege — not by the West, as bin Laden would have us believe, but by modernity. Could the end possibly be approaching for a major world religion with over a billion adherents? Yes, an inflexible Islam is in danger in the same way that in the face of a storm the tree that cannot bend is snapped off or blown over. Almost two centuries ago Alexis de Tocqueville noted in his *Democracy in America*:

> Muhammad brought down from heaven and put into the Koran not religious doctrines only, but political maxims, criminal and civil laws, and scientific theories. The Gospels,

on the other hand, deal only with the general relations between man and God and between man and man. Beyond that, they teach nothing and do not oblige people to believe anything. That alone, among a thousand reasons, is enough to show that Islam will not be able to hold its power long in ages of enlightenment and democracy, while Christianity is destined to reign in such ages, as in all others.

Christianity can better weather the storm of modernity because it is flexible and can bend before it breaks. It can safely retreat from the public square and still find a home in the hearts and minds of men and women of faith. But can Islam do the same and remain true to itself? What do such stark realities portend for the war on terror? That question leads me to another point: *the war on terror is not a war on terror*. It is a war on Islamism and the jihadists.

I prefer to avoid calling bin Laden a "terrorist" (not because I care about his feelings), because it is an inaccurate label. A terrorist, by my definition, is someone from the West who knowingly operates outside the Western rules of the game. Bin Laden is not of the Western world. He is a Muslim, and within his ethical context, he is perfectly justified in commissioning the acts that he does. We feel more comfortable branding him a terrorist because, in our minds, that makes him a criminal and allows us to separate the man from his faith. Further, many in the West prefer to view the current struggle as a vast police action against individuals driven to terror because of the ravages of poverty and the scars of Western imperialism. To acknowledge that bin Laden is a jihadist, motivated by a legitimate interpretation of a faith with more than a billion adherents, is rather frightening; but it is the first step to understanding his motivations, the types of actions the jihadists undertake and will conduct in the future, and why bin Laden finds support throughout such a wide swath of the Islamic world. Bin Laden is "of Islam." His actions are taken in conformity with his interpretation of Islam, an interpretation that, while not universally accepted by Muslims, is nonetheless a viable one. His legitimacy will ultimately be determined by how well he fares in his war against the "crusaders and Jews."

How long will this war against the jihadists last, and how is it likely to end? The nature of the conflict, both in operational terms and as a struggle for Islam's future, suggests a prolonged contest that will, at best, be measured in decades. I expect that the conflict will grow increasingly harsh as the years pass. I wish I had a prescription for victory that I could offer in this book — other than all nonbelievers converting to Islam — but I do not. The great difficulty of fighting terrorists or, in this case, jihadists is that if you do nothing, you appear weak and foster more attacks; whereas if you respond forcefully, you inevitably kill people, look like a brute, and induce new converts to replace those you have slain. No matter what course the West pursues for the foreseeable future the jihadists will find a ready source of recruits. If the United States does nothing or little, jihadists will find recruits because people will be convinced that the United States *is* the paper tiger that bin Laden claimed it was. If the United States responds forcefully and takes the fight to the Middle East, then the jihadists will gain recruits because we will have exercised our power on Muslim soil.

But the jihadists and those Muslims watching from the sidelines should understand that engaging the United States, and eventually the West as a whole, is likewise a problematic undertaking. If the jihadists do not attack for a given stretch of time, they will appear weak, disorganized, and ineffectual; but when they do strike, their attacks will outrage Westerners and harden their resolve.

The jihadists should also understand that Americans are inscrutable people. Throughout the Cold War the United States wrote off various areas of the globe — for example, Iran in 1946 and Korea in 1950 — but then intervened diplomatically or militarily to the great surprise and chagrin of Josef Stalin and the Soviet Union. Possibly during the 9/11 planning, bin Laden, who noted that killing "tens" of Americans had been sufficient to force a U.S. withdrawal from Somalia, was convinced that killing thousands on their own soil would lead the United States to withdraw entirely from the entire Middle East. If he did, he made a grievous mistake.

Warfare, Martin van Creveld has written, is one of the most imitative forms of human behavior. Inevitably as this struggle continues, the United States, and eventually the West, will respond in an ever-harsher fashion. In the fall of 1941 Americans considered unrestricted submarine warfare something immoral, unethical, illegal—something conducted by the likes of Hitler and his Nazis. Nevertheless, on December 7, 1941, the Commander, Submarines, of the Pacific Fleet issued the following order to all American submarines: "Conduct unrestricted submarine warfare against the empire of Japan." In 1941 Americans were appalled by the Nazis' terror bombing of Warsaw, Rotterdam, London, Coventry, and Belgrade. By 1944 the United States was doing the same thing—firebombing German and Japanese cities and dropping nuclear weapons on Hiroshima and Nagasaki. On September 10, 2001, who would have believed that famed Harvard Law School professor and civil liberties defender Alan Dershowitz would, shortly after 9/11, write about situations in which torture would be justified?

Bin Laden's campaign is aimed at destroying the United States and ultimately the West. If he is successful and the jihadists undermine "the West," what will remain but human beings stripped of the Western veneer that stands between them and their savage nature? If the jihadists succeed in Iraq or in conducting some new terror strike on U.S. soil, all they will have done is ensure a nastier outcome for themselves and their brothers and sisters in the "*ummah*."

Bin Laden warned the Americans shortly after September 2001 that Muslims were "the Nation of Martyrdom; the Nation that desires death more than you desire life." He was not the first to make such a fundamental miscalculation. Hanson W. Baldwin wrote of the Okinawa campaign of 1945:

> Human will in war is still in this mechanistic age *a*—and
> perhaps *the*—fundamental intangible which makes the
> difference between victory and defeat. The Japanese
> possessed the will to fight to a high degree, but it was
> built on a negative philosophy—a fatalistic will to die. At
> Okinawa the will to die and the will to live met in head-on
> conflict; in this instance the will to live—aided by far su-
> perior material—won. Yet it is well to remember that the
> will to live must, in war, have more than a selfish context,
> or men who are willing to die for a cause will defeat
> those who put life ahead of their cause. In the case of
> the Japanese the kamikaze represented more than a tech-
> nique; it might be called a self-destructive urge, a death
> wish. And in the long role of history the sole reasons for
> man's persistence has been that the will to live has tri-
> umphed through the ages over the will to die.

The same will hold true in this current struggle, whatever its length and vicissitudes. The questions now center on how long will it take and how many lives will be spent before the inevitable is realized. Yes, nature has ensured that the will to live is superior to the will to die, but in 1945 Americans still had to weather the Kamikaze storm at Okinawa, obliterate Japanese cities, prepare an invasion, en-sure the Soviets' entry into the war, and drop two atomic weap-ons. How far the West will have to go to win this present conflict will depend on how quickly and surely the Western powers go about their work. Unfortunately, at present, they are far from united—many refuse to even recognize the war as a war—and sup-port for the United States, for myriad reasons, is faltering. Does that mean that the West is losing? No, but it does give the jihadists strength and legitimacy, which, in turn, will cause the struggle to persist. As it continues, it will reach new levels of barbarity.

The real danger is that the longer the conflict lasts, the more likely it becomes that the West, with its unlimited means of destruction, will shed its self-imposed restrictions and adopt an ever-more brutal and unlimited response. Al-Qaeda has shown, even if it has not yet played, all of its cards: it has threatened to use nuclear weapons against American cities. Conversely, the United States, let alone the West, has yet to reveal its entire hand.

I often ask my students if the United States has ever won an asymmetric war. They inevitably start to mumble about our failure in Vietnam. Then I remind them of the "Indian Wars." In that conflict, which spanned several centuries and pitted primitive peoples waging an unlimited war with limited means against more modern people armed with far more powerful means, Americans threw away the Western "rules of warfare" and adopted more vicious tactics. They targeted not only Native American warriors but also their women and children and very way of life. In the end the conflict became, depending on one's political view, either a near or an outright campaign of genocide.

The longer the GWOT continues, the more likely Islamist terrorists will get their hands on WMDs and use them. If they do and an American city is incinerated and hundreds of thousands of citizens killed, any U.S. administration—be it Republican or Democrat—will be hard-pressed not to respond in kind. What might be unthinkable the day before such a terrorist strike might well seem far too doable the day after. Just such a scenario led Fred Ikle in a June 2002 opinion piece in the *Wall Street Journal* to hypothesize about the nuclear destruction of Mecca and Medina.

The key to avoiding such a scenario is to end the war against the jihadists as quickly as possible. We must begin the modernization process in Iraq and stand up a government that is at least partially representative. Regrettably, despite their enemies's overt utopian, totalitarian, and anti-Semitic nature, political divisions in the West continue to undermine those efforts in Iraq, to sustain the dreams of the jihadists, and to ensure the uncertainty of the

Muslims who cautiously watch from the sidelines to see if Allah will fight on the side of the "big battalions" or alongside the faithful. Further, the longer this conflict continues, the greater the strain on those restraints that bind the West. A Germany willing to secure the freedom of one of its citizens kidnapped in Iraq by releasing the Hezbollah terrorist who murdered Robert Dean Stethem—the American to whom this book is dedicated—could one day intern Muslims in camps. Never! you say. Who in the 1920s would have believed that a people who had produced Bach, Beethoven, Schiller, and Goethe would one day establish camps at Dachau, Sobibor, Treblinka, and Birkenau? The abyss beckons, and the disunity of the West only deepens the chasm.

Bibliography

A note on the sources for the Qur'an and the Bible: I used online sources for both. For the Qur'an, I used the easy to search site hosted by the University of Michigan's Humanities Text Initiative, http://www.hti.umich.edu/k/koran/. For the Bible, I used the also easy to search King James version at Bible Gateway, http://www.biblegateway.com/.

Primary Sources

Lawrence, Bruce, ed. *Messages to the World: The Statements of Osama bin Laden.* New York: Verso, 2005.

Miller, John. "Interview with Osama bin Laden." John Miller (ABC News) interviewer. *Frontline*, PBS, May 1998. http://www.pbs.org/wgbh/pages/frontline/shows/binladen/who/interview.html.

National Commission on Terrorist Attacks upon the United States. *The 9/11 Commission Report.* Washington, DC: GPO, 2005.

Al-Qaradhawi, Sheikh Yousef. "The Prophet Muhammad as a Jihad Model." Special Dispatch Series No. 246. Washington, DC: Middle East Media Research Institute (MEMRI), 2001.

——. "'We Gave Up on Haifa and Jaffa': I Am Opposed to Attacks in Islamic Countries." Special Dispatch Series No. 531. Washington, DC: MEMRI, 2003.

——. "We Will Be Victorious, Allah Willing, Despite [the Traps] Set by Judaism and Crusaders." Special Dispatch Series No. 1045. Washington, DC: MEMRI, 2005.

United Nations Development Programme. *Arab Human Development Report, 2002: Creating Opportunity for Future Generations.* New York: United Nations Publications, 2002.

——. *Arab Human Development Report, 2004: Towards Freedom in the Arab World.* New York: United Nations Publications, 2004.

United States Department of Defense. "Deputy Secretary Wolfowitz Briefing with Iraqi-Americans." March 28, 2003.

United States Department of State. *Patterns of Global Terrorism, 2001.* Washington, DC: USGPO, 2002.

——. *Country Reports on Terrorism, 2004.* Washington, DC: GPO, 2005.

United States Executive Branch. *The National Security Strategy of the United States of America.* Washington, DC: GPO, 2002.

——. *The National Security Strategy of the United States of America.* Washington, DC: GPO, 2006.

United States National Security Council. *National Strategy for Victory in Iraq.* Washington, DC: GPO, 2005.

Al-Zarqawi, Abu Musab. "Communiqué No. 8 Issued by the Attawhid Wal Jihad Group." Washington, DC: Site Institute, 2004.

——. "Al-Zarqawi Declares Total War on Shi'ites." Special Dispatch Series No. 987. Washington, DC: MEMRI, 2005.

Al-Zawahiri, Ayman. "Al Qaeda Leader Ayman Al-Zawahiri on Al-Jazeera." Special Dispatch Series No. 791. Washington, DC: MEMRI, 2005.

Secondary Sources
Books

Abdel-Malek, Kamal. *America in an Arab Mirror: Images of America in Arabic Travel Literature—An Anthology, 1895–1995.* New York: St. Martin's Press, 2000.

Ágoston, Gábor. *Guns for the Sultan: Military Power and the Weapons Industry in the Ottoman Empire.* Cambridge: Cambridge University Press, 2005.

Ajami, Fouad. *The Arab Predicament: Arab Political Thought and Practice Since 1967.* Cambridge: Cambridge University Press, 1992.

——. *The Dream Palace of the Arabs: A Generation's Odyssey.* New York: Vintage Books, 1999.

Akbar, M. J. *The Shade of Swords: Jihad and the Conflict Between Islam and Christianity.* London: Routledge, 2003.

Allison, Robert J. *The Crescent Obscured: The United States and the Muslim World, 1776–1815.* New York: Oxford University Press, 1995.

Anonymous (Michael Scheuer). *Imperial Hubris: Why the West Is Losing the War on Terror.* Washington, DC: Potomac Books, 2004.

——. *Through Our Enemies' Eyes: Osama bin Laden, Radical Islam, and the Future of America.* Washington, DC: Brassey's, Inc., 2003.

Ashtor, Eliyahu. *Levant Trade in the Later Middle Ages.* Princeton: Princeton University Press, 1983.

——. *A Social and Economic History of the Near East in the Middle Ages.* Berkeley: University of California Press, 1976.

Azzam, Abdullah. *Defence of the Muslim Lands: The First Obligation After Iman.* http://www.religioscope.com/info/doc/jihadazzam_defence_2_intro.htm.

——. *Join the Caravan.* http://www.islamistwatch.org/texts/azzam/caravan/caravan.html

Baldwin, Hanson W. *Battles Lost and Won: Great Campaigns of World War II.* New York: Harper & Row, 1966.

Black, C. E. *The Dynamics of Modernization: A Study in Comparative History.* New York: Harper & Row, 1966.

Blankley, Tony. *The West's Last Chance: Will We Win the Clash of Civilizations?* Washington, DC: Regnery, 2005.

Bostom, Andrew G. *The Legacy of Jihad: Islamic Holy War and the Fate of Non-Muslims.* Amherst, NY: Prometheus Books, 2005.

Bronowski, J., and Bruce Mazlish. *The Western Intellectual Tradition: From Leonardo to Hegel.* New York: Harper Torchbooks, 1960.

Bulliet, Richard W. *The Camel and the Wheel.* Cambridge, MA: Harvard University Press, 1975.

—— *Conversion to Islam in the Medieval Period: An Essay in Quantative History.* Cambridge, MA: Harvard University Press, 1979.

——. *Islam: The View From the Edge.* New York: Columbia University Press, 1994.

Buruma, Ian, and Avishai Margalit. *Occidentalism: The West in the Eyes of Its Enemies.* New York: Penquin Press, 2004.

Casson, Lionel. *The Ancient Mariners: Seafarers and Sea Fighters of the Mediterranean in Ancient Times.* 2nd ed. Princeton: Princeton University Press, 1991.

Cipolla, Carlo M. *Guns, Sails, and Empires: Technological Innovation and the Early Phases of European Expansion, 1400–1700.* New York: Minerva Press, 1965.

Clausewitz, Carl von. *On War.* Edited and translated by Michael Howard and Peter Paret. Princeton, NJ: Princeton University Press.

Cook, William R., and Ronald B. Herzman. *The Medieval World View: An Introduction.* New York: Oxford University Press, 2004.

Crone, Patricia. *Meccan Trade and the Rise of Islam.* Princeton: Princeton University Press, 1987.

Crone, Patricia, and Martin Hinds. *God's Caliph: Religious Authority in the First Centuries of Islam.* Cambridge: Cambridge University Press, 1986.

Dawson, Doyne. *The Origins of Western Warfare: Militarism and Morality in the Ancient World.* Boulder, CO: Westview Press, 1996.

Efendi, Huseyn. *Ottoman Egypt in the Age of the French Revolution.* Translated and edited by Stanford Shaw. Cambridge, MA: Harvard University Press, 1964.

Esposito, John L. *What Everyone Needs to Know About Islam*. Oxford: Oxford University Press, 2002.

Field, James A., Jr. *America and the Mediterranean World, 1776–1882*. Princeton, NJ: Princeton University Press, 1969.

Fisher, Sydney Nettleton, and William Ochsenwald. *The Middle East: A History*. 4th ed. New York: McGraw-Hill, 1990.

Gerges, Fawaz A. *America and Political Islam: Clash of Cultures or Clash of Interests?* Cambridge: Cambridge University Press, 1999.

——. *The Far Enemy: Why Jihad Went Global*. Cambridge: Cambridge University Press, 2005.

Gierke, Otto. *Natural Law and the Theory of Society, 1500 to 1800*. Boston: Beacon Press, 1957.

Guilmartin, John Francis, Jr. *Gunpowder and Galleys: Changing Technology and Mediterranean Warfare at Sea in the 16th Century*. London: Conway Maritime Press, 2003.

Hanson, Victor Davis. *The Western Way of War: Infantry Battle in Classical Greece*. New York: Alfred A. Knopf, 1989.

Houben, Hubert. *Roger II of Sicily: A Ruler Between East and West*. Cambridge: Cambridge University Press, 2002.

Hourani, Albert. *A History of the Arab Peoples*. New York: Warner Books, 1991.

Howard, Michael. *The Invention of Peace: Reflections on War and International Order*. New Haven, CT: Yale University Press, 2000.

Ibn Khaldun. *The Muqaddimah: An Introduction to History*. Translated by Franz Rosenthal. 3 vols. New York: Pantheon Books, 1958.

Jansen, Johannes J. G. *The Neglected Duty: The Creed of Sadat's Assassins and the Islamic Resurgence in the Middle East*. New York: Macmillan, 1986.

Jayyusi, Salma Khadra, ed. *The Legacy of Muslim Spain*. Leiden, Netherlands: E. J. Brill, 1992.

Johns, Jeremy. *Arabic Administration in Norman Sicily*. Cambridge: Cambridge University Press, 2002.

Jomier, Jacques. *The Bible and the Qur'an*. San Francisco: Ignatius Press, 2002.

Karsh, Efraim, and Inari Karsh. *Empires of the Sand: The Struggle for Mastery in the Middle East, 1789–1923*. Cambridge, MA: Harvard University Press, 1999.

Keeley, Lawrence H. *War Before Civilization*. New York: Oxford University Press, 1996.

Kennedy, Hugh. *Muslim Spain and Portugal: A Political History of al-Andalus*. London: Longman, 1996.

Kepel, Gilles. *Jihad: The Trail of Political Islam.* Cambridge, MA: Belknap Press, 2002.

Lambert, Stephen P. *Y: The Sources of Islamic Conduct.* Washington, DC: Center for Strategic Intelligence Research, 2005.

Landes, David S. *The Unbound Prometheus: Technological Change and Industrial Development in Western Europe from 1750 to the Present.* Cambridge: Cambridge University Press, 1969.

——. *The Wealth and Poverty of Nations: Why Some Are So Rich and Some So Poor.* New York: W. W. Norton, 1998.

Lawrence, T. E. *Seven Pillars of Wisdom: A Triumph.* Garden City, New York: Doubleday, Doran & Company, 1935.

Lewis, Bernard. *The Arabs in History.* New York: Harper & Row, 1966.

——. *Islam and the West.* New York: Oxford University Press, 1993.

——. *The Middle East and the West.* New York: Harper Torchbooks, 1964.

——. *What Went Wrong? Western Impact and Middle Eastern Response.* Oxford: Oxford University Press, 2002.

Little, Douglas. *American Orientalism: The United States and the Middle East Since 1945.* Chapel Hill: University of North Carolina Press, 2004.

Long, Pamela O. *Technology and Society in the Medieval Centuries: Byzantium, Islam, and the West, 500–1300.* Washington, DC: American Historical Association, 2003.

Lowney, Chris. *A Vanished World: Medieval Spain's Golden Age of Enlightenment.* New York: Free Press, 2005.

Maalouf, Amin. *The Crusades Through Arab Eyes.* New York: Schocken Books, 1984.

McDougall, Walter A. *Freedom Just Around the Corner: A New American History, 1585–1828.* New York: Harper Perennial, 2005.

——. *Promised Land, Crusader State: The American Encounter With the World Since 1776.* Boston: Houghton Mifflin, 1997.

McNeill, William H. *The Rise of the West: A History of the Human Community.* New York: Mentor Books, 1965.

Marshall, Paul, ed. *Radical Islam's Rules: The Worldwide Spread of Extreme Shari'a Law.* Lanham, MD: Rowman & Littlefield Publishers, 2005.

Maududi, Sayyid Abul A'la. *Jihad in Islam.* Birmingham, UK: U.K.I.M. (UK Islamic Mission) Dawah Center, n.d.

Metcalfe, Alex. *Muslims and Christians in Norman Sicily: Arabic Speakers and the End of Islam.* London: Routledge Curzon, 2003.

Musallam, Adnan A. *From Secularism to Jihad: Sayyid Qutb and the Foundations of Radical Islam.* Westport, CT: Praeger, 2005.

Padfield, Peter. *Maritime Supremacy and the Opening of the Western Mind:*

Naval Campaigns That Shaped the Modern World. Woodstock, New York: Overlook Press, 1999.

Pagden, Anthony, ed. *The Idea of Europe: From Antiquity to the European Union*. Cambridge: Cambridge University Press, 2002.

——. *Peoples and Empires: A Short History of European Migration, Exploration, and Conquest from Greece to the Present*. New York: Modern Library, 2001.

Palmer, Michael A. *Guardians of the Gulf: A History of America's Expanding Role in the Persian Gulf, 1833–1992*. New York: The Free Press, 1992.

Parker, Geoffrey. *Military Innovation and the Rise of the West, 1500–1800*. 2nd ed. Cambridge: Cambridge University Press, 2000.

Pipes, Daniel. *Militant Islam Reaches America*. New York: W. W. Norton, 2003.

Pryor, John H. *Geography, Technology, and War: Studies in the Maritime History of the Mediterranean, 649–1571*. Cambridge: Cambridge University Press, 1992.

Qutb, Sayyid. *Milestones*. http://www.youngmuslims.ca/online_library/ books/milestones/index_2.asp.

Ramadan, Tariq. *Western Muslims and the Future of Islam*. Oxford: Oxford University Press, 2004.

Record, Jeffrey. *Bounding the Global War on Terrorism*. Carlisle, PA: Strategic Studies Institute, 2003.

Roberts, J. M. *The Triumph of the West: The Origin, Rise, and Legacy of Western Civilization*. New York: Barnes and Noble, 1998.

Rosenberg, Nathan, and L. E. Birdzell, Jr. *How the West Grew Rich: The Economic Transformation of the Industrial World*. New York: Basic Books, 1986.

Said, Edward W. *Orientalism*. New York: Vintage Books, 1979.

Shaw, Stanford. *The Financial and Administrative Organization and Development of Ottoman Egypt, 1517–1798*. Princeton, NJ: Princeton University Press, 1962.

Shaw, Stanford, and Ezel Kural Shaw. *History of the Ottoman Empire and Modern Turkey*. 2 vols. Cambridge: Cambridge University Press, 1976–77.

Sicker, Martin. *The Islamic World in Ascendancy: From the Arab Conquests to the Siege of Vienna*. Westport, CT: Praeger, 2000.

——. *The Islamic World in Decline: From the Treaty of Karlowitz to the Disintegration of the Ottoman Empire*. Westport, CT: Praeger, 2001.

Spencer, Robert. *The Politically Incorrect Guide to Islam*. Washington, DC: Regnery Publishing, 2005.

Stead, W. T. *The Americanization of the World, or The Trend of the Twentieth*

Century. London: Horace Markley, 1901.

Strayer, Joseph R. *On the Medieval Origins of the Modern State*. Princeton: Princeton University Press, 1970.

Tibi, Bassam. *The Challenge of Fundamentalism: Political Islam and the New World Disorder*. Berkeley: University of California Press, 2002.

——. *The Crisis of Modern Islam: A Preindustrial Culture in the Scientific-Technological Age*. Salt Lake City: University of Utah Press, 1988.

Toqueville, Alexis de. *Democracy in America*. Edited by J. P. Mayer. Garden City, New York: Anchor Books, 1969.

Van Creveld, Martin. *The Transformation of War*. New York: Free Press, 1991.

Wasserstein, David J. *The Caliphate in the West: An Islamic Political Institution in the Iberian Peninsula*. Oxford: Clarendon Press, 1993.

Weigley, Russell F. *The American Way of War: A History of United States Military Strategy and Policy*. New York: Macmillan, 1973.

Yergin, Daniel. *The Prize: The Epic Quest for Oil, Money, and Power*. New York: Touchstone, 1992.

Articles

Argo, Nichole. "The Role of Social Context in Terrorist Attacks." *Chronicle of Higher Education* 52 (February 3, 2006): B15.

Bar, Shmuel. "The Religious Sources of Islamic Terrorism." *Policy Review* 125 (June 2004). http://www.policyreview.org/jun04/bar_print.html.

Barendse, R. J. "Trade and State in the Arabian Seas: A Survey From the Fifteenth to the Eighteenth Century." *Journal of World History* 11 (Fall 2000): 173–225.

Barkan, Omer Lufti, and Justin McCarthy. "The Price Revolution of the Sixteenth Century: A Turning Point in the Economic History of the Near East." *International Journal of Middle East Studies* 6 (January 1975): 3–28.

Bennett, Norman Robert. "Christian and Negro Slavery in Eighteenth-Century North Africa." *Journal of African History* 1 (January 1960): 65–82.

Burke, Edmund III. "Islamic History as World History: Marshall Hodgson, 'the Venture of Islam.'" *International Journal of Middle East Studies* 10 (May 1979): 241–64.

Cantor, Milton. "A Connecticut Yankee in a Barbary Court: Joel Barlow's Algerian Letters to His Wife." *William and Mary Quarterly*, 3.19, no. 1 (January 1962): 86–109.

Clark, G. N. "The Barbary Corsairs in the Seventeenth Century." *Cambridge Historical Journal* 8 (January 1944): 22–35.

Coolidge, Archibald Cary. "The European Reconquest of North Africa."

American Historical Review 17 (July 1912): 723–34.

Dols, Michael W. "Plague in Early Islamic History." *Journal of the American Oriental Society* 94 (July 1974): 371–83.

Earle, Edward Mead. "Early American Policy Concerning Ottoman Minorities." *Political Science Quarterly* 42 (September 1927): 337–67.

Eisenstein, Elizabeth L. "Some Conjectures About the Impact of Printing on Western Society and Thought: A Preliminary Report." *Journal of Modern History* 40 (March 1968): 1–56.

Faroqhi, Suraiya. "Social Mobility Among the Ottoman Ulema in the Late Sixteenth Century." *International Journal of Middle East Studies* 4 (April 1973): 204–218.

Findley, Ronald. "The Roots of Divergence: Western Economic History in Comparative Perspective." *American Economic Review* 82 (May 1992): 158–61.

Fisher, Sydney Nettleton. "Civil Strife in the Ottoman Empire, 1481–1503." *Journal of Modern History* 13 (December 1941): 449–66.

Fukuyama, Francis. "The End of History?" *National Interest* (Summer 1989). http://www.wesjones.com/eoh.htm.

——. "Has History Started Again?" *Policy* 18 (Summer 2002): 3–7.

——. "Second Thoughts: The Last Man in the Bottle." *National Interest* (Summer 1999). www.findarticles.com/p/articles/mi_m2751/is_56/ai_55015107/print.

Gilbert, Felix. "The 'New Diplomacy' of the Eighteenth Century." *World Politics* 4 (October 1951): 1–38.

Goldstone, Jack A. "East and West in the Seventeenth Century: Political Crises in Stuart England, Ottoman Turkey, and Ming China." *Comparative Studies in Society and History* 30 (January 1988): 103–42.

Gould, Mark. "Understanding Jihad." *Policy Review* 129 (February–March 2005). http://www.policyreview.org/feb05/gould.html.

Guilmartin, John Francis, Jr. "Ideology and Conflict: The Wars of the Ottoman Empires, 1453–1606." *Journal of Interdisciplinary History* 18 (Spring 1988): 721–47.

Haarmann, Ulrich W. "Ideology and History, Identity and Alterity: The Arab Image of the Turk from the Abbasids to Modern Egypt." *International Journal of Middle East Studies* 20 (May 1988): 175–96.

Heck, Gene W. "'Arabia Without Spices': An Alternative Hypothesis." *Journal of the American Oriental Society* 123 (January 2003): 547–76.

Hess, Andrew C. "The Battle of Lepanto and Its Place in Mediterranean History." *Past and Present* 57 (November 1972): 53–73.

——. "The Evolution of the Ottoman Seaborne Empire in the Age of the Oceanic Discoveries, 1453–1525." *American Historical Review* 75 (December 1970): 1892–1919.

——. "Islamic Civilization and the Legend of Political Failure." *Journal of*

Near Eastern Studies 44 (January 1985): 27–39.

——. "The Moriscos: An Ottoman Fifth Column in Sixteenth-Century Spain." *American Historical Review* 74 (October 1968): 1–25.

——. "The Ottoman Conquest of Egypt (1517) and the Beginning of the Sixteenth-Century World War." *International Journal of Middle East Studies* 4 (January 1973): 55–76.

Isani, Mukhtar Ali. "Cotton Mather and the Orient." *New England Quarterly* 43 (March 1970): 46–58.

Issawi, Charles. "The Christian-Muslim Frontier in the Mediterranean: A History of Two Peninsulas." *Political Science Quarterly* 76 (December 1961): 544–54.

——. "Europe, the Middle East, and the Shift in Power: Reflections on a Theme by Marshall Hodgson." *Comparative Studies in Society and History* 22 (October 1980): 487–504.

Keddie, Nikki R. "Is There a Middle East?" *International Journal of Middle East Studies* 4 (July 1973): 255–71.

Kennedy, Hugh. "From Polis to Madina: Urban Change in Late Antiquity and Early Islamic Syria." *Past and Present* 106 (February 1985): 3–27.

Khalidi, Tarif. "The Idea of Progress in Classical Islam." *Journal of Near Eastern Studies* 40 (October 1981): 277–89.

Kortepeter, Carl M. "Ottoman Imperial Policy and the Economy of the Black Sea Region in the Sixteenth Century." *Journal of the American Oriental Society* 86 (April 1966): 86–113.

Kraemer, Joel L. "Humanism in the Renaissance of Islam: A Preliminary Study." *Journal of the American Oriental Society* 104 (January 1984): 135–64.

Kurtz, Stanley. "The Future of 'History.'" *Policy Review* 113 (June 2002). http://www.policyreview.org/JUN02/kurtz_print.html.

Labib, Subhi Y. "Capitalism in Medieval Islam." *Journal of Economic History* 29 (March 1969): 79–96.

Lewis, Archibald. "The Islamic World and the Latin West, 1350–1500." *Speculum* 65 (October 1990): 833–44.

Lewis, Bernard. "The Muslim Discovery of Europe." *Bulletin of the School of Oriental and African Studies, University of London* 20 (1957): 409–416.

Mardin, Serif. "Some Notes on an Early Phase in the Modernization of Communications in Turkey." *Comparative Studies in Society and History* 3 (April 1961): 250–71.

Milbank, John. "The Gift of Ruling: Secularization and Political Authority." *New Blackfriars* 85 (March 2004): 212–38.

Neuhaus, Richard John. "The Naked Public Square." *National Review*, November 20, 1984. http://www.findarticles.com/p/articles/mi_m1282/is_v34/ai_3534833/

Parker, Richard B. "Anti-American Attitudes in the Arab World." *Annals of the American Academy of Political and Social Science* 497 (May 1988): 46–57.

Roberts, Priscilla H., and James N. Trull. "Moroccan Sultan Sidi Muhammad Ibn Abdallah's Diplomatic Initiatives Toward the United States, 1777–1786." *Proceedings of the American Philosophical Society* 143 (June 1999): 233–65.

Wilson, Gary E. "American Hostages in Moslem Nations, 1784–1796: The Public Response." *Journal of the Early Republic* 2 (Summer 1982): 123–41.

Short Papers and Reports

Blanchard, Christopher M. "Al Qaeda: Statements and Evolving Ideology." Washington, DC: Congressional Research Service, 2005.

Cordesman, Anthony H. "U.S. and Global Dependence on Middle Eastern Energy Exports: 2004–2030." Washington, DC: Center for Strategic and International Studies, 2004.

——. "The U.S. and the Middle East: Energy Dependence, Demographics, and the Myth of Oil Wealth." Washington, DC: Center for Strategic and International Studies, 2002.

Dankowitz, A. "Libyan Intellectual Dr. Muhammad Al-Houni: The Arabs Must Choose Between Western Civilization and the Legacy of the Middle Ages." Inquiry and Analysis Series No. 240. Washington, DC: Middle East Media Research Institute (MEMRI), 2005.

Ghazanfar, S. M. "The Dialogue of Civilisations: Medieval Social Thought, Latin-European Renaissance, and Islamic Influences." Foundation for Science, Technology, and Civilisation, 2004.

Ihsanoglu, Ekmeleddin. "Ottoman Educational Institutions During the Reform Period." Foundation for Science, Technology, and Civilisation, 2004.

IntelCenter. "Ayman al-Zawahiri Audio/Video Release Analysis." Alexandria, VA: IntelCenter, 2005.

——. "Osama bin Laden Message Analysis and Threat Assessment." Alexandria, VA: IntelCenter, 2004.

Ipsirli, Mehmet. "The Ottoman Ulema (Scholars)." *Foundation for Science, Technology, and Civilisation,* 2004.

Mearsheimer, John J., and Stephen Walt. "The Israel Lobby and U.S. Foreign Policy [Working Paper Number: RWP06-011]." Cambridge, MA: Harvard University/Kennedy School of Government, 2006.

Wolfowitz, Paul. "Briefing with Iraqi-Americans." Foreign Press Center briefing with Deputy Secretary Wolfowitz and Iraqi-Americans Emad Dhia, Zakiya Hakki, and Sam Kareem, March 28, 2003. http://www.defenselink.mil/transcripts/2003/t04012003_t328dfpc.html.

Yehoshua, Y. "Dispute in Islamist Circles Over the Legitimacy of Attacking Muslims, Shiites, and Non-combatant Muslims in Jihad Operations in Iraq: Al-Maqdisi vs. His Disciple Al-Zarqawi." Inquiry and Analysis Series No. 239. Washington, DC: MEMRI, 2005.

Zaimeche, Salah. "Al-Qayrawan (Tunisia)." *Foundation for Science, Technology, and Civilisation,* 2004.

——. "Aspects of the Islamic Influence on Science and Learning in the Christian West (12th–13th Century)." *Foundation for Science, Technology, and Civilisation,* 2003.

——."Baghdad." *Foundation for Science, Technology, and Civilisation,* 2005.

——. "Damascus." *Foundation for Science, Technology, and Civilisation,* 2005.

——. "Granada: The Last Refuge of Muslims in Spain." *Foundation for Science, Technology, and Civilisation,* 2004.

——. "Islam and Science." *Foundation for Science, Technology, and Civilisation,* 2002.

——. "The Mamluks in History." *Foundation for Science, Technology, and Civilisation,* 2004.

——. "The Question Is . . . ? Myths and Fallacies Surrounding the Decline of Muslim Civilisation." *Foundation for Science, Technology, and Civilisation,* 2004.

——. "Sicily." *Foundation for Science, Technology, and Civilisation,* 2004.

——. "Toledo." *Foundation for Science, Technology, and Civilisation,* 2005.

Magazines and Newspapers

Asia Times
Australian
Boston Globe
Economist
Guardian
Khaleej Times
New York Post
New York Sun
Times (London)
Wall Street Journal
Washington Post

Index

About the Author

MICHAEL A. PALMER is a professor in the History Department and the Program in Maritime Studies at East Carolina University. He is the author of two previous books that address U.S. policies in the Middle East, *On Course to Desert Storm: The U.S. Navy and the Persian Gulf* and *Guardians of the Gulf: The Growth of American Involvement in the Persian Gulf, 1833–1992*. He lives in Greenville, North Carolina.